WISE MEN FISH HERE FOR

poetry, prose, film, theater, art, new thought,
first editions, manuscripts, literary archives . . .

GOTHAM BOOK MART & GALLERY INC.

41 West 47th St. New York, N.Y. 10036 [212] 719-4448

CONJUNCTIONS

BI-ANNUAL VOLUMES OF NEW WRITING

Edited by

Bradford Morrow

Contributing Editors

Walter Abish

Mei-mei Berssenbrugge

Guy Davenport

William H. Gass

Kenneth Irby

Ann Lauterbach

Nathaniel Tarn

COLLIER BOOKS
MACMILLAN PUBLISHING COMPANY
866 Third Avenue, New York, N.Y. 10022

SENIOR EDITOR: Elisabeth Cunnick

MANAGING EDITOR: Susan Bell

ASSISTANT TO THE EDITOR: Karen Kelly

PRODUCTION MANAGER: Cynthia Anderson, for Tom Buhl Typographers. Assistants: Judy Neunuebel, Fran Setbacken, Joyce Hart

CONJUNCTIONS is published in Spring and Autumn of each year by Collier Books and Charles Scribner's Sons, Macmillan Publishing Company, 866 Third Avenue, New York, NY 10022. Collier Macmillan Canada, Inc. Editorial communications should be sent to Bradford Morrow, CONJUNCTIONS, 33 West 9th Street, New York, NY 10011. Unsolicited manuscripts cannot be returned unless accompanied by a stamped, self-addressed envelope.

DISTRIBUTION. Trade accounts should address their orders to: Macmillan Publishing Company, 100K Brown Street, Riverside, NJ 08370. Macmillan books are available at special discounts for bulk purchases for sales promotions, premium, fund-raising, or educational use. For details, contact: Special Sales Director, Macmillan Publishing Company, 866 Third Avenue, New York, NY 10022.

SUBSCRIPTIONS.
Single year (two issues):
$16.00 paperback, postpaid; $20.00 for institutions and overseas.
$45.00 cloth, postpaid.

Two years (four issues):
$30.00 paperback, postpaid; $40.00 for institutions and overseas.
$85.00 cloth, postpaid.

Patron subscription (lifetime): $150.00 paperback.

Overseas subscribers please make payment by International Money Order. Back issues available.

Printers: Edwards Brothers.

Typography on covers by The Grenfell Press, New York City. Printed by A. Colish, Inc.

CONJUNCTIONS is a subsidiary of the New Writing Foundation, Inc., a not-for-profit corporation. This issue is made possible in part with funds from the New York State Council on the Arts and the National Endowment for the Arts.

Library of Congress Number: ISSN 0278-2324
ISBN 0-02-035281-6 Collier (paper edition)
ISBN 0-684-587112-9 Scribners (cloth edition)

TABLE OF CONTENTS

Δ   Δ   Δ
READINGS: Reviews and Criticism

ABOUT THE COVER: Oil on paper, 12″ x 18″, painted by Gregory Amenoff for the cover of CONJUNCTIONS:12. Reproduced courtesy of Hirschl & Adler Modern, New York.

John Billy
David Foster Wallace

1. Was Me Supposed To Tell Simple Ranger

Was me supposed to tell Simple Ranger how Chuck Nunn Junior done wronged the man that wronged him and fleen to parts unguessed. Brought up the Ranger to date on Chuck and Mona May Nunn's boy Chuck Junior, closest thing to handsome and semi-divine we got here in Minogue Oklahoma, good luck bad luck man, who everything that hit him stuck and got valuable, but on whom of this late time the vicissitudes of human relatings had wrought grief and retinal aggravation to such a extreme that C. Nunn Jr. lost his temper to a nameless despair and got him some vengeance.

Told Nunn's tale to Simple Ranger, the damaged dust-scout, who is a old man, watched his farm blow away in the hard and depressed highwindy days of the Bowl, got farmless, but however angled some job out of F. Delano R.'s WPA and set himself up in a plywood shack on the Big Dirt between here and El Reno, drawing government pay as a watcher for major or calamitous dust. Stayed out there near on forty years til looking at the dust made him damaged. Now he's too old not to be back, roving the streets in a kind of crazy d.j. vu, Minogue Oklahoma's own toothless R. Winkle, wants to re-know the lives of his people and their children after forty alone years of trying to make out the shape of his farm in the air. Buys me my personal beers with the checks some Washington D.C. computer sends him too much of, and I tell Simple Ranger things about Minogue only he don't know.

Told him some facts about Chuck Nunn Junior, with whom even the high winds decline to mess. How the prodigiousness of his 1948 birth tore up his Momma Mona May's innards so bad that even today the woman can only fall asleep after hotpads and loud opera, and requires institutional caring. How Chuck Junior was swarthy and pubic by ten, bearded and bowlegged and randy by twelve; how his late Daddy tried to whip him just once, like to broke his belt to smithers on Chuck Junior's concrete behind. How C. Jr. flipped his cherry on our seventh-grade music teacher, a pale, jagged woman, but highly scented, who even today passes through Minogue

Oklahoma in a Trailways bus ever leap year, kneedlepointing and humming vacant tunes of love's non-requiting. How Chuck Nunn Junior's color was that of the land and how his sweat smelled like copper and how the good ladies of Minogue got infallibly behooved to sit down whenever he passed, walking as walks a man who is in communion with Forces, legs bandy and boots singing with the Amarillo spurs he won himself at the '65 State Fair in O. City for kicking the public ass of a bull without but one horn, but a sharp one.

Told Simple Ranger, whose rate of beer is scary on account of no teeth to hinder a maximal swallow, told Ranger how, while he was out on Big Dirt watching skies and eating peas out of cans, Minogue Oklahoma H.S. won the state H.S. football title two years back to back with Chuck Nunn Junior at quarterback and defense and myself at Equipment Manager. How in '66, in the state final versusing Minogue Oklahoma and Enid Oklahoma, our sworn and fatal foes for all time, how in the final game's final few competitive seconds Enid, down by five, granted the ball to their giant ringer nameless nigra wingback, who took off from the Enid eleven with the ball in his hands and wrongness in his eyes, meaning harm to Minogue Oklahoma's very heart and self-perception, this nigra blowing through Minogue boys like grit on big wind, plus getting interferences run by two cow-punchers' boys of human form but geologic size, plus a Canadian martial arts expert in a padded bathrobe and metal cleats, who played dirty and low. How (I'm seeing this now, mind) how after a climactic and eternal chase-down-the-field and catch-from-behind, a swift cruel red-bearded and glitter-eyed C. Nunn Jr. brought down the whole stadium house, solved the runner-plus-interference problem at our ten's Enid side-line by tackling the huge cow-boys, the low Canadian kicker, the inhumanly fast nigra, three Enid cheerleaders, a referee, and one ten-gallon cooler of Enid Gatorade, all at one cataclysmic time. Busted a igneous leg on a interferer's spine and healed up in just weeks, bandier than before. Got a hall of Minogue Oklahoma H.S. named Chuck Nunn Junior Hall.

2. CHUCK NUNN JUNIOR MORE GOD THAN NOT

Told Simple Ranger some data on how Chuck Nunn Junior, more God than not to those of us peers that lived for a whiff of his jet trail, ate up his school and town, left us bent and in mid-yearn, in his eighteenth year, and moved on to Oklahoma University, Norman, at whence he was observable throwing high-altitude televised spirals and informing his agriculture and range-management teachers of facts they did not know. Then how Nunn chucked it all to give time as a volunteer in The United States' Involvement In Vietnam, whence trickled down rumors of the glory and well-armed mightiness of Nunn: how he toted his unit's fifty-calibers up sheer and cliff-like impediments to conflict; how he declined to duck, never once crawled or ate mud, however never even once smelled lead in his cranial vicinity; how he got alone and surrounded by VCR's (Viet Cong Regulars) in '71, and through sheer force of personality and persuasion persuaded a whole battalion of sly slanted Charlies to turn their own guns on their selves. How etc. etc. How he sent me a postcard with a red bloom of napalmed jungle on the front, wrote how he wished my personal vision was better so I could leave the feed store and get over there to watch and whiff the trail of his jet.

Simple Ranger's eyes is the color of the sky. There's speculation hereabouts concerning if you look at something long enough, does your eyes take its color.

I profess to telling the grey-eyed Ranger, plus a Nunn-happy group of Minogue civilians, how Chuck Nunn Junior returned home from OU Norman and South East Conflict more theory than man. How there was a welcome parade, fussy and proud, with a tuba. How the immoderate and killer twister that hit in '74 (this twister old Simple Ranger, by then more than a tinch damaged, chased for twelve helter and skelter miles in his DeSoto, said he smelled his aloft land in every revolution, finally wound up upside down in phone lines and no sign of his car evermore. Didn't never come down) that hit in spring, '74, the day after Nunn's returning and parade, how that sucker ripped the roof off Nunn's late Daddy's machine shed, sucked two N. Rockwell prints and Nunn's late Daddy out a busted ranchhouse window to follow Simple Ranger's DeSoto in a straight-up, and how it took up the Nunns' TV's aerial antenna off the house roof and flew the electric javelin out a fair quarter mile, flung the pole down into Nunn land like a mumblepeg, and how up from this TV-speared ground, just inherited *ex officio* by Chuck Nunn Junior, come a bubbling crude. Black gold. Texas tea. How Nunn paid off his late missing Daddy's sheep ranch's mortgage with revenues, put his scrambled and operatic Momma Mona May into institutional caring, and took over the Nunn sheep business with such a slanderous cunning and energy, plus oil money, that soon amounts of CNJ-brand sheep was bulging straining and bleating against the barbed wire limit of Nunn's spread, mating in frenzies, plus putting out wool hand over hoof, plus fighting over which one got to commit suicide whenever Nunn looked like he even might

("*Might,*" I told Simple Ranger)

be hungry.

Was telling the dust-watcher how C. Nunn Jr. passed up multitudes of come-hitherish cheerleaders and oriental princesses to return to Minogue and enter into serious commitment with his childhood sweetheart, the illegally buxom and tall Glory Joy duBoise, closest thing to femininity and pulchritude that to date exists in Minogue Oklahoma, eyes like geometry and a all-around bodily form of high allure and near-religious implication, and just as I was commencing a analogy relating the shape of Glory Joy's hips to the tight curve of the distant Big Dirt horizon, the door to the Outside Minogue Tavern busted inward and there against the dusty sunlight was framed the tall, angstified, and tortured frame of Glory Joy duBoise, hand to her limpid and Euclidean eyes, hips (that was similar to horizons) brushing the trauma-struck frame of the busted-inward door. She stood like that for time, looking at me, then come over toward the table we was all at. Whereupon she stood, staggered, dropped, and flopped in a floor-direction, her wracked and convulsively semi-conscious frame moving in directions like the Minogue Oklahoma H.S. half-time band, spelling out Kicked In The Butt By Love, Or, Forlorn And Subject To Devastation Following The Loss Of Chuck Nunn Junior Due To The Hurtful Precariousness Of His Post-Accident Temper.

3. Nunn's Personal Undoing Was the Day it Rained Sheep

Nunn's personal undoing was the day it rained sheep, I outlined to Simple Ranger as me and several civilians carried the forlornly swooned and flopping frame of Glory Joy duBoise to our table, smeared cold Rolling Rock on her pulse-points, and propped her up in a splinterless chair to come round to the outlining of our mutual Minogue sadnesses and troubles.

Told Simple Ranger how the success of the Nunn sheep ranch, plus the devotion of the near-beautiful Glory Joy, had aroused the ire and jealousy of T. Rex Minogue, the antique and hermitically reclusive, also malignant and malevolent, Minogue Oklahoma sheep mogul, plus the manufacturer of the illegal and chemically unstable sweet-potato whiskey that kept our neighboring reservation's Native Americans glazed and politically inactive; and how following the spectacular rise of the Nunn sheep operation under the energy and Agriculture Degree of Chuck Junior, who was, remember, a-shtuppin' the little lady T. Rex himself had wanted to a-shtup since she was twelve,

how in light of all this it's comprehensible how T. Rex Minogue repeatedly and with above-average vigor attempted to financially acquire, legally finagle, then violently appropriate the Nunn sheep operation from Chuck Nunn Junior; how Nunn was too petroleumly rich, well and savily educated, and martially formidable, respective, for any of the attempts to fructify; how Nunn took all Minogue's shit with good humor, even the complimentary and ribboned jelly jars of yam liquor that T. Rex kept sending Glory Joy, each attached to a note headed NOTICE OF FORMAL WOOING, all with great and superior humor, until finally T. Rex, a man allergic to any distance between himself and his way (least here in this town his own Daddy built before getting fatally harmed by some politically active Native Americans), until T. Rex arranged for his younger antique brother V.V. Minogue—a benign however treatably alcoholic rangehand and poet (his stuff rhymed, I'm told) who was under the thumb of dependency on T. Rex's secret sweet-potato recipe, I informed the ranger—for V.V. and two humungous out-of-town cowpunchers' boys from Enid (yes the old interferers from the climax of the state football title game in '66), for them to explosively dynamite a large and bulk-like portion of Chuck Nunn Junior's ranch's flock-infested grazing land; how whereupon the land was in fact dynamited by V.V. and the geologic Enid boys; and how it rained various percentages of sheep in Minogue Oklahoma for one whole nauseous afternoon two years ago next Ascension.

As Simple Ranger sat up straight at this and informed myself and the civilians that he himself had heard a far-off thunder booming off the dome of Big Dirt space, plus seen a singular pink-white rain from clear out in his shack on Dirt two Ascensions back, and had attributed the experiences to theology, plus the effects of damage, Glory Joy duBoise fluttered her way into consciousness and arousal, smoothed her brass-colored and towering hair with a hand-motion of such special sensuousness that two civilians tipped back over in their chairs and was largely lost for the duration, and entered into the therapy of it all, getting on the outside of several beers and detailing for the Ranger how it had been, that dark, fluffy, and rusty day, running with C. Nunn Jr. through the blasted heaths of exploded former pasture, ruining her best silk umbrella for all time, watching her man move through turf, mutton, and gore like the high wind of madness itself, floundering bow-legged through gruesome fields of gruesomer detonated wool, catching plummeting major percentages of particular favorite sheep in a shearing-basket, Glory Joy watching his mood and attitude getting more and more definable in terms of words such as grief, sorrow, loss, disorientation, suspicion, anger, and finally *unambiguous and univocal rage.* How as coyotes and buzzards began to sweep in off Big Dirt and commence a scavengerial orgy unsurpassed in modern Oklahoma in terms of pure and bilious nasty, how C. Nunn Jr. unhitched his '68 souped-entirely-up Italian Sports Car from his OU Norman quarterback career and fairly flew off the ranch east on rickety two-lane 40 toward the gigantic and private T. Rex Minogue spread, without so much as a kiss my foot to Glory Joy, who watched her man inject his vehicle of light into the chewed-up straight-shot road to TRM, his mind on the noun, T. Rex Minogue, the near-gerunds confrontation, reparation, possibly even reciprocation (i.e. detonation).

4. So it Went Back and Forth

So it went back and forth, myself and Glory Joy, Simple Ranger gumming his bottle, his expression moving between vacant and preoccupied, the odd and frequent passing civilian patron getting pulled into the table, beer in hand, whenever Glory Joy rose her six-foot self up to tell what it had been similar to, those lonesome days of trying to run off carrionizers and mop up sheep percentages and run a ranch—admittedly, now a smaller spread by a good measure—all herself; she'd rise up in her purple satin pantsuit and pay public tribute to the resemblance the days after Nunn's undoing and accident bore to hell right up on the grey and psoriatic skin of this world's land.

So it went back and forth, me handling the historical and observational, Glory Joy the personal and emotive. Was me revealed to Simple Ranger how, after the rain of sheep, Nunn was fairly flying in his little Italian Sports Car east on 40 to present to T. Rex Minogue the gift of T. Rex's own personal ass, and how meanwhile, back at

Nunn's ranch, a good part of Minogue Oklahoma commenced to
arrive and gawk and Kodak and catch mutton-cuts in receptacles
("Honey," this one old Mrs. Peat in yellow rain boots and slicker and a
pince nez told me as she adjusted her hairnet she told me "Honey,
when it rains bread and fishes, you get yourself a bucket, is what you
do."). And how but *mean*-meanwhile, T. Rex Minogue's benign but
sub-digital brother V.V., steeped in post-explosion guilt and self-
loathing, plus not a little eau d'sweet potato, was speeding away
from T. Rex's enormous spread for the Deep Dirt of Oklahoma's
interior to commune with himself, guilt, pain, and a whole big truck
full of jelly jars of distilled yam, and was accordingly fairly flying
west on rickety 40 in this huge old truck, and at a ominous and
coincidental point in time V.V. subconsciously decided, in some dark
and pickled back part of his oceanic head, to see just what it was like
driving his gargantular three-ton IH home-modified yam liquor
transport truck on the left side of the hills, valleys, and sinewing
curves of two-lane 40, V.V.'s left side being Chuck Nunn Junior's by
right, course; and how here come Chuck Nunn Junior ripping up the
highwayed hill right dab equidistant center between the two
ranches, and here's V.V., driving in a pickled manner and a inappropriate lane up the hill's other side, and how there was impact at
high speed, of a head-on kind, between the two.

"Impact," I said to Simple Ranger. "Plus damage, in a non-small
measure."

And Glory Joy duBoise testified to the feelings she felt upon
arriving in my pickup upon the accident scene, some pathetically
few miles down 40, and seeing her Chuck Nunn Junior literally
wearing his little impacted car; how there was white steam whis-
tling out of his tires, out of the accordion that had been his engine,
and out of Nunn's head, which looked on first look to be minus a jaw,
consciousness, and two healthy eyes, in that order. How red lights
and sirens come emergencying out across Dirt; how the Emergency
Folks had to cut Chuck Junior out of his car with torches; how they
was scared to move him on account of spinal considerations; how
Minogue Sheriff Onan L. Axford announced to some press and
media that wearing a safety belt, which Nunn was, had been all that
come between Chuck Nunn Junior and a eternal flight out a punctured windshield.

She told how Nunn come more or less to, in his little wrap-around
car, his torch-lit busted eyes in blood like bearings in deep oil;

"Remember the eyes of Nunn," I interjaculated, and Simple

Ranger give me a watching look,

; and as Glory Joy finished up communicating the anger and justicelessness she felt, upon seeing T. Rex's brother V.V. Minogue, listing far to port up against the largely unharmed cab of his IH liquor truck, weepy, shitfaced, scratchless; how V.V.'s accidental ass had been immunized and preserved by how some old International Harvester trucks turned out had one of them air bags in them, that nobody knew about, from a IH experiment in the 1960's that didn't make the economic wash. But so the whole accident that was V.V.'s pickled fault and that impacted Nunn's hairy jaw and busted both his eyes, plus a pelvis, plus concussed the sucker into moral comatosity and undoing—the whole damaging calamity had consisted for V.V. Minogue of just a jillionth-of-a-second sensuous experience of soft and giant marshmallow (the white foaming lumpy bag was still filling up the big truck's cab, at this time, I remember, starting to jut and ooze out the busted windows, looking dire and surreal), of a marshmallow instant, plus a upcoming year of subsequent legalities. As Glory Joy climaxed telling how it felt, and took a deserved grief-intermission, a certain palate-clefted but upstanding civilian turn to me and he say,

"Sucker busted his eyes?" being real interested in physical damage, birth defects, accidental maimings, and the like.

"Sucker busted his eyes?" the Simple Ranger repeated in a rich gritty voice that croaked of advanced Grey Lung, the disease most specially feared by us who spend our lives on Big Dirt.

Out of a consideration for Glory Joy duBoise, who was wearing her pain like a jacket, now, I lowered my voice as I invited civilian and Ranger to picture what two cantaloupe melons dropped from a high height would resemble, if they wanted the picture of how Nunn's eyes got busted out his head via general impact and collision, hanging right out his head, ontologically insecure.

And was me told the table how except for the eyes, the jaw, and the pelvis, which to our community relief all healed up, *prime face*, in just weeks, leaving good luck bad luck Chuck Junior a sharper shot, wickeder dancer, and nearer to handsome than before, how except for that, the major impact and damage from the accident had turned out to be to Nunn's head, mind, and sensibility. How right there in the post-accidental car he suddenly got conscious but evil,

"*evil*," I emphasized, and there was shudders from civilians and Glory Joy,

and how a evil Chuck Nunn Junior fought and cussed and struggled against his spinal restraints, invected against everything from the Prime Mobile to OU Norman's head football coach Mr. Barry B. Switzer hisself; how even slickered in blood, and eyes hanging ominous half out their holes, Nunn'd laid out two paramedics and a deputy and shined up my personal chin when we tried to ease him into a ambulance; how right there on rickety two-lane 40 Nunn publicly withdrew his love from his Momma Mona May, me, the whole community of Minogue Oklahoma, and especially from Glory Joy, who he loudly accused of low general spirits and a lack of horizontal imagination.

"Chuck Junior was just in a moral coma from the accident, is all it was," declared a Glory Joy known from here to next door for the deepness of her loyalty toward Nunn. She told Simple Ranger how C. Nunn Jr. suffered six evil and morally comatose post-damage days, his sense of right and wrong and love and hate smithered to chaotic, but how the subsequent Nunn thankfully remembered none of those six dark and devilish days of screaming and vandalizing in the Minogue County Hospital, where he was at, as restrained as was possible given the personality and persuasiveness of Nunn vis à vis orderlies. How Nunn woke up familiar and normal on the seventh day and asked about location, which is always a real good medical sign. How we was all relieved.

5. NUNN'S SURFACE HEALED UP, BUT WITH SOMETHING INTERIOR ASKEW

Got dark outside, gritty afternoon dark that means serious wind through high dirt, movement of soil in sky, a swirl that fakes twister once a week and keeps the tourists minimal, and there was a peculiar but occasional black flutter at some of the tavern windows, and Simple Ranger got aroused, disquiet. Me and G.J. was telling the Ranger how Chuck Nunn Junior's surface healed up as fast and fine as the town could expect, how he was back on his post-explosion ranch and inside Glory Joy's affections and limbs by six weeks time; how his broke cantaloupe eyes got put back together via skill and laser by Drs., paid for through V.V. Minogue's subsequent legalities (V.V. was in institutional caring and de-tox up in El Reno, by this time), how the eyes healed together so right and improved that Nunn could claim to spot dust-movement against the sky's very curve. No small claim.

15

But how something inside Nunn got left by the impact askew, his interior self messed with, hurting, under strain, all due to the lingering insecurity of the previously busted Nunn temper and moral sense.

"We got frightened of his temper and moral sense," Glory Joy told from a window she was at, standing, curious and distracted, looking out against dark at something against the seam of land and air that stretched tight across the Dirt. "Chuck Junior got scared of hisself."

Ever get scared of your own self? Painful. Glory Joy had mummed up to Nunn, from concern and such, but Chuck Jr. got subsequently informed by friends and civilians about his six-day moral coma, about things he'd done, said, and implied in the privacy of a special padded Hospital wing, things he did not recollect; got told of a unnameable evil and rage directed at the universe in general, one that was diarrhetic and fearsome to see in a previous semi-demiurge, larger than life. It got known around Minogue Oklahoma that while his quality Italian seatbelt had saved his exterior, the impact with V.V. following the rain of sheep had knocked something loose in the center of Nunn. Chuck Junior got informed on this fact, and it chewed at him.

"His temper got scary," Glory Joy said. "It got precious and valuable to us, like only something you is scared to death to lose can get." She'd got to carressing the peeling frame of the window she was at with a mournfulness and musing that repercussed among the civilians piling up in circle at our little table. "His temper got insecure. We lived in around-the-clock fear of when Chuck Junior might possibly lose his temper."

"Focus in on that verb *lose*, S.R.," I told Simple Ranger. "The lady means it special. Whenever C. Nunn Jr. lost his post-accident temper, he lost the sucker real and true. It became gone. Absent. Elsewhere. Blew away to unfindable locations. A state of nameless and potential eternal rage and evil ever time he but stub his toe or some such shit." I put a earnest hand on the Ranger's deep grey sleeve, tried to get his eyes off the air outside the window. "Chuck Nunn Junior lived in fear of, plus alienation from, his own personal temper."

Was Glory Joy duBoise told us in emotive terms how collision and concussion and coma had left Nunn's interior bent. How the bow-legged pride of Minogue Oklahoma had to scrutinize and rein his own emotional self each minute, for fear that upset or anger could loop him back into a blank white comality of evil and meanness.

16

How his tender gentleness toward G.J. duBoise got so extreme as to crowd pitiful, so scared was he that if he stopped loving her for a second he'd never get it back. How the rare times when a vicissitude of human-relating, sheep-shearing, or pasture-status pissed him off, he'd get positively other-, under-worldly with anger, a bearded unit of pure and potent rage, ranging his sheep's ranges like something mythopoeic, thunderous, less man or thing than sudden and dire force, will, ill. How the bright blank evil'd stay on him for a day, two, a week; and Glory Joy'd shut herself in the storm cellar Chuck Nunn Junior hisself had lined with impregnable defensive steel, and she'd stay put, drinking bottled water and watching out for Nunn-activity through a emergency periscope Chuck Jr. had punctured through the storm cellar's roof for just such episodic periods; and how, after time, Nunn would come back out of the blind nameless hate, the objectless thirst for revenge against whole planets; how he'd find his spent and askew temper on some outer range of detonated Nunn land and return, pale and ignorant, to a towering, quivering, forgiving Glory Joy.

"Chuck Junior steered way clear of even thinking about T. Rex Minogue's place for fear he'd kill the old man," I told the Ranger. "Got terrified of even the concept of what T. Rex might could do to his emotions and sensibilities."

"The tenderness and caring Chuck Nunn Junior showed me were inhuman," Glory Joy semi-sobbed, her eyes resembling a St. Vitus of red threads. "Superhuman; not of this landed earth."

Simple Ranger got moved, here, at something.

6. Was Buzzards That Had Stayed On

Now, the peculiar darkness and peculiarer fluttering outside the Outside Minogue Bar was in fact buzzards, two civilians at the busted-inward bar door told us. Glory Joy and the Ranger nodded absent to theirselves. We took looks outside. There was buzzard-presence and -activity of thought-provoking scope. The air was dark and agitated with wings, beaks, soft bellies. The suckers soared round. The air around the Outside Minogue Bar was swirling and influenced by regiments of the buzzards that had got drawn to Big Dirt by the rain of Nunn mutton two Ascensions past, and had stayed on.

It was like something giant was coming out of the Dirt to die, the

Ranger said in a gravelly whisper, staring his eyes past civilians, door, into a swirling soiled grey, looking for signals, his land, his car.

"This sucker's damaged," whispered a civilian, low.

But I commenced to revelate to Simple Ranger about Chuck Nunn Junior's special and secret post-accident strain.

"You knew about the secret post-accident strain when I didn't til it was too late and Chuck Junior was temperless and gone?" asked a disbelieving Glory Joy, pale, tight of lip, hip-shot. She come back over, toting menace.

I sympathied Glory Joy, told her how Chuck Junior had suffered a spell of his optical dislocation over to the feedstore once after I once slapped him on his back over a humorous joke, and how he'd dislocated, and I'd seen, and how he'd swore me to a eternity of silence about his secret,

a sworn promise I kept til he wronged T. Rex Minogue and vameesed. I told Simple Ranger and the civilians about the hidden and subterranean strain, suffered by a already askew C. Nunn Jr., caused by his post-impact-with-V.V.-Minogue-spontaneously-detachable eyes. Told some historic facts: how the Drs. sewed up Nunn's busted bearing melon eyes with laser and technocracy and left him farther down the line from blindness and blear than ever, but with a hitch: those eyes, sewed with light, was left smaller. Aint hard to see that the Drs. at the Hospital had to take them some slack up from Nunn's busted eyes to laser-stitch the busts with, and how the deslacking of the eyes left them tight, small, rattling in the sockets, insecure.

"They'd fall out his head," I told the company of men that was round our table about three deep, countless bottles of Rolling Rock already dealt with, stacked in a pyramid and headed for ceiling. "Be like the accidental impact all over again, at times: slap Chuck Junior on the back, or maybe he'd bend down after a untied lace, or

(worst)

if he'd sneeze at all—ever see the man sneeze, personally, a post-accident sneeze, Glory Joy?"

Glory Joy's powdered and geometry-eyed face got singular, loose, looked like Walter Matthau a second, out of my stimulating of a old but sudden recognition (unclear, but true). She got smaller in her chair, too interested by half in the label on her ninth Rolling Rock.

Was me told Simple Ranger, who kept coughing and sniffing, nervous at the special smell of interested buzzard, how Chuck Nunn Junior commenced to buckle under the emotive strain of two little post-accidental eyes that exited their sockets and dangled by cords down his bearded and near-handsome face at the slightest gravitational invitation. How the twin pressures of fear that the possible sight of his insecure and A.W.O.L. eyes could repulse the love clear out of Glory Joy duBoise, plus how the fragileness of his coma-inclined and skittish temper might at any time dust from Nunn's concussed head any sense of ought, right, love, or concern for men, man, woman, or Glory Joy, how all this shit wore on Chuck Nunn Junior. How he got wore: thinned out, legs bandier, skin loose and paler than land, copper sweat verdigrised, rattling eyes milky and other-directed.

"Interior and progressing damage," I summed.

7. AND, PENCLIMACTICALLY,

Glory Joy revealed how, some weeks back, the infamous pollenated dust of pre-Ascension springtime Minogue Oklahoma brought on a hay fever that had Chuck Junior woolly and writhen with secret strain, plus mysteriously excusing himself from her every few minutes to go out to the privy to sneeze,

"And to reinsert his recalcitrant and threnedic eyes," she moaned, "I understand the total picture now, God bless his soul and mine together,"

(tears, by this point in time)

; and how, the torpid grey three-days-past morning of Nunn's temper's final debarkation into vengeance and fleeing, Glory Joy revealed, a fit of uncontrollable and pollenated sneezing had reared up out of the dusty land its own self and overtook a tired, tattered Chuck Nunn Junior there at breakfast, at the table, and how to Glory's combined horror and pathos he'd sneezed his keen but tiny eyes right out into his bowl of shredded wheat, and milk and fiber covered his sight, and Glory Joy'd rushed over to his sides but he was already up, horrified and swinging the balls, the twin cords the color of innards, Nunn fumbling in a wild manner to refit his lariatic eyes, healthy ears keen to the sound of the horror, pathos of the gasps of Glory Joy, temper bidding adios altogether to the flat grey world of the limited but steady-keeled mortal mind.

"And off he flew for the second recent-historic time," I climaxed, "this time in the impact-proof and souped-up used cement mixer he'd bought with V.V.'s legalities, off he flew east on rickety two-lane 40, blank with hate and optical mortification, to reciprocally wrong old T. Rex and V.V. Minogue."

"Who'd malignantly through willful and explosive machinations and vehicularism caused Nunn the twin insecurities of eyes and moral temper," Simple Ranger finished up for me, in a curious plus haunting voice that was not

(more I reflected there the more I got convinced that those polysyllables were not of his gravelly Grey Lung voice, somehow)

his own, somehow.

Was telling Simple Ranger how C. Nunn Jr., blood in his eye, plus cereal, roared out on that military mixer, in mood and stature similar to a demiurge, a banshee, a angry mythopoeum, roared out east on four-O to deprive T. Rex Minogue and wretched V.V. of their animate status, how he left the tall, forlorn, and quivering Glory Joy duBoise to watch the ever-tinier fog of his thunderous exhaust, his dusty final jet trail, three days past, and how Nunn never got seen no more. How the rumorous talk around town was that he'd forcibly detached the Minogue brothers' malignant/benign, reclusive/alcoholic asses, reattached them in inappropriate and harm-conducive locations, left the two of them twisted, bent, wronged, full of gnash and rue and close to expiration, and fleen the state and nation in his unimpactable mixer, taken on down the last road to fullness, redemption, and temper.

Any old civilian at all can conceptualize Glory Joy duBoise's crumpled Walter Matthauness by this revelational and recapitulatory time, but it's something just other to visualize how she refilled, smooth and animated, in a negative manner, toward the sight that now half-filled the busted frame of the door of the Outside Minogue Bar, appeared against the swirling swooping light through soil outside. The sight, dressed and draped in a dusty black, was the ancient and all-around ravaged frame of T. Rex Minogue, appearing publicly for the first time since the wool-price crisis of '67. He was seated in a dirt-frosted wicker and electricity-powered wheelchair, which hissed a low electric hiss as T. Rex made, first entry, then his way over to near the plywood bar and the combined and uncharitably disposed sight of our whole crowded three-deep pyramided table. Was me whispered to Simple Ranger, "Minogue, T. Rex, first public display since '67, crisis, wool," and the Ranger nodded, his eyes more full of knowing than sky, a second.

Glory Joy duBoise, here, was getting hostiler-looking as she stared at old T. Rex, by the bar in his chair, covered by a black blanket, with crumbled old cheesy brown boots protruding from under, a white

National Cancer Society cap on his skull-shaped skull, a curved and immense and hopefully domesticated buzzard on one shoulder, plus besides all this a device for electronic talking he was trying to put to his throat in just the right spot, for folks with throat dysfunctions. One of the civilians Glory Joy had proned to the floor swears later how he seen out-of-town dirt caked on the tattery soles of T. Rex's boots, seen a tiny and scripted IMPENDING glowing fire in T. Rex's one eye, a also tiny DOOM, CANCER burning cursive in the other; and this supine civilian was the first saw the rich orange of the jelly jars of illegal unstable sweet-potato whiskey that T. Rex commenced to pull out of a soft sheepskin satchel he had with him under that unwholesome blanket. Got the jars out and tossed them to the Ranger, who passed them around.

We passed the jars around and unscrewed Minogue's bootleg lids.

We was silent at our table, expected T. Rex dead, or at least twisted, traumatized, Nunn-struck.

"Hi," he said.

8. WAS THE MALIGNANT AND MALIGNIFIED T. REX MINOGUE

told us and Simple Ranger how Chuck Nunn Junior did flee to unknown and foreign locales. Manipulated his wicker-chaired plus disease-ridden self to where we all couldn't avoid but look right at him and his bird. Held his little vibrator-esk talking tube to his gizzardy (liver-spotted to hell) throat. Lifted a jar of potato whiskey to the dusty light. Told us some facts on how C. Nunn Jr. pulled up at the lush and isolated Minogue homestead in his heavy cement mixer, freshly re-fit eyes, moral unconsciousness, and a fine fettle, not respective; how Nunn right off laid out the two geologic Enid ranchhands, who was on their way off the TRM spread to take their women skeetshooting, how Nunn laid them out, kicked them where they laid, and rogered their women; how subsequently (not very), Nunn manufactured a unarchitectural and spontaneous entryway in the bay window of the front of T. Rex's Big House; and then how Nunn, on the spot, performed for T. Rex Minogue, in his wheelchair, in his front parlor, a uncontrolled and optically hazardous dance of blank white mindless rage that turned out to be one complex and complete charade for some words bore semantic kin to Wrath, Damage, Retaliation. So on.

Now the buzzards outside the Outside Minogue Oklahoma Bar

21

was down, sitting row on straight and orderly row on the edge-of-Minogue land stretching off toward dirt. Appeared to us through the windows like fat bad clerics, soft and plump, teetery, red-eyed, wrapped up tight in soft black coats of ecumenism and observation. Had orange beaks and claws. Was a good thousand orange beaks out there. Double on the claws. Lined up.

T. Rex Minogue was asking us to drink to his death;

"To death, gents, lady, civilians, Ranger,"

he said in a rich electricity of mechanical voicebox. He hefted a jar of yam liquor, up, and Glory Joy grinned unpleasant and right off lifted hers up with a enthusiasm I got to call sardonic. Upright civilians commenced to lift too, and finally myself, and under the pyramid of bottles on our table there was a quiet community toast to the publicity and temporariness of T. Rex Minogue, who explained while he poured rounds—his IMPENDING-DOOM-ravaged face dry brown and wrinkled as a circus peanut, hair hanging out his cap thin and white as linen off the deeply unwell—explained that when Chuck Nunn Jr. come three days past to damage and maim T. Rex and V.V., he got informed in the parlor by T. Rex that the benign and pliable V.V. had already previously ceased and succumbed, in a institutional-caring facility in El Reno, months back, to hostility of the liver and smoothness of the brain. That Nunn, in mid-rage-charade, declined to show either sympathy for the late V.V. or any sort of compassion or Christianity to the soon-to-be-late T. Rex; expressed, instead, through interpretive amoral dance, his own personal attitude toward T. Rex Minogue, plus some strong personal desires that had to do with the nullifying cancellation of T. Rex's happiness, gender, life.

Jelly jars or no, we was objectively and deeply unclear on how Chuck Junior and T. Rex got spared iniquitous criminality and grievous harm, respective; and was me asked T. Rex Minogue, who was attending a itch between his buzzard's wings with the corner of a tie clip, how and where Nunn had spared T. Rex and gone, plus whether the moral coma and eye-and-T.-Rex-centered rage and vengancelüst still now had hold of the fleen and missing Chuck Nunn Junior.

"A titanic plus miraculous scene to see," grated T. Rex's vibrator. He detailed the titanic plus miraculous struggle of minds and wills that proceeded to take place in Minogue's front parlor that vengeful dancing day: Nunn cataloguing such T.-Rex-offenses as jealousy, neighbor's-wife-coveting, avarice, manipulation, illegality, explo-

sions of turf and lamb, loosenings of eyes and consciousness, de-
securings of abilities to love and requite; T. Rex, in his wicker chair
and blanket, countering with a list of Nunn's putative virtuous
qualities headlined by charity-via-might, -main, altruism, Christian regard and duty, forgiveness, other-cheek-turning, *eudaimonia*,

sollen, *devoir*, [handwritten symbols] 壘 . Told how he, T. Rex,
due for consumption by his own malignancy in just time, anyhow,
refused to yield up fear or resignation to Nunn's blood-eyed
blankness. How T. Rex's ravagedness, will, and wind-blown statuses
saved his life from a thoroughly amoral and fatal-minded Nunn.

Now "To life," intoned the Ranger, nose full of dust and buzzard,
eyes to quartz glitter by vegetable hooch, face shining with a odd and
ignorant presence. Voice was still different, smoother. Young. Also
familiar.

T. Rex Minogue and his personal fowl looked at Simple Ranger.
Asked him some soft and intimately acquainted questions about the
variable various shapes of the dusted Big Dirt air patterns. Asserted
he could hear the special whistle of the Ranger's aloft land in certain
storms of darkness, grey. Ranger done nodded. His face come and
went.

"But not a bad career, Ranger," T. Rex continued, referring here to
the governmental dust-watcher job Simple Ranger had had for a solid
forty. But except T. Rex said wasn't actually the Ranger who had got
hisself the cushy WPA angle; fellow with the real cushiony arrange-
ment was a certain old and hold-out government clerk in Washington, D.C., who'd got his antique job under the original F. Delano
R. Clerk was the one had himself the cush: his entire and salaried
career was just sending Simple Ranger, plus this certain blind
octogenerial Japanese sub-sentry in Peuget, Wash., their checks ever
month. Clerk lived in big-city Washington and owned TV, T. Rex
revelated. Simple Ranger commenced to feeling along his own jaw,
thrown by new fits down into a jelly jar of introversion and temporary funk. And just internal theorizing on how T. Rex Minogue
possessed these far-off historical facts sent some civilians into a
state of shivering that had T. Rex's vulture agitated and hissing, plus
opening and closing its clerical wings, thus hiding and revealing by
turns the spectral and disquieting (calm, though) face of T. Rex
Minogue, making his IMPENDING eye show red fire. The rows of
audobonial Dirt-scavengers was still outside, now a tinch closer to
the bar windows, watching, lined up.

23

Things was threatening to get surreal until Glory Joy duBoise rose up, tall and shaky, looking the worse for a mixture of Rolling Rock and yam whiskey, which your thinking person don't want to mix, and proclamated in a falsetto of disbelief and anger that: one) she disbelieved T. Rex's sitting here, leguminous cool and unscathed, if her own Chuck Nunn was as desirous to scathe him right there in his parlor as T. Rex implied; and that: two) she was angry as a animal, plus forlorn and subject to devastation following the loss of Chuck Nunn Junior due to the hurtful precariousness of his post-accident temper, plus eyes, angry as a animal at the galaxy in general and T. Rex in especial for his causal part in the above precariousness, forlornness, and devastation; and that the malignant T. Rex Minogue just better come out clean about the whereabouts of Nunn if he didn't want his wrinkled and senescent butt to make the acquaintance of Glory Joy's high-heeled shoe, but good. And T. Rex, whose historical thirst for the self and corporeality of Glory Joy duBoise is the stuff of Minogue Oklahoma myth—a whole nother story, I informed the funked and othered Ranger

—T. Rex, whose passion for our town's lone arm-wave at beauty is legend, glanced, gazed, and stared at Glory Joy, til we all of us got skittery. T. Rex and G. Joy faced each other cross ten feet of plywood room like fields of energy, all energetic with lust mixed up with regret, on one hand, rage and repulsion mixed up with a dire need for knowledge of Nunn, on the other. Simple Ranger's face had checked entirely out: the old and historical and adental man was dreaming out through the window into the geometry of bird and soil that stretched to the sky's tight burlap seam.

"I took the boy upstairs," T. Rex croaked into his box. "Took him upstairs to my own boodwar and to the window and I showed the boy what was outside, is how I come out of the titantic plus miraculous struggle." Addressed himself to Glory Joy, plus to Simple Ranger, who besides looking checked-out now was looking also strangely odd, bigger, eyes both here and not, his head's outline too focused, some deep wrinkles in his face, stained by dust for all time, like slashes of No. 1 pencil. T. Rex touched his fowl's claw with speculation, rue:

"Took the boy to my own window and opened her up. It was mornin. Three months exact since we buried my brother, who got consumed by my liquor, by poetic burnings and yearnings, by grief and legalities on account of under-influence driving and the eyes and mind of Chuck and Mona May Nunn's boy."

24

"What I see," whispered the big sharp clear new Ranger in a smooth new clear young voice, his paperskinned hands steady around his jar of liquor. There was non-spectral colors in his eyes.

"Ranger?"

"What was outside?" said Glory Joy.

"Was and is," vibrated T. Rex Minogue. "Showed the boy where it all blew to. Showed him what his seatbelt done left him to look at and be." Looked around. "Made the sucker sniff and see." Drank up.

"Made him smell death on your own wind? Death he'd missed by a impacted whisker, zif that was a prize? Made him read IMPENDING and DOOM, CANCER? Introduced him to buzzards and such fowl?"

The birds was at the windows, now. All over them. Ranks broke. Bar all dark. Each window covered and pocked with a mabusity of cold red observational buzzard eyes. Dry rasp of orange claws going for purchase on the dusty frames and panes. We was on exhibit to animals.

"Miss Glory Joy," T. Rex said, "I knocked that boy upside the back. Out come the eyes, hangin. The eyes Drs. me and V.V. paid for put back together after they was busted."

"Made him think he owed you his eyes?" I incredulized.

"Ranger, tell John Billy here he's missin a point," said T. Rex.

"Don't owe my eyes to nought but the clean high wind," whispered Simple Ranger.

Glory Joy stared. "*Your* eyes?"

"Knocked that boy's eyes loose, out they come, hangin," recollected Minogue. "I lean his puppy ass out the window so he's dangling his eyes out over the land. Wind blows them eyes around. Sucker can see straight down into everything there is."

We was all looking at the new Ranger, tall and straight and other. Each window a smeared tray of cold red watching marbles. Glory Joy took back her seat, dizzy with mix. T. Rex Minogue lifted his jar of deep orange up to the fly-speckled overhead light, swirled it round.

"You brought Chuck Nunn Junior's eyes out his head and made him look at dirt and brush and soil and fowls?" I said. I was pissed off. "You show him the waist-deep shit we all grew up in, like it's a gift from you to him? Grey sights and greyer smells we can't get out our own heads, and for that he declines to scathe you?"

"Something like that."

"Don't believe it for nothing," Glory Joy wailed. (Woman could *wail*.) "T. Rex done something sinister to Chuck Junior, is what happened."

I agreed loudly. Plus two civilians, as well, with the sinister part.

The ceiling commenced to creak and precipitate dust, on account of the immense and shifting clerical weight on top. We was in the belly of something black and orange and numerous.

Now: "Where it all blew to," whispered the smooth steely Ranger. I remarked how his jelly jar's colors was overhung with lush and various floras. Was me asked Simple Ranger how floras got in his liquor.

"Gents, lady," smiled T. Rex, "in regard for your community selves I'm here today public to say that me and Chuck and Mona May's boy's struggle ended where all things titanic end. In meadow physics. We done some together, that day. Some macrocosmic speculation."

This one previous civilian, cleft palate, red iron hair, up and levitates. We look up at his Keds. He asks the air in front of him: "Where did Minogue Oklahoma blow to?"

Commenced to just *rain* ceiling-dust.

"Boys, wrap yourselves around something affirmative," said T. Rex, his domestic bird now holding his box to his throat with one savvy claw. "Remember what's the next world and what aint. Minogue blew to Minogue, neighbors. See you selves. You, me, the corporeally phenomenal Glory Joy, the Ranger especial, we been swirlin and blowin in and out Minogue land since twinkles commenced in our Daddies' eyes."

"Minogue is you, Minogue?" slurred Glory Joy duBoise. I couldn't say skank. We was all sleepy with vegetable fuss.

"Minogue blew to Minogue," Minogue said. "Under Dirt's curve she's whirled and fertilized her own self into a priceless poor. Lush, dead, elsewhere."

"So where is it at, Minogue," asks the palatal man, aloft in a cumulus of webs and dust and creak. "Where's the meat of the bones we crawl on, plus eke out of, plus die and sink back in without no sound."

"Aint no difference," sighed the Ranger. He'd growed him half a beard in just time. He sniffed at his liquor.

"Where you at, there, Ranger?" smiled a uncertain and far-off T. Rex.

"At the window," whispered the Ranger, at the window. He stared into a wormy and boiling black peppered with eyes, red. "Me and Mr. Minogue is at the window looking down at what the life and death of every soul from Comanche to Nunn done gone to fertilize and plenish."

"Showed him what we own," said T. Rex. He smelled at his old hands. "Showed what we all done gave via the planetarial actions of movement, wind, top-soil artistics, to the landed spread my own personal Daddy first plowed. That I first fertilized to humud black with the juices of his arrow-punctured self and my grief-withered Momma."

"Aint no Chuck Nunn from Minogue Oklahoma that aint eternal and aloft," sighed the Ranger at the window. The cleft rigger got levitationally joined by some more civilians.

Things was dark and singular.

"Aloft," intoned the damaged man. "My eyes are free of my head and flat grey temper and I am able to see directly below my dangling self the plumed and billowing clusters of the tops of trees of meat, dressed and heavy with the sweet white tissued blossoms indigenous to Minogue, fertilized by the wind-blown fruit of the toneless Curve on which me, my woman, my people move."

"Indigenous?" I slurred.

"That voice there, John Billy, that voice there is Chuck Junior's voice," said Glory Joy, flat, toneless, curved, Klan-white.

"When the high winds blew off Country," the Ranger said, "I was able to hear the infinitely many soft sounds of the millions of delicate petals striking and rubbing together. They joined and clove together in wind. My eyes was blowing everywhere. And the rush of perfume sent up to me by the agitation of the clouds of petals nearly blew me out that window. Delighted. Aloft. Semi-moral. New."

Glory Joy duBoise up and levitated. Also myself. Soon we was all uncommitted except to air and vision. T. Rex stayed where he was at, under us, by our pyramid of bottles studded with jars.

"Shit," he said.

Buzzards was gone. Flown home with a violence that set the edge-of-Minogue soil to lifting and tearing, twisted and grey, only to get beat down by a sudden plus unheard-of rush of clean rain from a innocent and milk-white sky. It fell like linen-wear, strings of technological light. Other such things. Windows ran smeared, then clear, then the rain shut down as abruptly as it had etc. etc.

The land commenced to look wounded. Dimpled puddles stretched off into nothing, outside—coins of water bright and clean and looking like open wounds in the red light of the low hurt red sun.

"Fore I die," whispered the malignified T. Rex, "I need to know where y'all think you live." He looked up. Around. "It's why I'm public today. Think what this is costing me. I need to know where y'all think you *live* at," he wailed. (Sucker could wail, too, gravelly vibrator or no.) His fowl got ornery.

"Maybe we'll just have us some fine new liquor first," whispers a aloft Ranger beside me, old, unbearded, sky-eyed. I saw for the first time how cataracted he was.

T. Rex commenced to hand up jars. "Tell me, Ranger," he said.

"Lord but don't it look clean," I was saying over and over.

"Show me the Chuck Nunn Junior I love, plus need," Glory Joy petitioned to a T. Rex maneuvering into a position for looking up her dress.

I grappled with some unsayably fearsome temptations to tell Chuck Nunn Junior's loyal and near-lovely woman who in all this landed world I loved.

"What's all that again?" said the Ranger in a flat grey gurgle.

"Have some liquor."

"Tell me where y'all think you live at."

Should of seen me grapple.

9. MY NAME IS JOHN BILLY.

Was me supposed to tell you how, on that one fine dark day a pentacost's throw from Ascension, we all of us got levitationally aloft, moving around the seated form of Minogue Oklahoma's expired T. Rex Minogue. How we passed, hand over hand, jar after jar of his unstable sweet-potato medicine, each jar deeper in color, duskier, til it got like the washed bleeding land in the colored outside. How we all, even and especially Glory Joy, got glazed and apolitical, also torpid, docile, our minds in a deep loose neutral gear; how I started the story how Chuck Nunn Junior done wronged the man that wronged him all over again; and how at a point in time,

which is where we live at, if the sucker'd asked me,

we all, me and civilians and Woman and old lone listening sky-eyed Ranger, we all crossed the thin line and slept. Aloft. How we dreamed a community dream of Chuck and Mona May Nunn's good luck boy Chuck Junior, riding his own mixer and might and absent purpose high, chasing a temper, a Daddy, Simple Ranger's deSoto and farm, an everything of flora, sheep, soil, light, elements, through the windy fire of Oklahoma's roaring, watching stars. Now go on and ask me if we wasn't sorry we ever woke up. Go on.

28

Itinerary's Control
Norma Cole

FORMS OF THE VERB TO MAKE ALMOST ALWAYS INCLUDE THE EYE
for instance the bird is watching the eye or the eye is looking
at the bird
presence of the eye in the text is witness to having done
the other is the stolen eye remembered
the eye is often in the hand
or is provided with a hand
which might introduce light, a double chandelier
permanent, ephemeral, the eye is what touches things

collusion: to doubt is to touch
so the hand supports the eye
being an eye the hand can penetrate line or skin
surface or space
being in the eye
tending towards vision

use: let it be a drawing
being careful
a world without color
sense is opposed to the literal sense hidden in it
figure is description of world with portrait in it
first geometry then portrait

number, space, emotion, gift
custom is our nature
by nature so different
numbers imitate space
experience study

Norma Cole

PARABOLA LEADS TO FABLE, COUNTRY AS THEATER, HISTORY AS SCENT
call it itinerary or complication it exists for urgency
a corresponding distraction expanding from what to
theory makes its heroes
a yellow curtain blocks the view of the lake
the flowers formed a yellow curtain
attracting force absorbing available forces
hid them and wore them stormed willed maintained
thinking act towards acted thought is bait

Don't look directly at this skin between the wood and the bark
baited thought surprises blocks bruises take location will separates
charm reorganized is recognized just so setting out
owe that work disorder to exasperation
found a body in the lemony depths of the frozen lake
and later in the center of Rome the same body
windows cut through walls on one condition only mountains
photographs setting out one or two little things
weather framing for margins adorable definitions forfeit

Double as much as you like traversing glacial alpine sands
its specific balance active diffuse it's these who enter dreams
handwritten grottos and castles placed a name on the line
of rupture and defense opposition's annihilation a modest hill
serve as stepping stone to city's base without the same defenses
ready all projections from ambush dialectical profile of these hills
managed water compensates for walls red rock tower barrier
time winds invisible lines connecting knowing almost certain
smiling station stretch to middle tremble honey so strong it burnt
long after the sound its order none asleep in ritual fair watch

———————

MARGINAL COVERED GRANITE BACK TO MAINTENANCE
little to front water without depth
single anthem long and bitter
history come from cultivation
lightning hit the cross or dust nearby

30

terraced surface of roads palm divided song elided
salt notes orange of algebra
objects remote out of itinerary's control
water horizon rockbed specific to time as to place
first sight second sight does ego pictor hold the tone
full stop like being sung to
and after a time the landscape stamped permanently on her
never to think of it again

TIME IS SLEEPING IN THAT WHITE STONE SENTINEL
dark content
and comes back
shakes shadows value
words inconlusion
white amidst the other
simple present

THE SKY IS BUSY WRITING WRENCHING
night and left is not enough
which world is this—
busy sky
animals walking by

Let nothing go unsaid
slashed did not go unsaid
although the music is intermittent
wrists must be named
daughter and son
(they married young)

Norma Cole

The sky is burning
writing wrenching night
and left is not enough
which world is this—
burning sky

ATTRIBUTE A THEORY OF DIRECT AND DISCONTINUOUS ACTION
to actions of a place without volume
the children have gone with the driver or piper
into the daily less flat thoroughly walked
unable to isolate matter from its phenomena
discontinuity jumps even out of time
increasingly articulate that matter in flight
consider the notion of ether
struck by its character of artifice
by definition limitless, a continuum
these are its properties, it surrounds us
we're surrounded by absence of mass
it has not been permitted mass
but continuity having been denied matter
they're even

REJECTS FROM VINCENNES (DFA)

operant and cooperant ironed to ice I plead your case to dust

meet the hand that burns

notes in another hand: these notes are in the hand reflections
towards reading

an excellent soup I will not repeat this qualification the soup
must always be excellent

regarding the deception of numbers

but the heart spoils, nature turns . . .

so long kept naked in danger of being entered robbed the dampness
will cause the contents of the lower room to spoil most becoming
to my state send complete or not at all this language found at the
bottom of the stair to disavow for the last time listen I repeat

a new number placed in the blank does it mean a number if it does
mean something write it in white if it does mean something put in
the blank space that I'm brilliant if not that I'm crazy I won't
let on that I know but will act crazy as usual

never forget you have longer to spend living I know it's been decided
a number at the head of a letter I've decided to sign nothing do
everything sleep on the floor stone and enclosed a date mouth is
all I can say look you transposition fucking illusion universe entire
isn't delicious were the styles improved everything would be improved
sometimes giving what we do not have but we do not hold to that
fanciful little lesson

———————

Norma Cole

ROSE EYES

"And I as metteur en scène am inferior . . .
realizing as I go to fold this letter that (they)
absent in the beginning are present in the end
having without my mentioning it returned while I wrote
pleased, dotted with confetti."

ether having been formed in the image of matter
commas to reconcile the irreconcilable
fire keeps matter in volume, something displaced, something unresolved

rose eyes leaf countless music stem center
berthed full dream or weeping
bend to moving sleeping

"swiftly as waters flow down the Rhône" nothing this foam turns
undesignated distance universe drowns sails cutting winter's thunder
"what price" solitude's white priceless considered canvas

black wind
foot any way
climb without sticks or jars

sun on sand
sleeping battle
one a landscape

figure either worth a breath
shadow pipes horizon's downpour
riddled quicksand "That I cut here . . .

threshold's emblem
black receding pace
a window

here is the ritual—extinguish this fire
with your hands—locked in a vault
clarity's voice alters space

a change of climate
reasoned real or not
the second time aloud

I am not cured and I don't know why
other hath not the world nor stars
a stone to itself

whence the initial figure is recovered
modelled creature of its work
literal creature measured

whose wings finally
water or light meeting without recognition
having walked in the waters of that certainty

resistance as far as the island
water or light pouring out of that tree
am for working

small change to place in your mouth
an elementary task
"connoissant l'attachement"

to transform them into channelled cities
what clearer sign than
water or light being first

"here I am in the process of changing
this temporary home for another
also temporary"

this elemental task
so little corresponding
to our restricted life

certificate of professional aptitude
from the public instructor
X indicates the capitol

Norma Cole

rose eyes muscle some laziness work rests
silence's rock called iron gate
that music holds up

almanac of illusion
not from as you said
looking at the moon

meaning squared
blows stars off course
fort de l'est

rose eyes minus music
meet resistance muscle covers

The Way Home
Trevor Winkfield and *Harry Mathews*

IMAGINATION MOVES BY ANGLES, along a black line inscribed on a white ground that is itself bordered by blackness. The mind rests when it comes to identifiable objects athwart or alongside this line: chewable wood pellets, for instance, or a woman catching minnows. The imagination then faces, after many other obstacles, a choice it cannot avoid: whether to engage the identifiable object—that is, face its identity as a clear or coded sign that will help the imagination round the next angle—or to accept it as no more than an occasion for rest, something to lean an elbow on while drawing fresh and not necessarily metaphorical breath. For instance, the woman catching minnows may be simply an image of pleasantly inconsequential country work, hardly significant to the passerby except as a pretext for pastoral-minded relaxation (an effect heightened by the

37

skirts drawn up in her right hand above her bright, reflected knees); or she may turn to him and speak.

One class of objects provides the imagination with peculiar confusion and, perhaps, opportunity: the class of objects that can be recognized but not named, that strike the voyager as having every right to claim a place in the real world (the real world of the imagination) but whose context he cannot remember or conceive of. Think of a rectangular box whose six sides, made of composition board, are separated from each other by spaces five-eighths of an inch across. No magnet, twine, or loosened screw connects them, and yet the box keeps its shape in front of our eyes without straining our reason or our belief.

Can we associate objects such as this with the moment in which desire is conceived? Are they desire's catalysts or its companions? In the real world, the real world of the imagination, the appearance of such objects operates, or allows the voyager to operate, a reversal of elements: for example, day will turn to night, and not necessarily the night of dreams. More simply, darkness will replace light, as though the white ground, out of some sublimely appropriate courtesy, had surrendered to the blackness bordering it. No loss is felt at this moment, and no confusion. The reversal and the surrender produce, it is true, a surprisingly new context, but clearly this context has been created in response to an imperious need. The voyager knows that in the reality of his imagination he cannot hope to understand his need except through an exploration of the context that has been created for this very purpose. So he has no sense of confusion. He may have a sense of desire, and of the fear that goes with desire (that school of flitting minnows). More probably, he has little sense of anything except the darkness that gives the new object such frosty brightness.

At times objects will distract and finally disappoint him. They will give rise to graceful or interesting explanations. Thus a group of inanimate, irregular solids will be seen through a screen of swaying vines, and the traveler, who has after all not slept for days or years or even since the time of his birth, will rest his eyes (and his nose, his tongue) on these vines, becoming ridiculously pleased with himself when he discovers they are not vines at all but the little green clusters of bastard toadflax or the slender blackish stalks of some fern he remembers from moister, warmer climes. He forgets the chewable wood pellets.

Mr. Maltmall had spent the greater part of his life, perhaps every moment since his birth, in shadowy, imaginary voyage. He flitted precariously at the hub of time's wheel like a hummingbird motionlessly voyaging at the center of a spoked, nameless flower. The spokes of the flower sharpened his engagement with life, hovering pointedly on the periphery of his vision like the figures on a clock face or the circle of constellations on an astrological calendar. They reminded him that he had committed himself to a ceremonial of limited duration, so that while they did not confine him, out of the knowledge of his finiteness he kept his enthusiasm at a whirring pitch, like a partisan mounting guard on a quiet night in territory occupied by the oppressor, like a mandarin rewriting salutary laws that neglect and misrule have left a shambles.

He held himself straight, with a slight bend of alertness in his knees. Not lean or fat, he gave an impression of despondent strength, with his wide, bent shoulders. His beard, once thoroughly black, had turned brownish and was mixed with sparse white hairs. When he was offended, his lips and the tip of his nose looked blue against his florid face. He gestured and walked with considered slowness, as if not to offend in turn. He spoke in a harsh, broad voice pitched agreeably low.

Sometimes, as he considered deeds, prospectuses, contracts, an apparition would form in the chinks of the print, delineated by the cascade of spaces flowing through terms of payment and mortgage allowances. (The words by no means bored him, lively as they were with promises of building, exchange, and newly roofed lives.) Amidst these technicalities first a white haze, then a white possibility emerged in the background of the page: a waterside of reeds and redwing blackbirds, sun-warmed shallows glittering beyond, apparently roiled by the swoop of an oar—but it was too shallow there for an oar, something else was being dragged through the fertile water, a pole, or the bared foot of a wader. Beyond the reeds, beyond the fine bunched type, Mr. Maltmall assembled an event out of whiteness and light, the way a starwatcher connects a constellation from dispersed bunches of stars.

The scene he had thus encountered or constructed in his attentive, imaginary travels provoked a sense in him less of desire than of hopeful curiosity. He felt that something new had been promised him, new, agreeable, and perhaps illuminating. The promise immediately restored his gift for noticing small, attractive anomalies in the course of his ordinary life. At lunch his place was set with a fork to the left of his plate, another fork to the right of his plate. On his way to the beach, a short clothesline sagged inexplicably with the weight of a single stiff, fluffy diaper.

Some of his friends were already smacking a ball over the volleyball net set up on a level area of off-white sand. "Walt the Malt!" they cried when they saw him. He took his place among them. His teammates appreciated the sharp accurate smashes that he made using the outside of his fist. He played willingly enough, although he was never completely absorbed by the game. He liked best the moments when he tossed the ball high in the air to serve and looked up into the hazy summer sky. That afternoon, turning away from the net after a point-winning smash, he saw a boy and girl down the beach hitting a shuttlecock back and forth in high, slow parabolas and wished that he could join them.

The whipped paddle, the shuttlecock's lazy flight: real play. After the team changed sides, the children were constantly in view. The

sun drooped behind dunes; one swipe sailed the white-plastic feathers into its tilted rays, which seemed to catch and hold them at the apogee of their flight. Walt was reminded of a high note near the end of a solo by John Coltrane, sustained with sweetly inhuman intensity. The volleyball hit Walt on the nose. He clenched his eyes. In blackness, lines of brilliant light streamed outwards from a twirling, shadowy center that he longed to cling to, at least until his nose forgave him. He wiped his eyes. Bouncing from his face, the ball had been retrieved by an alert teammate. He had not lost the point. It was his turn to serve.

Subsiding twinges in his buffeted eyes looped red, readable strands against the gold-showered sky: an old woman with a staff was prodding three sheep towards a marketplace. He blinked and tapped the ball far into the opposite court. The red scene, quickly gone, recalled to him the morning's waterside apparition. It had been very different. The red scene held no promise, he knew it at once to be only a relic of some childhood story, of no use to him now even as a place to rest and breathe. The battledore partners were calling it a day.

The air cooled, and evening cooled the tones around him—pale gray sand, blue-gray ocean, black-and-whitening beach grass, the volleyball black when tossed against the sky. Walt Maltmall: he silently pronounced his name with bitterness and contempt. Playing ball looked to him like playing at still-growing childhood; and he resembled rather the aged, disheveled, waddling gull that was methodically exploring litter on the emptying beach. After his friends said goodbye, he shut his eyes, making literal his feeling that he was losing his sight, his feeling that the only living sensation in him was a thoroughly blind urge to follow something—something that was running away from him, something tender that might be caught, torn to pieces, eaten, held against his tearless cheeks. He hated this urge, which had the reddish blackness of rage, and hated his self-hatred. Stars faded against the maroon depths of his eyelids.

Fading or not, the stars restored a sense of space outside the restricted corridor of his imagined pursuit. He considered the new space opening around him, soon huge enough, and the objects it presented as they slid past him. He saw a baby fastened to the nipple of an adolescent girl's breast, poking it compulsively and regularly with tiny fists. The capital letter *S* stood alone and high against a landscape of pale orchards and vine-covered hillslopes. A solitary joker in cap and bells lay on a wooden table painted a brownish shade of maroon. His father was showing him how to thread a rod used for fly fishing. An ad he had once placed in the Sunday *Times* displayed a photograph of a thirty-room shingle house with broad lawns surrounding it. Seen from behind, a young woman dexterously plugged and unplugged the connections of a hotel switchboard. A cake encrusted with green rock candy proposed a bright red plum at its center.

There is no object so soft but that it makes a hub of the wheeled universe. There is no shadow so slow but that it makes a wing of the wheeling soul. There is no thought so precarious but that it makes a word of the drenched shadow. There is no pit so shallow but that it

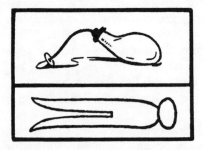

makes a chasm of the sensible intelligence. There is no drink so wet but that it makes a desert of the dying voice. There is no sonatina so short but that it makes a fluency of the chartered streets. There is no brood so scattered but that it makes a hearth of the dying miser. There is no man, no woman so lost but that she makes a goal of the attentive will. No book so sold but that it makes an expectation of the obsolescent barman. No dish so bland but that it makes a lesson of the deserving dog. No Walt so Malt but that he makes a shadow of the universal wheel.

And that woman, that young woman picking mallows, if that is what she's doing—in a vague way, he dreaded banishing her to the hillsides, where he would no longer hear the fretting of her corduroyed inner thighs. He had reached an angle of his black line and was afraid of becoming stuck there. He did not want to rely on her to help him around the angle, to turn his journeying gaze down the next stretch of black band. What he somewhat less vaguely imagined he had to do to negotiate the turn was to step away from what lay in front of him, to turn his back on it and then keep turning until he had swung around into the direction of the next straight passage. He imagined her helping him if he chose this more extensive but more yielding shift onto his new course. She would broaden or even complete his intended revolution by providing an angle of darkness equal to his own darkness. Addressing it, he might have to relinquish breathing completely, his mouth buried in blackish fern, his nose pinched shut in her pleasurable native grasp. Such symmetry made no sense, it meant not vaguely but precisely dark to dark, his eyes (whether open or shut) also stifled by beach balls—hers. He followed her into the hills.

Deep into the night, he told himself that he had no excuse not to be at work on time. His imaginary journeying demanded actual common-or-garden movement, not sitting around contemplating the situation. Perceptions came as accessories to keeping appointments, to reading the fine print. Movement meant shuttling day after day between familiar places, which all the same were tinged with a kind of mental dye if they promised to coincide with his secret itinerary of desire. It had been the same during his childhood when places to go meant the rooms of his parents' apartment or at most the buildings on his grandmother's farm. His grandmother had built a sheepfold with a protective cupola over it and had painted the cupola with green polka dots scattered across a coal-black field. Walt as a boy knew the minute he saw it that the covered fold would be a refuge; and he soon settled himself inside it in moments of neglect, crouching and daydreaming among stuffy ewes and lambs, many of them shorn and ticketed for sale and slaughter.

Was there truly a black angled line, inscribed on a white background, along which he perceptibly moved? Or was he still at his point for departure, the readiness of departure forming the substance of his life rather than any calculably real advance? He pictured himself as a runner in an everlasting crouch, one foot on the starting block; or launched into a first stride, neither foot touching the ground and destined never to touch the ground. Whom was he racing against? All those he knew stood behind him or along the nearby sidelines, while those he imagined knowing were waiting on the far side of the finish line.

A foot straining with the promise of motion: can that ever be called motion? Shouldn't the foot disappear entirely in the swift blurred revolution of the runner's stride (and there was no stride either, only the race)? Walt said to himself and to some others, "I say that's what it's all about." Then why did he insist on feeling like a mere foot, and sometimes like a shoe, full of the best and most useful intentions?

He lay down in the moist, black ferns. He had hoped to reach a lake, but he'd stumbled into this marsh in the darkness, which fell so quickly these mid-September days. He didn't really mind. The marsh mud was like lake-bottom mud in its warm clayiness and its sweet, mulchy smell. He wiggled his fingers and toes into it, his nose, his pelvis, and at last his tongue. (He expected the mud to taste shittily bitter; it proved almost bland.) He bit down into the clay. He thought: now stop breathing, keep burrowing your face into this muck, let yourself go, let it all go. Would that be so bad? The mud still kept some of the sun's warmth, its squelchiness was consolation made matter. Where else is there to go? And if I go there, how will I explain the way I look?

He nestled in the mud bed like a shoe tree inside a closeted black shoe. He knew he could not stay there. He had lost the least intention of motion, of travel, he had forgotten the daylight and the succession of amusing days. He became aware of this himself because against the dark lining of his eyelids he saw nothing but mudlike darkness. He was enjoying himself. He found it ecstatically soothing to be able to look at what could not be called nothing, since there was a blankly black something there, but a something shorn of every physical and metaphysical detail, a mass of empty soft flat indifferent darkness. When he was through enjoying himself (a moment he had to pick willfully), he stood up out of the mud and returned to the living world of his imagination.

So much remains to be told, so much remains to be disguised in order to be told. The image of the black shoe cannot be right, even to describe a condition of solitude. There is never a condition of solitude. It is as if a cat arrived in a town and discovers that it has become a ghost town. Signs along the main street indicate that the town is now in the power of mouse ghosts, who threaten all cats with suffering and death. And the newcomer cat is duly made to suffer and die. He becomes a ghost in turn; he is thus able to reassert his predominance over the mice who had so gleefully persecuted him. So Walt Maltmall, glittering blackly with the muck of oblivion, returned with no apparent stealth to his bungalow and breakfast.

A moment occurs in the dawn twilight when the oppression of darkness and the oppression of light are symmetrical, although our dread of light is greater because we know that is what now threatens us. At that moment Walt diverted himself with abstract concepts, like dialectic, process, or signification. These concepts became or replaced the familiar wayside objects of the category "things to lean against." To emerge from this state of abstraction, Walt needed certain omens: a red knot, a patch of windlessness, an agreeable stench, something conspicuously if loosely recurrent, like the displacements of a lawnmower outside the deli he was now passing. He could conveniently adapt what he came across (the knot could be one in a painted board) but he needed to focus on these reassuringly tangible things in order to realign the disordered self he had knowingly left to one side when he resorted to generalities.

Walt was modern enough in his way. He knew that the money he made was no more than worldly acknowledgement of his commitment to playing the work game. He disliked poker because, when he played the play game, he resented having his decisions judged according to the same principle. (He also hated losing.) He knew

45

perfectly well that work and play were fictions, mirror-faceted shoes on the runner's feet; whereas knees, nude and evasive, promised more genuine significances.

But when Walt began looking for omens, he found his awareness obfuscated by anticipations of matters and people to be dealt with during his forthcoming day—matters of money and pride. The anticipations then revived memories: memories not of material events but of old fantasies, which replayed themselves as black-and-white movies in an utterly dark, undefined space. Once, taking the form of an adolescent girl, he opens the door of the guest room and finds his grandparents in gravely ecstatic copulation. The young girl does not know whether to shut the door as softly as she opened it or to drape herself like a film of cream across their grizzled bodies. Their grizzled hair and skin have stirred her by reminding her of the skin on the faces of ewes as they entered a domed fold at twilight. In another movie he finds himself in a junkyard littered with battered although almost new pie tins and old knives of widely differing sizes but identical design. This movie has an obsessive voice-over: "The very word is like a knell, the very word is like a knell . . ."

As he approached home the needed omens manifested themselves. When he reached his front door he spent a moment looking through the peephole, which offered him a slightly blurred but undistorted view of the interior, with at its center the ball on the newel post, reflective as a mirror, shadowy as a closed eye. He was looking forward to his breakfast, after possibly a quick washup: frozen tangerine juice, Del Monte peaches, instant coffee with a drop of Carnation milk in it (remember not to cheat and suck a delectable jet out of the punctured can), a cigarette between coffees, the smoke at his elbow rising tenuous and straight towards the ceiling. He longed to have a mutt that would sidle up to him at such moments and lie across his feet. He was aware at the same time of bristling with aversions to all the pure and impure dog breeds of the world. He opened the front door and entered his home contentedly. He stopped to consider his barely distinguishable reflection in the varnished globe on the newel post: it looked like his memory movies before they coalesced into objects limp or stiff.

He took off his mud-caked shoes, washed off the mud, filled their insteps with crumpled newspaper, and set them out on the west deck to dry. He straightened up too quickly after putting them down, so that the blood drained out of his head and he had to lean on

the railing of the deck. Shutting his eyes, he had a glimpse in the maroon darkness of the woman at the waterside, the minnow fisher, standing up to her ankles in the glittering pond. She raised her skirt to her hips, pointed her right leg a little to the side, and loosed a sun-spangled quivering shaft into the roiled water at her feet. And ever shalt thou yearn. At least he hoped to. Or rather he expected to look forward to—he mentally and quickly made the correction since he knew hope to be no more than a barb on the hook of desire; he had no intention of ending up like a trout on his father's line, even if he knew that soon he would be considerately released.

Miss Minnower! She probably got along with all kinds of dogs, knowing when to leash and unleash them, when to let them chase cats and when to let the cats chase them. If only she would look back, cast wide her arms, let her frizzled hair fall behind her ears and show her face to him and the generous sun! Teeth and all.

He knew that he must move on from this scene. It too now belonged to the past, the past of expectations. Nothing wrong with that. Half way through his peaches he sensed that light had begun shining on the path in front of him. The view remained one of gloom and murk, but he was fairly sure of a division of the dark grayness into lighter elements withdrawing right and left and blacker elements starting to concentrate in the center of the picture, soon to become a way, his way. He sat and waited for more light, or more clarity, as though waiting for a roll of the dice in Monopoly, which as a boy he had played addictively if never with much intelligence.

He did not have to wait long. In the dissolving grayness a black band led straight ahead of him towards the next angle. He could even see what awaited him there: a familiar scene, a country fair, in the midst of which he noticed a broad, slowly turning wheel connected with some game of chance, a wheel segmented according to the succession of the constellations, with what seemed to be a captive plastic hummingbird fluttering in a shaft of air expelled from the center of the wheel. He had barely started down the path when he felt a light tap on the side of his head. Looking round, he discovered his beloved grandmother in her red cloak and pointed red hat. She was leading him and his fellows to the fair, prodding him considerately behind his ticketed ear, leading them to the country fair past freshly winnowed fields.

Four Poems

Laura Moriarty

In the new environment in real time
The question of material means
The actor carries his piece of the city
Of facades and columns, faces
A hand holding a letter
Without intonation, without length
Squandering words and money
There is no accumulation of time
In the new meaning acquired by common
Phrases like we don't all come from there
But are made to seem the same by longing
As a way to engender a situation
The eager sacrifice of our more complex
Rhythmic needs to putting down this form
In the new version we give it all away

*   *   *

We here become citizens
The ordinary quality of the sun
Makes our day indistinguishable
From what you see to what you want
To see exaggerated as a decision
The appearance of which was among
Our rights the only inviolable
Illusions preserved by our constitution
We here appeal to you as if you
Framed by the force of your caption
Were able to make those determinations
We now know are made on the basis
Like a street in the middle of nowhere
Of interest because it is present
We here see nothing beyond our control

*   *   *

Fitting this shot against one including
The uncontrollable desires of others
Through any degree of distortion
Or of oneself for the material
The speech without response they speak of
Luckily not us we think in unison
Starting again they don't count
The transparency assumed between us
Fitting against itself with a consciousness
Of being live which is more than life
Allowed to go unspoken indefinitely
As now the mouth seems to form
Around the stuff given then taken up
But less than what was actually swallowed
Fitting as it does against the heart

CUENCA

Someone real dies
Being reminded of dying

The crowd gave way around them cheering. Children marched. She spoke in two languages. There were echoes and distortion. The word for eye in her language was like the word for gold.

As I imagine her she is already gone. She had a place in mind. She went back to the other world. That night I saw her again in a report. She spoke as if of the future. Her features were indistinct. They were in a square in the corner. Heads filled the picture. I couldn't recognize myself. I could have been anybody.

We see her through screens and lenses flattened out and framed importantly as if in gold. I couldn't see her. Felt numb. Saw nothing. Every few seconds the picture changed.

I realize how little I know

She describes her home. It's like a wooden bowl. It's hot in the valley. That spring we came across. The bodies out of the river. The movement. You can see in this portrait behind my head indistinctly but it's green and clear. I was a writer in that language.

Or alternately I am not that one
Going mindlessly forward

Wearing a flower in her chest she spoke to the assembly. Later in the makeshift hospital. There are records. There are sheets taped to the walls. As if bronze were poured onto the whole. There was a stiffening of waves. Her culture also uses the rose in this way.

There is no private life. She looked back at me with that oddly televised stare. Her name for the last set of notes. The radio was powerful. The other radio came in under it. One can often hear her on the local station. There is continuity. There is an absence of rhetorical pathos.

But does how you go
Matter is what you become

A badge or name card or something else written. The script was a personal one. A second image as of a repeated portrait occurred as a fault of reception. That was the memory of what was to become the event. Perhaps it was the same. The infectious power of a sequence including what was not planned. I thought it was torture to see her that way.

Her dress and hair stand out against the gold. An entire room is pictured. I had imagined someone. She was that person. At places the light made the gold look silver. The black was static. What was going to happen had happened.

The crowd gave up, putting its head in its hands. They lost their identity as a crowd. They were each identifiable. Others were in love. Crowds can love. Perhaps it was only crowd love as when a woman like a painting or a country dies in its ruins.

The picture they have of you
Someone real caught

So that later in its houses before its televisions the crowd could still

51

be seen in thought as well as mechanically. Or in words. Another in a long line of deaths. She made a beautiful report.

There is a portrait in a broken gold frame. Glass or plastic is held in front by tape. It seems makeshift. It is a reproduction. The face is indistinct. There are two faces. Paper or gauze or a fine plastic mesh sticks to the face in layers. The ink is smeared. The process stopped. It seems to continue. The portrait doesn't reach to the edge of the frame. The flower can be seen clearly between her dress and her chest.

> Without a time or place
> Decisions unmade plans
> Being taken so completely

You own voice played back approaches the effect of the remembered speech of someone absent. Questions are asked by rote as in a catechism. The responses from another catechism change the tone. They are wanton. The children got through by chance. They were stunned by the attention. I wonder how to interpret her constant cheerfulness.

> This has been called dancing

Equally absent I am interviewed in a dream. I know this writer. The questions are a source of control like happiness. We accede to it gladly. We react. We are the public facts.

There aren't any children in the next version. They weren't really like children. The event or act was given as if she were present. We knew her so badly we are mistaken in imagining who is left. The new person reads a list of demonstrations.

> But we are the same
> Someone real gets older

The crowd opens up before her. Seeing is entering. We believed it. Having invented a character we miss her as she looks back at us. Without a body except by inference. Smiling perpetually from there. I am not here. We endow her with everything she doesn't have. We include life.

From The Letter Left to Me
Joseph McElroy

THE WOMAN HOLDING, then handing over the letter to this poised, dumbfounded fifteen-year-old: is the letter also *hers*? She's been busy, her hands are anything but idle here in a room of a city apartment, but today what belongs to her hands? The words are echoey-bare—a room, a city apartment—they sound rugless, not yet moved-*in*, don't they?—which is not this place at all.

My father has written a letter to me, a letter *for* me. He isn't here—which is the way with letters, I think, (like an alarm signaling my distraction from whatever I ought to be thinking about). But this letter *has* been here. How long? (I'm building backward naturally.) Was it waiting for him to be not here? It's been in a drawer of the desk right here in the living room, that open lower drawer there.

A drop-leaf desk made by an early-nineteenth-century cousin of my mother's. I would sit and lean my elbow on it—write a letter, say, that I'd been reminded of more than once—though I don't forget things—a thank-you note—which could have been why I wrote it at my parents' desk, on the spur maybe of being asked again. This desk reacted to me with an experienced give but a subtle solidity in its joints and grooves and finished sockets, its dark-glossed grains. To close it up, with its pigeonholes and miniature drawers, you raise the drop leaf. So its underside, with a tiny brass lock that shines like gold, becomes the front panel banked into a groove along the edge of a mantel-like top. A China vase—orange, with two or three flowers in it, and nearly taken for granted by me—stands on that top surface, which, I see, roofs the pigeonholes below whether the desk is open *or* closed.

But when was it not open? I would put my hand under the drop leaf and find the dingy key where it hung half-turned in the lock and I would lift the drop leaf and close the desk and slide the two narrow boards that had been supporting the drop leaf in out of sight except for their brass knobs, and I would work the lock. The desk was not kept locked. The lower drawers had locks, too, but this same key.

Did my mother know of my father's letter?

She didn't need to say a thing getting up from the desk lightly and alone and turning to me in the same just and discovering motion. (*I* knew what must be in the envelope.) When she wouldn't normally have *gotten* up. Though might turn halfway toward me in her *chair* as if a part of *her*, natural and questioning, had come into the room.

She didn't need to say a thing. And it's as *if* she didn't. The January winds off the harbor ripple certain windowpanes, the living room paled around us half-wittingly. My impatience I keep hidden, it is mean and my own. This open lower drawer of the desk tilts downward full of folders. Jammed-looking is what it is—inner monument to recordkeeping, this weighty, rather beloved (at the moment) drawer, stricken, threatening because of being temporarily just left pulled out. She's terribly energetically systematic, she is managing, but so finely that it is like silence or an absence similar to that. Who was it called me "poised"? Someone—a woman who didn't know my father and came to the funeral because of my mother.

My mother hands over the envelope and I feel her. What happens now? Is it already in our living with each other? Nothing's up to me unless I think I can now have anything I want. I am standing *with* her; this is about all I am doing. I'm sure it's some deal between us, she'll do her part. I could be on stilts assimilating into this living room where she is; but I'm the one this envelope is meant for. Am I to make something of my "envelope" now?

She sees that I get my envelope. We live here; but this is an appointment, her voice out here in the living room a minute ago called my name, it had me in mind in part: I thought of whole intentions outside me, of penalty, the floor plan, her voice when she sings.

But that summoning sound of activity elsewhere turns out to be honor, not fresh danger days and hours after my father's amazing death. For when I call, "Yes?" and locomote briskly from my room into the living room, I get this envelope.

Is it some paper of release, Graduation a year and a half ahead of time? (But my diploma when the time comes will be like everybody else's, and this isn't the headmaster, grizzled, pink cheeked, a "Doctor.") This dear woman and I are unbalanced equals; I might spell it out. My living, wildly valued mother. As I take the envelope, my thumb below my name, I just pick up elsewhere on the envelope her hand, her fingers leaving it.

Fingers of someone else. And her *husband* has just about vanished. He is "no more no more." He is gone. A goner! What about it? I have the words, some; and I can say I loved and admired my father. (I "wished him well," if I am to be listened to.)

In the living room, the first day of the letter, I don't want to be *in* this silence of his. But then I do—I know it, I know that much. It's closer than my mother's waiting scent, his absence, the dumb plummet of his absence. Closer upon me than my clothes—this brown corduroy shirt I got for Christmas that I like so much I can practically settle for it. The room lives with her own near scent, clean, speaks it, or holds it, it is *about* her, I wouldn't know what it is, it isn't just "scent" or soap, I might name it like some olfactory microscoper. I know *his* smells, I kiss his cheek. But what *is* his smell? Now lost to this room, these cold windows, he who liked "the way" my mother "lived."

Words better than mine into the phone to a woman friend of my mother's calling to see "how he's doing"—three, four days ago (what's fast and what slow here?) And I said, "My father passed away last night." *I* who of all people know enough to say "died": yet said "passed away." I'm on the phone, I feel that person's good surprise, the push of her spirit at *my* end of the line—welcome her wide, generous mouth!—a musician calling from "out of town," her eyes easy, strong (lazy? happily remembering sleep?), her heavy gray hair created with big veins of black color, which are hair too. Curly bangs, bang curls upon her forehead; last summer's coarse, tanned throat and blue work shirt, too: a *musician* (the skill and beauty in that do take your mind); a confident, pointed force of a person but less quick on the phone the other night; a *blunt* "nice person"— "hard," it comes to me—who gave me a message for my mother, said things to *me*, says my mother's first name to me, *and* doesn't ask to *speak* to my mother. This fleshly woman-voice, her husband was my mother's mentor once upon a time, bushy-haired conducting in a summer barn in Massachusetts and crazy in a way about tuning up and "making music" and telling others what to do.

I've come through those quite powerful words I had with his wife, phone call's over and done with, one of many, a sort of business; so now three days or so after I broke the news to the friend of my mother's powerfully, I finger the long-size business envelope, it has my father's voice in it, I fear. Never mind *passed away* (my mother wouldn't say that either—but my father's family *would*, I see, as if those ready words, loathed and officious as I spoke them, *relieved* us of words). Yet words *in* me: "passed away": maybe he hasn't "died." I'll bet he has.

My father is not so much dead as not living. Or not here. This sizable room was sometimes his — reading, reading so well, so sweepingly, books, flipping pages; aiming his frown, commanding himself, one trousered leg crossed over the other, his black shoe stirring from something going on in him, like a smile: for he, and not only he, can smile as he *frowns*. When it is the newspaper he's reading, his head moves defendingly, welcomingly, strategically at large in the scope of the shoulder-wide page and its columns: I can tell he's looking at a picture, I come behind the couch, it's a photo of a Jap atrocity, I put my hands on him, the molded shoulder padding, he's home from work, bending over him I smell his sweet daylong scalp.

I've seen lunatics stand in this room. Beside furniture somehow. A wing chair to the elbow, lampshade to the tits, coffee table to the shin, drop leaf to the fly. I'm measuring the room as ours, my mother's and mine. Standing is one thing people do in the living room. Its size has a spirit, too, a room with openings into other rooms.

I am inside and at least get the idea that I could be standing outside. If she gave it to me, the envelope is mine. Mine to open anyway.

We're polite. But every few hours she's different, too, amid my father's death, which schedules everything to perfection and puts yesterday on top of tomorrow if I try to think when things happened, though I don't at all think her different when all has stopped or has left us as if she would now be just her.

Yesterday cooks a moistly good-to-look-at meal "with her left hand" practically, as *he* noted her airy motions at dinner time: food heals the insides where my *father* is, actually — oh "helpings" we say are "generous." She gets it onto the dining room table with my help; doesn't tell me to sit up straight, I'm hungry politely in my *father's* place; and I speak, and she nods with a blind courtesy, or such learning nearness — and I'm at a loss facing her reserved grief, scared, tempted by it; talks with me, we can't believe the "behavior" of an elderly battle-axe by marriage who showed up late to drive with us to my father's church for the funeral, griped about my mother's directions, condemned the trip over here from Manhattan, the subway ride that had been full of doubt (who was twenty-three years in China, her late husband my mother's cousin with Standard Oil, and now doesn't have a husband to have a funeral *for* or children to bury her — quite separate from all others, it came to me yesterday at the table as our interesting meal went on and it came to me that we had eaten alone together often). My mother will talk on the phone out in the hall and I can hear her not exclude me, she says "we"; she's been writing at the desk, I'm afraid to see her cry as if she has no right to, and I have not seen her cry.

What will we do now standing in the living room? We would take a trip, my mother said at the hospital, a cruise, when "this" was "over": he had "improved"; it was two days before he died.

But what will we do *now*, standing in the living room? I know, apparently—for I don't *feel* I *don't* know. I'm half *free.* You have time to spend with this. I am hearing a lot about what you do at a time like this. You live through it. You go on. You do things. I give some of it back, saying things and *hearing* things as if I've known them before. Yet am a distinguished personage right now and don't care. I am "doing my part." She lets me know this in looks more unspeakable and businesslike than sentimentally approving—yet presently recalled as unyielding tender, dryly like the faintest down upon her cheekbones.

I'm building, but backward naturally. As if this envelope upon being passed to the dumbfounded, poised fifteen-year-old is passed right back, because anything can happen if you don't know what it means. Shouldn't my mother and I open it together?

Or, standing here in the living room with an envelope in my hand, I'm free in one breath like I've achieved an unquestionable thing so beyond my *known* gifts that people in my vicinity go along with their awe in the event. Yet it's no more than entering a room to join some friends of my parents having drinks after church, and a man with a silly thought smiling on his face tells me out of the blue, "You should go to law school." Why was my father not there? He came late, from services at *his* church in another part of Brooklyn. She is a beautiful —my father said she was "a beautiful woman" and he was right—beautiful legs, "slim" (slim-*boned,* I would think for myself perhaps while he was actually talking), "tall" (which means "tall for a woman"), very dark-haired but not dark, sometimes a reserved person (come to think of it), my mother, very often so charmingly welcoming she's not generous at *all* but maybe just enjoys it. A kind person ("soul") like my father. What she did for "others." He was also stern (in his quickness) with a gentleness unwavering that could have scared me I almost grasp with the envelope and its contents in my hand held not low at thigh level or high near my face like something to talk with but at belt level: wasn't *she* some of these things? but no punster or connoisseur of slips of the tongue like him, or light quoter of things that stayed with me or I let them. "A daydreamer," he called me, speaking to another man in this living room, with me here, so I knew he had thought it before. I *saw* he had.

Maybe now she is different. (But this can't occur to me slowly and sort of fully even now when she's what she is just to me without my father to see her.) With people she's *not* reserved sometimes. Yet I don't especially know this—don't much bring it to mind standing beside her in the living room with the unchanged but comfortably empty furniture: equals, equals through being of different *bodies*, I think this is what my fingers dream moist and casual on the envelope—client/lawyer, *that* was it, but *she's* the one that needs the lawyer—and *has two*!

There's going to be more breathing room in the apartment before long but there's less now, the thought's already gone from me, for *I* go on. The light from the view is very smart light, too smart for me, her hands don't touch me, I have this envelope from my *father*. I don't know it's from my father. My mother has said, I think this was from your father. A trace of novelty outlines my skin or heart. A shiver of wit, once my father's, offers to cloak me. "Less noise from the cheap seats," it means not noise primarily, it means you don't have as much right to speak, you're young ("to say the least"). The two of *them* could be loud. Or "silly" *they* called it. A reaching, breaking laughter I happily received from my room, shouted all together at a dinner party by them and their friends and then names nearly shouted, as if for minutes on end the words I couldn't really hear in between these bursts equaled a grownup surprise-party game of silence until it couldn't be contained.

But the two of *them* weren't *wild*-loud, or loud-awful, and were admirably silly, I grasped. They "get me up" to listen to the Joe Louis fight: as if I am going in at ten o'clock to see it, a two-man (two-name) fate glittering with night, the sheerly bright living room like new weight, and the distance of a radio voice's closeness, all reported bit by bit to us who were not there with an unfolding and building and completeness of waking life, which, coming to it from bed away from this group of relaxed grownups, smelling of comfortably spicy stinky sweet drinks and smoke, I felt to be reliably thrilling, "explosive" but bleeding, or bruised, but not cruel.

Joe Louis runs his words together as if he's talking fast in the interview after the fight. He says hello to his ma, she wasn't there, she was far away listening to the radio, the grownups laughed in a friendly way, they said, *H'lo, Ma.*

The fight was an execution in its high preparation and late-night time, in my garishly awake state an entertaining side of tomorrow which I had gone some distance toward already in sleep: still, a right given me by my parents jointly, in return for Sleep First, and I never could sleep (I thought) from seven-thirty until ten, but more or less did, and woke up fast, *part* of me, as if nothing held me back for a time—I wanted my father to be happy, I always knew—and an hour later went back to bed and to sleep readily, the champion visible and quiet, hardly out of breath, amid the announcer's voice, voices near the announcer, things I could see from listening to him, not from my father and the guests commenting knowingly. The Brown Bomber looked less big in newspaper pictures, it was his smooth-shaped proportions.

It was a relief that Louis had won again. It was excellent. I went back to my room myself and slept. My mother let them talk, I felt, she's smiling, and smiling so sociably, lovably, entertainingly, or bringing in someone's glass. He liked the way she *lived. She* told me once that was what he had said. All the rooms are hers. Also hers and mine.

What do my mother and I do *different* today, this envelope in my hand? It's back to regular life, is it? But today it's a cold late-January morning, and my mother didn't have to say it—but then I figure she did—that it's from my father.

The envelope isn't birthday money from an uncle; or to be greeted like Christmas. It isn't my birthday. It is January. ("Your *envelope*"— "your Christmas envelope"—"I have your Christmas envelope upstairs," she said to the doorman Christmas Eve afternoon because he would be going off duty. He has grayish silver stripes, two, just above the cuffs of his grayish-green uniform jacket sleeves. It might be just an envelope, "*your* envelope"! My father was upstairs reading in his slippers and his bathrobe and regular clothes, alive.) Christmas was with my *father;* so it seems cheatingly months ago; but no it doesn't, it's recent, his voice is around somewhere, like Christmas: wrapping paper, slashing, ripping (yet care, polite love in the glad suspicion of "I *wonder* what *this* is") to the scent of pine branches, the aroma of sausages, coffee (which only my mother drinks), her unusually crisp buckwheat cakes that don't get soggy in syrup (How do you make them like this? my father said with his mouth full. Oh, with my left hand, my mother says) —and the two-second gasp of silence as the "loot" is exposed. (It's *just* what I *want*ed!, or she, You shouldn't have—it's beautiful.)

I'm electrified—he's in it.

Rip it open, find out what he wrote, what he said—what am I waiting for? It may be for all of us. It has my name on the envelope. I have to open it. Names aren't changing. He wrote a letter to me—*for* me—to be left for me. He left a letter. The letter is given to me three or four days after he died. She has done the job of getting it to me and I should open it here. She handed it to me. *You shouldn't have*, I think.

I have it; so my father left this for me. (I know what it is.) I'm *called* by my name on the envelope: my two initials and "last" name, and the "Jr."

This letter was typed. I *see* him typing but then I don't. I don't think he *ever* typed. I typed from the time I was seven. I should know if he did. He worked in an office high up in Wall Street, wrote figures and words in pencil on lined pads. "Tablets" the stationery store sometimes calls them. They got to be like books. He doesn't tear the sheets off them, or *I* never saw him; and they thickened with his writing. Did someone else type "up" this letter, I can't think so. What's the right thing to do? Time is fidgeting, according to my father.

Did my mother know of my father's letter? Maybe I will ask her. When was it written? I will never place anything on top of it. It was never mailed. There's no postmark, no stamp. The sender is not far away.

Together we think he was a good man and I am lucky. What is outside the room comes back and was always there. I believe that's true—thinking that way—but not coming out with it is a little like not thinking it, but it can't be.

The solid paper of the envelope on my fingers, from where we stand for a moment or two my mother and I have the embracing distances of the inner harbor, sights belonging to us if we wanted them. Right out the front windows. The Battery at the lower end (this end, where you can tell Manhattan's an island) right in front of us across the East River—large-scale, not-to-be-*trusted* nearness. "Battery" as in "stored electrical energy" (I decided). The ferry terminals low-scaled on their piers point outward—they *are* their piers. We have piers on this side, freighters loading, loading what? —for South America. I'm supposed to do something with the letter. *Have* it, maybe. Across the river, edifices of the Wall Street financial enclave gather tall-ly, where my father went to work. Noble and subtle or thin and to be taken for granted, and unlike landscape not graspably all there, those buildings are not "fine" as *people* were said to be "fine." As my *father*, who's now become the writer of this letter, was called "nicest man," and "fine," and ("to say the least") *"gentle*man" (a man in good clothes, black Chesterfield, velvet collar—lifting his hat—a derby, black and velvety hard—stiff-brimmed—on the street).

The *colors* here become ours, they're like *her*, like my mother: calm upholstery pine-green; the soft dull reds (found also among the chalks I draw with in my room somewhat messily but draw less and less); lemony greens of morning—and of *choice*, it comes to me somewhat foolishly; and pink that's really not pink because it's darkened by dusty light inside the cloth; and *dark* green that sends my eyes, my hands, to dark wood carved and used as if mined richly; and patterns in strong silk. The room is hers, she did this. My father didn't make this living room at all. But my mother made this living room for not just my father and her; yet anyway did it alone, I now see. She will "entertain" in it. The room holds the size it had but not the paint smell when it was being "decorated" a year and more ago before my mother and father moved in.

The view swung past the Statue clear to The Narrows, where the outer harbor waited. "The Narrows" is what my father calls it. Then looking around to the right with ease, we love pointlessly the Brooklyn Bridge. Though we looked beyond it.

Bounded by this grandeur, my mother's the *silent* arguer, stubborn, and delicately so, more something than I know. Others' words she might want to share—the poetry, the words, she is a poet, or poetic, *I* know, but would not come out much with old story-memories. She would seem to warmly bear the enthusiasm of others, nod with pursed-lip jollity and actual warmth at what came out of their mouths at the sights from our living room windows, the vision of Wall Street right over there, choppy waters, the Statue at night, the Bridge. She will warm to *jokes*, I will tell her a couple when I get home from school, and she secretly with a potential unpleasantness insisted on humor. I don't know if I should read her the letter here and now.

Whatever *I* decide. She didn't get one.

She did not wear a veil at his funeral. She is a "widow." That's not young enough to suit her. I think of saying with the letter in my hand, Well let's see what he's been doing—maybe he's got some news! "Woman" sounds in this slowness of the pause of my father's death, not "gal," which the women of her acquaintance will say with a casual vim comradely not so much with one another as with their whole set.

I don't know how to put it, how to get from here to my room with my letter. Time isn't short at all, but I'm stupid, I'm a dead duck: I think of him coming back, not *right* back, but it's how I happen to feel. We're looking at the letter, the thing in my hand, not each other.

My thumbnail below my name, I turned the envelope over and ran my thumb up under the flap, and I slit the envelope raggedly, methodically open with my finger. I opened the two sheets of paper and they are typed, and there's my name.

The contents were in his mind, his eyes in *front* of his mind. I feel his handwriting, his "hand." In mine.

I speak. And in my armpits to a heart on each side close to these touchy ribs comes a thought from my mother, not in words—only its twoness comes in that minute of attachment; it was maybe that love was "only" this or that—which I so can't imagine her voicing, that I *believe* it as a dangerously clear act *un*said, some sentimental vying.

The letter is dated February 22—why, it's Washington's Birthday! The letter's been in the house for months, well hasn't it? Months of his *life*. But three years ago almost! Here all the time. He had it, he might have gone and looked at it, recalled it, opened it, he's taking action but taking his time: what was *I* doing?, it was still his, his fingers took it out, unfolded it, stretched it taut, he did not scrunch it and lob it into the wastebasket that's covered in red leather embossed in gold like my bookends.

A line waits, two lines, they terribly ask something of me, or nothing, for he won't speak out loud again, I saw them, I might know them at a glance. I am afraid. That after all he *is* dead. To this my mother who does love me would say in gentle embarrassment, No— the way *her* mother used to say, Pshaw. *And* I could take it or leave it: or think I am not about to read it standing here or read it aloud. And they are *not* "lines."

I take in a *few* lines. My father's been dead three days or so, I don't for a moment know how many days. I think *"been* dead." I don't sit down, I don't read it. My mother's twin thoughts do exist, and somewhere in me they are to do with the letter being in my hand.

Now, on the day my mother has given me the envelope, I see that Gertie comes Thursdays: because my mother said, Are you going back to school tomorrow?, Gertie's coming. The letter might as well hold the answer to her question—but why *ask* me? Gertie comes every week, our not really Negro cleaning lady, small, busy, softly quick-talking, with glasses, part-Shinnecock Indian. I once called her "ma'am," trying it out wrongly. I am never here at the moment her key in the lock softly cracks the silence of the faraway front door. Come to clean "the house," run the wash through the machines and the wringers in the basement, and at the end of the day iron swiftly under the ceiling light in the kitchen; before she changes her "costume" (it occurs to me), puts on her overcoat while my mother, so much taller, pours two somewhat statuesque slender cut-glass glasses of sherry from the dining room decanter and they have a chat. My mother puts *her* glass on the enamel top of the stove, doing things. Just two *women* I fleetingly interest myself "thinking," the tall one standing, the small one seated. Family tribulations Gertie summarizes not in stories, the organ they've collected money to buy for her minister may not materialize, he may devote the money to some other purpose. Gertie ties her kerchief; it enshrines her cheeks. She is respectfully affectionate, is loyal, unquestioningly loyal is what I see I face.

But my mother has asked if I'm going back to school tomorrow, and Of *course* I am is the answer, and the letter has nothing to do with it. This is a woman who's handed me the letter. O.K., let's find out what he's been doing—find out his news! (But since when?)

But I took it away to my room, it and its envelope, he kept his torn-open envelopes with the letters in them.

I tried to read the letter slowly and it meant *too* much. I might be building something that's built, and wouldn't *that* be stupid. My forearms on my thighs, somewhat powerfully alone sitting on the edge of the bed—like sitting on the john—I'm reading with not much language of my own loose and sounding in my head—with a dramatic horror at this potential Victrola record, and with relief in the action, with fearless trivial hope—yet what can I do? I learned, I taught myself, to read, to read this page in two hands, the suspense wasn't killing me, I got up and went and closed the door.

My eyeballs became sore and hot. My face retched. It retched across its bones and life, eyesockets, pointless and hopeless. My face closed and opened with grateful helplessness. Sitting on the bed in the same position, I wept over that letter. I was in my room. I dripped on the paper. I held it in front of me. I had his voice and *had* had it. "In retrospect I am appalled by my neglect of the vistas which life has opened to me." My thoughts caroused. He would not knock. And I became *interested.* If my father had gone back to take another look, he'd have had to slit open the envelope and then use a new one. But he didn't need to lick the envelope to begin with. Did he show it to *her*? I believe he didn't.

She will still read to me. But will read letters or amusing newspaper items, a birth at the zoo, or a rave review of a play that may make her voice quaver with sentiment—will read to me in the kitchen or in the living room. To my father she will read in the living room and the bedroom. He'll say, "Let's have a little light on the subject." There's more going on in his mind.

I had plenty of time, unless there was a thing I must do at once. I'm sitting, he's gone. I know that I don't know what's quite happened to me. Which meant it had to be more than my father dying; because I did know that that had happened. Others act like they know what's going on. I accepted what had happened like a dope. ("You dope," he said out on the street, when I had left something home, a jabbing humor as if we were a larger family.) The violinist on the phone the night after my father died gave me a message for my mother, that she's thinking of her, she "loved" my father—when we come to Connecticut they have a dog now, a "too large bear-sized mutt" they found sleeping on a mountain. Did this woman on the *phone* know what had happened therefore?—when *I* was only *acting* as if I knew? I swear I felt no one else knew either. But not as some failure in them. I "knew" all this with a decided clearness of ignorance accepted by me. It was a little thrill to weep. Cry, weep—it was spasms or really gluts lifting from my stomach region down to my wretchedly ready legs. My door would never be knocked on and still I was alert to it and to the hall outside because it might be my father coming to knock and to say my name. But not while I'm reading his letter.

It said my name. It expressed the hope that I would make the most of my abilities as he said he had failed to do. It identified the two things he could leave me. A healthy constitution was one; a good education was the other. From the very first dreadful, instinctive, true time through, I could tell he was asking of me something in his *absence.* Do I mean "hard work"? The weight of this letter's gift is its giver's real absence. I will tell my mother when I come out of my room that it is a fine letter. Then I will give it to her. Or I'll say nothing and look into her eyes like a hug.

My father cited Abraham Lincoln. Lincoln made me sad here. He was himself. My father included among Lincoln's achievements "in the face of adversity" having succeeded despite being married to "an impossible woman."

I had read about Mary Todd Lincoln, I'm sure, and heard about her; I had seen her in a movie, her eyes oval, awfully dark, a small, intent person—best movie I'd ever seen, with "a story to tell," as my father once said of a musical he and my mother went to. My parents and I went to Washington. The Supreme Court opened inward like a church, glitteringly bespectacled justices far away but right there exhibited for the few minutes we stood just looking.

My father said I'm to keep a notebook, the cherry blossoms will be out, I imagine them red, we'll be away four days beyond the week of my vacation. Neat-domed, the Jefferson Memorial was new. I didn't actually write down how the seated Lincoln's knees were like cliffs but real knees with bones. At Gettysburg it got cold. George Pickett's Virginian division lost three-quarters of its men—the skinny guide didn't stop talking to take a breath—until my father couldn't wait any longer and asked where the corrals for the battery horses had been, but it was a question the guide didn't really know the answer to. Getting into the car, my father called him an "old geezer," and my mother gave a delayed, low-pitched laugh starting the car and looking to see if there was anything behind us so I thought, What was she thinking the moment before she laughed? I thought it was a mysterious liking for my father. In my desk drawer is a cardboard box of paper clips and an eraser in the shape of a parallelogram; and in the same drawer a dented, powder-seared shell from Pickett's Charge nailed to a little block of grimy pine. I am only remembering him.

He must have thought about his death. He said in his will that he might die before I reached "maturity." My mother showed me the will one day, *gave* it, it seemed, to me—to read, to take *away* and read. How personal his prediction seemed, or how reliable. A will wasn't like a talk. My father's great vim (which could flag abruptly, calmly) was the vim of a *reliable* man.

My letter *had* been in the safe deposit box, I learned from my mother; but it had been "found" by her in the living room desk. She knew the envelope.

It was him; I felt his voice.

I was overmatched, yet with an answering privilege that I picked up just holding the letter, sitting privately on my bed with my feet on the rug. When do I *do* something with this? My face feels this crying with a relief of crying itself more than interest. It's my gift, I don't try to remember it. It is a story told. Or is it hard to remember? I've read it again and again. I love it. It ends like a story.

> ... try to remember that, however keen the disap-
> pointments of youth may seem, there is nothing as
> bitter as a middle-aged man's realization that—

I could hardly get through the next words, I feel I have been told a whole life, and I do not want the letter to end. So much talk goes on, and this ends—this always ends. In grief, maybe I know grief is "about" remembering a middle-aged man's realization. But how am I going to do *that*? I want him here. What have I without him here? I felt for myself that he was more light *and* I mean more swiftly smart than other grownup men, and never-turning-away friendly. Coming home along the street in early evening and greeting me across the street where I'm playing, alive to me but not taking me away from my friends. I happened to see him race a man along a bathhouse boardwalk once, I was still in my bathing suit, splintery thin boards under my feet and grains of sand. But he is dressed, his dark blue trunks just visible rolled in his towel, and without warning, his body dropped lower, or his hips and haunches; it was not a straining sprint like mine, it covered the ground in one rush and he was dangerously laughing on the spur of the moment like loud breaths of power; and happening to come barefoot around a corner, I saw him with these others.

He was capable of being nervous, but was not jumpy, as *I* see him. His aliveness came my way in near-complete attention moderated by its everlasting thought but by patented seriousness going on here *and* elsewhere.

He plays lacrosse at college and afterward on a nationally important team in Brooklyn; I easily see him, I probably waste time seeing him, running like blazes down the sideline all by himself, like a joke, absorbed, but he is not alone, he knows where everybody is, and then down there he reaches up his stick, snaring out of a higher layer of air a long pass into the corner, twisting his stick to hold the ball and centering it all in one catapulting hammer-motion so the ball bends back across towards the goal and my father's teammate and the goalie who has come out too far hit in mid-air and the ball is somewhere else, loose, taken by someone else, who is sometimes on one team, sometimes on the other.

He had rheumatic fever as a child (a boy)—was there reliability in *that*? It left him with slight (I am always told) heart trouble and there was a "slight" defect in his heart that was referred to in the family as a "leaky valve," though I don't ever hear my mother say "leaky valve." To me it was wrong to speak of it like that. Like a mechanical thing or as if it were anybody's business. I would say "crude," and I mean "embarrassing," "dumb," "not right," "awful," "vulgar" (to use a word of my mother's). Rheumatic fever on my father's side wasn't quite diphtheria in my mother's family (*she* never came down with it)—outdated diseases, old as potions.

My *father's* mother remembers true stories and tells them with slow, southern glee. No describing of places or bodily acts, she quotes personages as if she's hearing their roundabout speeches for the first time so their words threaten us with wonders. My father's family, so much more frankly obligatory, had their ups and downs. These days of his death I'm aware of knowing more than I know in that quarter, an idleness in me or laziness whose nagging I will ignore, threatener that I could be. My father's family—secrecy didn't seem their way. He "helped" them.

They took a powerful interest in the letter left for me. They did not live with the same colors or smells, or at all as we lived.

My father wears his pressed trousers crisply; he *eats* with dispatch, he shifts his fork from one hand to the other, the day has darkened the room, it's Saturday lunch, and he rises and goes to the wall switch—"Let's have a little light on the subject." We're talking something over. In the letter he says to me, ". . . time-wasting trifles caused me to lose sight of my objective."

This letter event between me and Mom is one he won't be talking over. Was there anyone who wasn't worth talking to? *Hitler* you don't waste time with probably. (*Probably*? he says. Probably, I think. Make up your mind, one way or t'other, he says.) He got tickets to Forest Hills and we sit on a concrete level like a large step leaning forward above the grass court. Grass? but where are the bumps?, a scuffed, not-at-all lawnlike moss, we're quiet in the luxury of tennis that is a vision, no work—"effortless" is what my dad calls it. Afterward we're at a restaurant sitting on spinnable stools at the counter (it's right across the street from the steps up to the train station), but the counter man didn't act interested in bringing us the menu; he didn't actually say anything when my father asked if we could get something to eat; then my father spun around and got a menu from a booth, and he asked the man if he could find a couple of hamburgers for us. The man was scraping the grill and didn't look at us. My father shut the menu and stood up. "This fella doesn't need our business," he said. With that, we walked out, to say the least, and took the train.

His letter in my hand, I think I find his hand, his palm on my shoulder, his fingers pressing a little in on my collarbone, as we have no more of the counterman and his "behavior." I study murder cases. I investigate the earholes of a crippled bird in New Jersey and think if birds can smell. I store behind my desk an anatomy chart and know some of the muscles, know ligaments, know the hamstrings; I don't talk about it, I don't want this knowledge of mine taken note of. I know that some memories are with you and come back: and this *also* is having a good memory: which my mother and my father's mother separately tell me I have. But you think of homework and tests, a reliable *display* of memory; but it's also things to think *about*. So I just recall and recall, now when the letter in my possession with its advice re the future is what I should be thinking about, that I got down on the floor when I was four years old and looked up my Brooklyn grandmother's skirt in her and my step-grandfather's bedroom, and under their bed over on his side dark against the light his carpet slippers were side by side: so she said, He likes the ladies. "In retrospect," the letter says, "I am appalled by my neglect of the vistas which life has opened to me."

My father, I knew without hearing it said, was pleased with the living room of this fairly "new" apartment of ours. I, too, think it's better than other living rooms. I have not discussed such matters with him. And now he is not here to impress me. And I try to think, Is that right, what he said?

On wide winter mornings it is a seagoing living room in Brooklyn Heights, and "we" have, in addition to the bank of windows fronting on the East River end of the brilliant harbor, one single north window, "opening" north as if the builders thought they were done but then decided to knock a window out of the brick right here.

Here was the Brooklyn Bridge—too near (our fence, our majesty, our show; scale itself, but of events, how about that, Dad? But he's not here, he and I are halfway across it, hand in hand, smelling the harbor, I let go his hand, tilting our heads back to follow the mass above while he told of the men who worked on it underwater and suffered for their wages, hand in hand again); but upriver *past* the Brooklyn Bridge, the *Manhattan* Bridge (working alongside the Brooklyn but far from a copy), the envelope in my hand tells me I have daydreamed, I can know some of this half-pondering, this other bridge has the subway trains eight cars long exposed along it like workings rattling along the rails at their own speed below the cars, a

bridge not noble except as all bridges are—which I think my father'd
say he didn't really understand, though I haven't tried it out on him,
having not *thought* it until today—or do I see that *he* said bridges
were noble?); the *Manhattan* Bridge is more like streets, the jammed
grimy work of the boroughs. Midtown Manhattan looked as far off
as the sky, or parallel—the record height of the Empire State, the
sun-mined, sky-sharpened vehicle shine of the Chrysler Building, let
this be a little vague in the absence of my father. Views are overrated, *all* views, my mother's chain-smoking cousin drones, coughing, who lived for years in China. Children don't like views, she says.
Don't foist views on children, they couldn't care less.

My room and my parents' room *also* offer a quiet eye on this
harbor acreage. I go on about it as if I'm recommending this large
apartment we might move out of, though there's no rush.

And I'm drawn to it most before I left for school. At my own
windows. From my own desk in this apartment we had moved fairly
recently into so my room was known only to me.

And at four in the morning when a horn on the river, a clank of
couplings on the docks out below my windows, *something*, would
disturb me with messages, with word, and I would be awake.

Or when my father called me for dinner.

Or out in the street I'm drawn to the view in the "midst" of a
hockey game standing on roller skates tall-ly bottom-heavily at rest
when the leaden black-rubber puck skips over live on end and runs
like a lost wheel or black-rubber gasket under a parked car on a street
whose dead end *is* that view.

What was I lured *from*? (Why should I think it someone's speech or
meaning?) From voices close by—soft ones, complaining ones, too.
The gentlest of voices. *I* had a voice, edgier; and in my mouth
smarter—or faster when I heard it played back on a thin and bendy
little record I and two friends ad-libbed for a quarter in the slot of a
machine at a local hotel.

I used to get up early on the new spring mornings when I was
eight, nine, *seven*, keeping quiet among the created outlines of the
household. Knowing my parents in bed, listening for my mother
listening, I let myself out the front door and pass down the stairs of
our apartment house so as not to be with the elevator man and found
real freedom in the street, a street of my city, and "took a walk"
myself along sidewalk after sidewalk, street after street, each next
familiar one not quite enough. I'm unknown—out of the house—
and listen for myself to the suave whine of electric power rolling the

69

milk truck past me to the corner, where it turned, *powered* seemingly by this sound, keeping quiet so as not to wake people, inner and minor and smoothly recreationally simple so *I* could have driven that truck. Two dogs meet, and a third. The crazy man who normally projected his large, regular play-type false teeth almost out of his mouth at us when we were running around in the street in the afternoon I could meet now with his teeth hidden. He's snapping two fingers and looking straight ahead, he's going to work earlier than my dad, who likes to stay in bed a little longer after my mother gets up.

I told my dad about the crazy man's teeth while he was getting dressed. He laughed: "What makes you think he's crazy?" "Take my word for it," I answer and he laughs.

As a child I investigate many "matters," but I don't think my father's leaky valve is among them. I am amazed by his death, it's an action he has taken. In motion, turning, speaking, sitting down to a yellow pad, in the same voice. He has surprised me. I don't *say* this. The way I say things I pick up as I know them, or would know them.

"I didn't think you had it in you," a classmate said. I gave a speech to assembly. How easily people will say they are amazed. But maybe it happens a lot, because there is reason to believe them. If he was asking of me something in his *absence*, was it his absence itself? He wasn't *tired*. Though yes he was. Yet not of us.

You can tell from the letter that my father thought about an early death. It was in the subjects of waste and time in the letter. He expressed his hopes for me. "I have written all this because I earnestly wish you to be a better man than I am." One of his scholarships lost at the end of his first year at Harvard. A freshman alone. Really? I *felt* him alone, separated from his high school victories, his family almost. His *beliefs* painfully intact.

What got him started writing the letter, it said, was a talk he had had with a neighbor. What could they reasonably expect to leave their children? Having had that talk, my father was taking action. The letter is, I know, well *written*. It's signed in longhand, "Your affectionate father." I did not see my mother actually find the letter. Come across it; locate it. I came into the living room to that lower drawer out. I'm building backward again. I can make my father ask what *that* means. She had the blanket chest that had belonged to her mother open one day when I was a child and she pointed out to me fitted, snug, but not squashed into a corner two packets of my father's letters before they got married, tied with blue ribbon. She pulled out one packet and I saw the beginning of one. It said, "My dearest darling," the ink endless, swift, slantingly certain with a proud unthinking rounding in some letters like the swell of a sail.

I can begin over again with the dark-eyed mother in a room of a city apartment handing the letter over. "*Building* backward?" I can just hear my father inquire. Dark-*haired* generous mother in a spacious room handing over the letter without any flurry of mood to this not *visibly* sleep-walking son. Is any of this except the names true? No one was telling me to do anything. Not that they had to. Just be like my father, that's all *I* had to do.

How rosy on the puffed bed of the coffin's white satin lining. How of-another-material his hands, crossed. I know I'm sorry for him there as if he's missed out on things and it's not his fault. The eyelids were complete. My hazarded guess embedded far away in my sense of the occasion was that he still had a brain. Yet not that he was in any way, shape, or form asleep.

My mother's hands understood what they touched, reading a book of some composer's letters or lifting the silvery, a bit loose knob of a Dutch oven to pinch the crackly-jacketed potatoes baking on a burner; or with unthinkingly supple wrist holding with her fingertips the end of her violin bow, or with a finger of her bow hand so hastily flipping the page of her music that snatching a corner of the page it's violent, and an emergency met by a quite other personality. One I take for granted. But I can barely see her handing me the letter. The truth is I can't. Her hand is her mind now, or my mind.

There was talk of the safe deposit box. There was strength and fact, architecture, good metal and a newness in the safe deposit box, and my mother wants me to have a key to it. There it is across the river imprisoned in the barred stages of a gleaming gray basement of the Seaman's Bank, Wall Street. I have no use for a key, and am touched even more. Is the letter to be kept there, when I'm finished "with it"? I don't ask such a question, which might be a very stupid question, because there's nobody to ask. That safe deposit box, my mother had said, was where the letter *had* been; I heard her. At the extreme bottom of one of those towering edifices, somewhat key-like. But then, no, it passed from there to a lower drawer of the desk in the living room, when she located it to give to me, a drop leaf of dark cherry.

The letter was typed. I don't see somebody else doing it; not the secretary who typed the "Market Letter" my father composed over the weekend. I'm asked to see him at a typewriter, but I don't.

Though I can see him sitting up straight. I had played with typewriters seriously from an early age and from my eighth birthday had had one of my own.

He wrote on the *long* yellow pads. He wrote fast with dark-brown (*-painted*, I saw,) Number 2 pencils with "Brokers Special" stamped on them in yellow gold. Why don't I recall seeing one of these without a sharp point? There are two on the large green blotter on the living room desk. He wrote a hand so swift with that concentration of his that its absorbed regularity gained a decorative flourish. Is it, then, *not* modest? Modest maybe in a drive that looked active, useful. Reading his letter I could grasp more about time and waste than I would try to say.

The truth of "Haste makes waste" I find is in the word *makes*. My father laid down his words on paper fast. He measured them unhesitatingly, didn't he?

His hand had a flair, a looping flourish on the capitals large-scaled; I fell into it, it was an awfully smart hand, it meant what it wrote. He said, That's too fancy, when he saw my hand imitating his. I don't see him typing. I don't imagine someone else typing my letter either.

The letter was here all the time. It could wait.

The words of my father's letter come as soon as my mother hands it to me, and point at me not from his voice like a magnificent demand or thing but more from his head or his malleably gleaming scalp-line above the square front of his forehead that, a few days after he dies, can still speak; and his awesomely fair *I have to say . . .*, "I'm sorry but I think you . . ." "Hey *you're* a better interrupter than *I* am" (smiling) voice is a voice that I don't think *through* enough to come at, though later I imagine needling him. (As once, and only once, playing late in the street outside our building, and seeing him come striding home, his newspaper under his arm, I called out an unthinkable insult, showing off, that I cannot imagine myself not saying no matter how hard I try to resay the scene.) That voice came from his eyes too, which must have fixed me more than I could help with their gray, part-colorblind *young* gaze. He sometimes gazes at me when he looks at me. *My* father had "trouble" with green and gray. It's what I can think of, as I wordlessly read his letter's words for the first time. Christian courtesy he spoke of, as if saying the words gave back some inner impress or name he could bring himself to know he had, or a conservative vividness.

I'm right: his words didn't come only from his voice. (But from his mouth, putting intentions into shape—*mouthing* them and his "civil tongue," his excellence; civil *feelings*, it comes to me.) He's an elder of his church out there where his family *used* to live, he and his cousin Esther still go there, to sing lustily, pray that way too, it's a happiness, receive each week as if every day thoughtfully each sentence of the sermon as Dr. Arms spoke on and on. It is something of a trip out there from the Heights, it's "church," and my dad goes Wednesday evenings sometimes, too, whereas I go to Sunday school a few minutes walk from my home, my street. On the Heights, Brooklyn Heights.

I went out to that other old gray church of big pale blocks of gray stone in another part of Brooklyn rarely. Now that he is dead, *my* not going there falls through. "*Old* church," but mine on the Heights is older. Near Henry Ward Beecher's church where Lincoln spoke. I didn't know the Sunday School kids out at my father's church and as for my father's church friends, they spoke differently, old Bedford and Flatbush people, jovial, embarrassing for what they supposedly knew of me through knowing all about *him*, about my father. He had grown up with some of those people, they admired him, *I* knew they admired how he *spoke*, it was their faces *behind* their words greeting me jovially as his son and a fellow-*Christian* at eight or nine or ten years old and welcome because they had known my father "all his life" and more prone to refer to Jesus Christ as "Him," like my father's cousin Esther in a pink cardigan sweater. They valued and prized my father. He was better than they, I believed they thought.

"Learn to do well ... relieve the oppressed": they believed the Bible. They said "Amen" out loud in church—"A" as in *aim*, as in ABC—which people on the Heights I felt did not. It was conversing with the minister up front, I felt. My mother said, "Ah-men" at the end of a prayer the way you *sang* "Ah-men." I heard and even *had* words, or positioned them sometimes to see they aimed, like a railroad switchman closing and opening track, though he would not have had all the time in the world. And reading and sustaining my father's letter, I have to read it and read it as a week passes—as if I've written it.

But once it was a Sunday *evening*—no radio programs that night, and my mother and father and I journeyed out to his old church to hear him give a Talk. We proceed, with a superior, pleased hopelessness, my mother and I, into a Sunday School room. I'm looking forward to it ending, to being back home. He sat at a broad, shellacked, schoolroom-activities-type table and talked across it to everybody sitting in rows of chairs. Once, he indicated me and my mother, and he said we were an example of the "love" he had been talking about. I did not like that, I thought about it and didn't speak of it.

My father would kiss me, and kissed his step-father—*my* step-*grand*father—and kissed his brother, my uncle, who was five years younger; and hugged, too. Though hugging and *kissing* is more with the women. "It's endless, all that kissing, coming and going, they bear down on you." It's my mother talking to *me* now. Though isn't she sort of that way, too? With *her* friends, and gaily, at the front door like an offer to dance.

With the letter in my hand that could not reach me until my father had died, I was hit with interruptions. I had a sneaking understanding that interruption was OK, though I did it. Should I think about anything that came up to do with the letter? He wasn't here. But he was nowhere else. "Believe me, my boy, I am deeply concerned for your happiness." Was he in the letter? *If* he was, was it in the words?—or what I could make of them? I'm doing what I always do, nothing's changed, you do nothing when you're sad, you daydream, maybe you go out or you read. When will this stop happening to you?

I really treasure the letter. Delivered like that, it has an ensured force. It has been in the desk. He means those words.

My father took out not a *huge* policy or gambler's amount, like the man whose young widow my parents knew. But the insurance company was going to lose on my father. I imagine him learning of this. I don't dwell on money except my own, but life insurance came to the fore. Why did I, at the age of eleven, undergo an insurance exam? We're in a smaller apartment, then, where I walked in my sleep: right to the open window of my bedroom where my mother in her nightgown and bare arms intercepted me, with cars rolling along Henry Street six floors below. One night the insurance company doctor sat at my desk; my goose-neck lamp was the only light, but my father is present. The doctor's hair was near my chest. I was being examined *standing*. Heart, pulse, chest, blood pressure—who knows? Could I have failed? The taking-out of that five thousand dollar policy guarded me in some way. It was an adult event that included me and singled me out. A household or *community* event. Like shots at the doctor's; like the fingerprinting they did on us at my Quaker school one morning. Who knows? Is my not-knowing really letting things happen? I had a life-insurance exam when I was eleven. Was it good of my father? He took care of things. He looked ahead.

In the Light
Robert Kelly

Where did I see you? In the mistaken light
between competence and performance

in the protestant light I cherish
dusty scarlet, light of a high church modest candle,
sanctuary light, real presence,

in the protestant light of presence,
in the presence of light, light
is always adequate

in the light between desire and performance,
in the mistaken light between
the rule and the sentence, the bleak
light over Kaminstein's Hardware,
lost marriages, all our olive natures
ancient, goat-gnawed,
in the dawning light between
desire and the expression of desire,

in the episcopal light
that makes you take off your violet shirt
and still your skin shows that color,
morning light coming in off the snow

in the snow light between danger and desire,
for lust driveth out terror
in the urbane light of South Kensington
between a museum and what it shows,
between a replica and an original, a door,
light of a door, light of your areoles
purple in the fluted light of my mouth
kissing them tight, in the light

that rides inside us on our tongues our hands
in the interpenetrant light between
Shakertown and Harrodsburg, in mountain light,
in the light inside a glass of wine,
a wine I never drink, light of absence,
where is your mouth to me

in the light of absence I pray all distance
become our one same house, stone chimney
in the light of burning wood, light
between syntax and intention,
light between how you excite me
and what I answer,
crimson light of expectation, in the soft
light of commercial arrangements, in the moneyed
light of pleasant restaurants in snowy suburbs, with ferns,

in the lesbian light that touches every woman,
in the light that finds you, in the orange
light of dissidence, lambda light, the ruddy
light they serve in catholic churches, in glasses,
in Mary light, blue light, in the brown
light of leather, of lore,
yellow flowers of woad light,

in the light of books you give me
in the light of your love understanding me
in the light of my darkness receiving—

And on the other end of the pier,
the part called Night,
there is a light now everybody knows
though everybody goes there and that light
is in every body. The knowers know
and the be-ers are.
Here the waves are sharp,
rims etched against the lower sky,
light carved into light,
intaglio light showing through in cloud,
amber light of rainstorm, crimson
light just before sunset, sideways light,

mother light that nothing sees
mother light that all forgives
mother light that wounds, or wounded light
meat light, Greek light,
eye light is skin light, light
of the oldest languages you speak,
low-waisted light, light of a belt around your waist,
light of silver thread in silk,
light around the earth, zone light,
house of tragedy full of comic light,
my arm around you light what do you see,

tree light snow light everything
washed away by that ocean they call Night now
I call it nothing it doesn't
see me it forgives my caress,
virgin light, palpable, pure
as a flag, pure as an unknown word
in an unknown language spoken by your mouth,

speak it, pure as my sleep, pure light
and North Sea coast light, pure
light and California light, light
of every street I've ever known,
light of every house and every car's light,

pain light, light inside bones broken or whole,
cheap light of understood ideas,
bad light of getting what I want, fierce
light of wanting, dear light of unknown roads,
light of someone at the door.

Into the Arms of the Man on the Moon

Yannick Murphy

THERE IS THE MAN on the moon. Go to him. Get bread from him, drink his water. Take your dog, Blue to him. Take your mother. She is skiing outside around the house. Stop her, tell her that Blue is going also. Take the gander, Henry. He is short in the legs. Leave me Iris. I have seen her eat feed in a pattern.

Tell the man on the moon I am out with the dogs. I have loaded them up. I am not without ointment for my lips. This is an occasion. Harnessed the dogs are mindful of the pregnant bitch. Tell the man on the moon I think she will whelp seven. Ask him if he can know those kinds of things. Ask him if he is like God. Ask him if he knows if God knows how many the pregnant bitch can whelp.

I will miss your hair. Cut some for me. Leave it inside my boot. When I pull it out I will see summer. My foot will stay warm. Tell the man on the moon we have summer here. If he asks, show him your hair. If he asks about stars, laugh, then if he asks again, show him your mother's eyes.

Your hair will not feel the same in my boot as it does on your head. Tell him how I would kill for you. You know already the scream a rabbit makes when it is killed. That is the most frightening sound of all. That is only what I think.

The dogs are loaded up. Go look at them first. Tell me they remind you of the time we climbed the mountain. I do not know why. I am thinking of the mountain.

Ask him not to sleep with your mother, my wife. Tell him I would even send the man from the moon into next week. Tell him we say things like that here. Try and draw next week. It always looks a little like last week, this is because we never know.

Take your mother's skis. I could not bear to watch them up against the wall with the snow melting off them and her not here. Tell her to wear them when she meets the man on the moon. If he asks, say she is sick in the foot. It could be gangrene. Let us think about the mountain again.

It is up there on the mountain that I saw the bone in your foot. You took off your shoes and we rested and I saw a bone on the side of your foot that I had never seen before. I thought you had put it there, at first. It took you away from me. I was watching evolution. You were going down the line away from me. There is no bone in my foot like that. There is no bone in your mother's foot like that.

I will eat bark. I will pull out your hair from my boot and I will see summer. O.K. I will tell you what summer is. Although check the dogs, they tire when I talk about summer and I cannot have them tired. Tell the man on the moon your father does not know what he is talking about. Tell the man on the moon your father would say he saw summer in his son's hair because it sounded good. Tell the man on the moon your father would kill for you. Tell him again. Tell him because your father sent you. Tell him to send back my goddamn wife. I like your foot. Open your ears. Tell the man on the moon we say things like that. Your foot is daring. It is breaking the line. My dogs are lying down. They are ready to go. I have to remember the ointment for my lips. If your lips are too dry you cannot call the lead dogs that you have named Peter and Bristle because you cannot make that "p" or "b" sound with lips with big pieces of skin like shutters hanging off one hinge and flapping in the wind.

Who can say he has truly seen the man on the moon? Go to him. This is the first I have seen of him. Here, sitting. How many times have I done this. Just sat. Imagine all the people who have said — "Oh, can you see the man on the moon?" I like him better than God. Everybody says they have seen God. "I have seen God," this is a familiar line.

There have been men who have done it with dolphins. Ask the man on the moon if he knows if these men have done it because they want to commune with an intelligent being. Ask the man on the moon if these men do it just because it feels good. Tell me you understand all of what I am saying so I don't have to tell you that yes, men do it with animals.

He is a stroke of luck. I want to send you into the arms of the man on the moon. Yes, I am leaving you. Every day. Do not deny your foot is still growing. That bone, I take it back, is ugly. Ask the man on the moon if he is going to be like God and expect us to put up with these things. Show him what you are made of. Show him your teeth. They are the same as my teeth. They are the same as my father's teeth.

So you are in love. You cannot sleep at night. Is this bigger than me having seen the man on the moon? Do not answer that. Neither of us knows. It is good to see you tuck your foot under your leg like that.

Your mother skis outside around the house. She waves when she sees us sitting. She has bet the pregnant bitch will whelp ten. "You cannot take a dog with her pups," your mother has told me. "If the food is low the others will eat the pups," your mother has told me. I have not told your mother that I already know this. Tell the man on the moon I am a man with a guilty conscience. Tell the man on the moon I do these things nevertheless.

When you were young you could not say your name. Tell the girl you are in love with this and she will love you forever.

Tell people that I am crazy. Tell people that I have seen the man on the moon—ask them if they can say that of themselves. Go to him. I am not one for signs. This is a sign.

Ask the man on the moon what will become of you. Tell him your father does not know. Lie to him. Tell him you are dying and you have to know. If he looks down at your foot, at your bone, what will you say? He will ask if you have been running away from your father. He will ask is that why you have come to the moon. He will ask your mother and she will say that she and you were sent by me to the moon. He will spread out his arms and he will say but there is nothing here. He will offer you only bread and water and you will be standing there holding Henry the gander, Blue by your side, and your mother standing still in her skis on the moon.

I will be sitting out here resting my hand in the dark on a place I will imagine to be your head, feeling your hair, but it will not be here. I will look up, I will see the man on the moon and I will see my wife on the moon and I will see my son on the moon.

The Winter Journey

Georges Perec

Translated by David Bellos

IN THE LAST WEEK of August 1939, while Paris was overtaken by rumors of war, a young teacher of literature, Vincent Degraël, was invited to spend a few days in a country house near Le Havre belonging to the family of one of his colleagues, Denis Borrade. On the eve of his return, rummaging through his hosts' library in search of one of those books you've always meant to read but never have the time to do more than flick through carelessly by the fireside before making up the fourth hand at bridge, Degraël came upon a slim volume entitled *The Winter Journey* whose author—Hugo Vernier—was completely unknown to him, but the opening pages of which made such a strong impression on him that he took scarcely a moment to make his excuses to his friend and the family before going up to his room to read.

The Winter Journey was a kind of story told in the first person and set in a semi-imaginary land whose overcast skies, gloomy forests, gentle hills, and canals with greenish-watered locks were heavily and surreptitiously reminiscent of the countryside of Flanders or the Ardennes. The book was divided into two parts. The first, which was the shorter, recounted in sybilline terms a vaguely initiatic journey, each stage of which was marked, so it seemed, by a failure, and at the end of which the anonymous hero (a man, and by all indications a young one) came to the bank of a lake shrouded in thick mist. A ferryman awaited him there and carried him to a steep-sided isle in the middle of which stood a high, dark, barn-like house. Scarcely had the young man put his foot on the narrow floating jetty which was the only form of access to the isle, when a strange couple appeared: an old man and an old woman, both draped in long black cloaks, seemed to rise from the mist, took their places at either side of the young man, grasped his elbows, pressed as closely to his sides as they could, then—almost soldered together, as it were—the three climbed a crumbling path, entered the house, climbed a wooden staircase, and came to a bedroom. There, as inexplicably as they had appeared, the two old folk vanished and left the young man alone in the middle of the room. It was sparsely furnished: there was a bed with a flowered cretonne spread, a table, and a chair. A fire burned vigorously in the hearth. A meal had been served on the table: bean soup, and a lean shoulder of beef. Through the tall window the young man watched the full moon appear from behind the clouds; then he sat at the table and began to eat. And on this solitary supper the first part of the book ended.

The second part alone made up nearly four-fifths of the whole and it soon became obvious that the short tale preceding was only an anecdotal pretext for it. It was a long confession, acutely lyrical, larded with poems, enigmatic maxims, and blasphemous incantations. Vincent Degraël had scarcely begun to read it before he felt an uncanny sensation he could not precisely define, but which only grew as he turned the pages with an ever unsteadier hand: it was as if the sentences before his eyes were suddenly familiar, started to remind him irresistibly of *something*, as if on the reading of each one was imposed, or rather superimposed, an acute but uncertain memory of another almost identical sentence that he had read somewhere else; as if these words—sweeter than kisses or more treacherous than poison—these alternately limpid and hermetic, obscene and heartfelt, dazzling, labyrinthine words, swinging incessantly like a demented compass needle between hallucinatory violence and fabulous serenity, were sketching out a confused configuration in which you could find (perhaps) in random array Germain Nouveau and Tristan Corbière, Villiers and Banville, Rimbaud and Verhaeren, Charles Cros and Léon Bloy.

Vincent Degraël, whose special interest was precisely in the field of late XIXth century French poetry (he had been working for some years on a thesis on "The Evolution of French Poetry from the Parnassians to the Symbolists") first thought that he could indeed have read *The Winter Journey* before in the course of his research, or —more likely—that he was suffering from an illusion of déjà vu in which —as when the mere taste of a sip of tea takes you suddenly back to England thirty years ago—a tiny detail, a sound or smell or gesture suffices (perhaps that momentary hesitation he had noted before taking the book from its place on the shelf, between Verhaeren and Viellé-Griffin, or the avidity with which he had read through the opening pages) to make a mistaken memory of a prior reading overlay the actual reading to the point of making it impossible. But soon his doubts had to be dismissed and Degraël was forced to admit the evidence: even if his memory was playing tricks on him, even if it was only by chance that Vernier seemed to have borrowed from Catulle Mendés his "lone jackal haunting tombs of stone," even if allowance was made for fortuitous coincidences, declared influences, intended borrowings, unconscious imitation, a taste for pastiche, a liking for quotation, and opportune matches, even if one took the view that expressions such as "the flight of time," "winter fogs," "dark horizon," "deep caverns," "misty fountains," "uncertain lights of untamed undergrowth" belonged to all poets as common property and that it was therefore just as natural to come across them in a paragraph by Hugo Vernier as in the *stances* of Jean Moréas, it was nonetheless impossible to fail to recognize literal (or almost literal) fragments—at every point—of Rimbaud ("I saw frankly a mosque in the place of a factory, a school of drums built by angels") or of Mallarmé ("lucid winter, season of serene art") or of Lautréamont ("I watched in a mirror the mouth mutilated by my own will") or Gustave Kahn ("Let the song die...my heart weeps/A dark smudge surrounds the light. Solemn/Silence rose slowly, it frightens/The familiar noises of individual waves") or, scarcely altered, lines by Verlaine ("in the endless ennui of the plain, snow sparkled like sand. The sky was the color of copper. The train slid on without a murmur") and so on and so forth.

Degraël finished reading *The Winter Journey* at four in the morning. He had spotted about thirty borrowings in it. It was certain that there were others. Hugo Vernier's book seemed to be nothing other than a prodigious patchwork of late nineteenth-century poetry, an outsize acrostic, a mosaic of which nearly every tesselation was the work of someone else. But just as he was straining to imagine this unknown author who wanted to draw the substance of his own book from the books of others, as he was trying to picture this senseless and admirable project in its entirety, Degraël felt the panic of a mad suspicion rise in him: he had just remembered that on taking the book from the bedside table he had mechanically noted the date of publication, following the reflexes of a young scholar who never uses a book without taking down its bibliographical data. Maybe he'd been mistaken, but he thought he'd read the date as 1864. With beating heart, he checked. He had read correctly: that meant that Vernier had "shouted" a line of Mallarmé two years early, plagiarized Verlaine ten years before the "Forgotten Airs," written Gustave Kahn almost a quarter of a century before Kahn had; that meant that

Lautréamont, Germain Nouveau, Rimbaud, Corbière, and quite a few others were merely the transcribers of an unknown genius whose single work contained the very stuff on which three or four generations of poets after him would feed themselves.

Unless of course the date on the title page was erroneous. Degraël refused to consider this hypothesis: his discovery was too beautiful, too obvious, too necessary not to be true, and he could already imagine the dizzying consequences it was going to bring, the prodigious scandal that public revelation of this "anticipatory anthology" would provoke. A huge field of literature would be affected; doubt would be cast on everything that critics and literary historians had calmly propounded for years and years. And Degraël was so impatient that he gave up sleep entirely and rushed back to the library to find out a little more about Vernier and his works.

He found nothing. The few dictionaries and reference works in the Borrade collection had no entries for Hugo Vernier. Neither the elder Borrades nor Denis could give any more information: the volume had been bought at an auction ten years before at Honfleur; they had glanced at the book, without giving it much attention.

The whole of the next day, with the help of Denis, Degraël examined *The Winter Journey* systematically, looking up its fragments scattered through dozens of anthologies and collections: they found nearly three hundred and fifty of them, shared among almost thirty different authors: the best-known as well as the obscurest poets of the *fin-de-siècle* and a few prose-writers as well (Léon Bloy, Ernest Hello) seemed to have used *The Winter Journey* as their bible, drawing the best of themselves from it: Banville, Richepin, Huysmans, Charles Cros, Léon Valade, alongside Mallarmé and Verlaine, and others now forgotten, whose names were Charles de Pomairols, Hippolyte Vaillant, Maurice Rollinat (George Sand's godson), Laprade, Albert Mérat, Charles Morice, and Antony Valabrègue.

Degraël made a neat list of the authors and the references of their borrowings, and traveled back to Paris determined to continue his research the next day at the Bibliothèque nationale. But events did not permit him to do so. His marching orders awaited him in Paris. He was posted to Compiègne and then found himself—he never grasped why—in Saint-Jean-de-Luz, whence he crossed into Spain and got to England, coming back to France only at the end of 1945. Throughout the war, he carried his list with him and managed by some miracle not to lose it. His research did not progress much, of course, but he did make one discovery of the greatest importance for him. In the British Musuem he had had the chance to look up *The Winter Journey* in the *General Catalogue of the French Book Trade* and his formidable theory was confirmed. *The Winter Journey*, by Vernier (Hugo) had indeed been published in 1864, by Hervé Frères, printers and booksellers, at Valenciennes, and as it had been lodged with the copyright office, like all books published in France, it was in the Bibliothèque nationale in Paris with the shelfmark Z.87912.

Degraël was appointed to a teaching post at Beauvais and henceforth devoted all his spare time to *The Winter Journey*.

Detailed research into the diaries and letters of most of the poets of the late nineteenth century easily persuaded Degraël that Hugo Vernier had had in his own time the fame he deserved. Notes like "today received letter from Hugo" or "wrote a long letter to Hugo" "read V.H. all night" or again the famous "Hugo, only Hugo" by Valentin Havercamp referred not a jot or tittle to "Victor" Hugo, but to the jinxed poet whose slim volume had consumed all those who had had it in their hands. Startling contradictions which criticism and literary history had never been able to explain thus found their only logical solution; and it was obviously with reference to Hugo Vernier and to their debt to *The Winter Journey* that Rimbaud wrote "I is another" and Lautréamont "Poetry should be made by all and not by one."

However, as he became more able to illustrate the dominant role that Hugo Vernier was going to have to play in the literary history of the end of the last century, he was less and less able to provide any tangible proof: for he never managed to get hold of another copy of *The Winter Journey*. The one he had read had been destroyed — together with the country house—during the bombing of Le Havre; the copy lodged with the Bibliothèque nationale in Paris was not on the shelf when he put in a request slip for it, and, after interminable enquiries, he learned that the volume had been sent off to a bindery in 1926, but had never arrived there. All the searches he had made by dozens, indeed hundreds, of librarians, archivists, and bookdealers came to dead ends, and Degraël soon believed that the five hundred printed copies of the book had been intentionally destroyed by the very people who had been directly inspired by it.

As for Hugo Vernier's biography, Vincent Degraël managed to learn virtually nothing. An unhoped-for footnote tracked down in an obscure *Biography of Notable Men in Northern France and Belgium* (Verviers, 1882) informed him that Vernier had been born at

Vimy in the Pas-de-Calais on 3 September 1836. But the registry of the town of Vimy had been burnt in 1916, at the same time as the duplicates kept in the county hall at Arras. Apparently, no death certificate had ever been made out.

For more than thirty years, Vincent Degraël struggled in vain to collect proofs of the existence of this poet and of his work. When he died, in the psychiatric hospital at Verrières, some of his former pupils took on the task of sorting the huge pile of documents and manuscripts he left. Among them was a thick ledger bound in black cloth, labelled in careful handwriting: *The Winter Journey.* The first eight pages recounted the story of his fruitless research. The other three hundred and ninety-two pages were blank.

The Asian Lectures
In anticipation of the question:
"Why do you write?"

Robert Coover

BECAUSE ART BLOWS LIFE into the lifeless, death into the deathless.

Because art's lie is preferable, in truth, to life's beautiful terror.

Because, as time does not pass (nothing, as Beckett tells us, passes), *it* passes the time.

Because death, our mirthless master, is somehow amused by epitaphs.

Because epitaphs, well struck, give death, our voracious master, heartburn.

Because fiction imitates life's beauty, thereby inventing the beauty life lacks.

Because fiction is the best position, at once exotic and familiar, for fucking the world.

Because fiction, mediating paradox, celebrates it.

Because fiction, mothered by love, loves love as a mother might her unloving child.

Because fiction speaks, hopelessly, beautifully, as the world speaks.

Because God, created in the storyteller's image, can be destroyed only by His maker.

Because, in its perversity, art harmonizes the disharmonious.

Robert Coover

Because, in its profanity, fiction sanctifies life.

Because, in its terrible isolation, writing is a path to brotherhood.

Because in the beginning was the gesture, and in the end to come as well; in between what we have are words.

Because of its endearing futility, its outrageous pretensions.

Because the pen, though short, casts a long shadow (upon, it must be said, no surface).

Because the world is re-invented every day and this is how it is done.

Because there is nothing new under the sun except its expression.

Because truth, that elusive joker, hides himself in fictions and must therefore be sought there.

Because writing, in all space's unimaginable vastness, is still the greatest adventure of all.

And because, alas, what else?

John Hawkes

An *Interview by Bradford Morrow*

After the fact—since during the process the "fact" was excruciat-
ing—I, at least, am grateful for the mechanical breakdown which
forced this conversation to take the eccentric, twisty course it took,
a course more or less faithfully reproduced here. Having returned
from the Palmer River Riding Club, where Hawkes takes lessons, we
had a couple of hours before dinner to sit down and (to be honest) get
the interview out of the way. Maybe it was the muscadet—an entire
bottle of which we consumed—but the conversation seemed to us
exceptional. When I rewound the tape, however, the "fact" presented
itself. The batteries'd failed twenty minutes into the interview.
Persistent if depressed, we used the half hour before the dinner
guests—Robert and Pilar Coover, Mary Caponegro and Sheffield
Van Buren—were to arrive, to try to recover some of the best
materials from the Lost Conversation. It was useless.

Coover brought fresh batteries and Albert Pic chablis, or Mer-
curie, and somehow during dinner collaborative spirit seized everyone while Jack flew off into an inspired monologue about how he
wanted to be—yes—a swamp. Only a crude Manhattanite could
contemplate putting a recorder in the middle of a dinner table in
Providence, but given the quality and even mystery of Jack's visionary flight against the fact that we had lost so much that afternoon, I
couldn't help myself. I would like to apologize in public and on
record to all present at that dinner for having shown such bad
manners; the results are transcribed here. The next morning,
Hawkes and I did sit down to attempt a more formal interview. That
conversation is also here.

After reading the proofs, Pilar Coover, in the same impromptu
spirit she showed that evening at dinner, made a needle-on-canvas
image, "The Swamp and the Rock." The embroidery is reproduced at
the end of the interview. I only wish we could have reproduced Pilar's
piquant, turbinated Catalan accent—the spirit in her rolled Rs
("rrrrrhock—") was of higher proof than even all the good wine
consumed at the Hawkes's table.

John Hawkes

Bradford Morrow: In your new novel *Whistlejacket*, the narrator Michael is a photographer whose great compulsion at the beginning of the book is in working through the etymology of several words, an interest which seems to disappear as the novel progresses. I was wondering whether the novel began to formulate itself for you within the context of certain words, and what the connection might be between that and his saying, "I am a carnivorous watcher and I pursue them all," his obsession with seeing.

John Hawkes: The novel begins with Mike's concern for words, mainly with *corgi* because in his boyhood the little dog was constantly with Virgie, and was suggestive of an erotic world that was denied to Michael since he considered Virgie his sister, therefore inaccessible. The dog followed them everywhere.

Morrow: Sexually inaccessible?

Hawkes: Yes. Prohibited. As a child, Virgie was constantly thrusting herself on him; he felt that she was dangerous because she was an incestuous creature—although it's not put in those terms—and so he came to hate the dog as suggestive of, or identified with, Virgie's pursuit of him.

Morrow: What does "corgi" mean?

Hawkes: Dwarf, in Welsh. It's a Welsh dog, a squat thing with legs like sausages, black and white—

Morrow: They were bred to go down holes, I think.

Hawkes: I'm not sure, Brad—with very long ears, it's a strange looking, pathetic little dog and I myself am attracted to the strange and pathetic. But for Michael the dog is an image of obscenity. He knows that it means dwarf. And that's exactly what he wants it to mean.

Morrow: How did you get from the word "corgi" to obscenity when you were first working on the book?

Hawkes: The dog is either like an adumbrated penis, a sort of walking sausage, stunted, marred by long ears, or it's a dwarfed dog walking on partial phalluses. It's a grotesque rendering of male sexuality and all its power and horror. By the way, *Whistlejacket* derives to some extent from my books *The Lime Twig* and *Travesty*. Like *The Lime Twig*, it has a killer horse, a dangerous, unusual, fabulous horse. At one moment in *Travesty* the narrator says, "I love the dark night. Through the thick green lens of the night I see only the brightest light." *Whistlejacket* begins by repeating the same idea, except that the narrator substitutes a camera's lens for the dark night: "Through the thick transparent lens of my camera—cameras I mean to say, but one will do for the metaphor—I see woman. Not women. Woman. Although I see both." For me, every act of seeing in *Whistlejacket* reflects the night of *Travesty.*

MORROW: Are there other origins of *Whistlejacket*?

HAWKES: The book grew out of Peter Greenaway's film *The Draughtsman's Contract*. That film is set in the eighteenth century and involves a wife and her daughter who murder the husband-father and a draughtsman who makes drawings of the house they live in. I loved that film and began to be obsessed by it, which hadn't happened to me before and hasn't since. It was my editor who suggested that my next novel after *Adventure in the Alaskan Skin Trade* also be set in America. I didn't think that I wanted to set any more fiction in America—

MORROW: Why not?

HAWKES: I'm not very excited by American landscapes.

MORROW: What do you mean by landscapes?

HAWKES: Places, sounds of language. I simply don't know America very well. It rarely occurs to me that I'm American. I am, of course. But if I think about it, I consider myself an alien in the country, someone born here but not assimilated into the culture. I was born in Connecticut, lived in New York, didn't go to school at all, except to St. Agnes School on 91st Street where I went just long enough to be humiliated by having to play Jack in "Jack Jumps Over the Candlestick." In 1934 my mother and I ended up with my grandmother in Old Greenwich, Connecticut, at that time called Sound Beach, when my father went off to Alaska to investigate the possibilities in coal mining there. He came back a year later and took my mother and myself up to Juneau. We stayed five years, until I was fifteen. Then came the war. I went to school in New York City for about a year (my father was still in Alaska), then my mother, who was afraid New York would be bombed, moved us up to Pawling. I attended the high school in Pawling for a year and a half, went to Harvard and failed Chemistry and German. At this point I joined the army but was discharged for asthma after six weeks. Then I drove an American Field Service ambulance in Italy and Germany. By the end of the war I was back at Harvard. But my nine months in the war gave me a life that had nothing to do with America. I don't know anything about baseball, as a child I never collected baseball cards. At best I was mystified by Jack Armstrong, the All-American Boy.

91

MORROW: All the landscapes you've lived in, though, are obviously American.

HAWKES: They didn't seem to matter. I was never able to swim, never able to participate in sports. We moved around just enough to prevent me from being "from" anywhere. I had more than the usual distaste for school, for gymnasiums, for gym teachers, and so on.

MORROW: How would you define America, or American?

HAWKES: Mainly as knowing its language—dialects, jokes, slang, comic strips, speech as heard on radio and television—which I never did understand. Now, at sixty-two, I take at best a negative interest in America. I could never write about this country, its politics, its history. Except for *The Beetle Leg* and *Adventures in the Alaskan Skin Trade* and half of *Second Skin*, it had never occurred to me to set any of my fiction in America. I was so moved by and really obsessed with Europe in the mere nine months I spent in Italy and Germany, seeing a glimpse of Holland and France, all of it ravaged during the war—and in its semidestroyed state it was horrifyingly compelling; I felt erotically drawn to the unknown, and to languages I didn't know, couldn't speak.

MORROW: Eroticism is always the central component or aspect to your reaction to something, isn't it? And you don't think that America, in all its chaos of detail, reveals itself, finally, as erotic?

HAWKES: It's a chaos of valueless amorality. Most cult figures in the United States are bores, and rather unpleasant and disgusting.

MORROW: *Whistlejacket* has an interior landscape that seems to be anywhere, and this has been the case before. *Travesty* is set in a car. There is a workable interior setting that myth requires, myth being again crucial as you pointed out in a recording that was made of one of your readings at Stanford. Enclosure seems to be a place in which you work well, where tension is heightened by the very field it is working within.

HAWKES: *Travesty* was a pleasure to write because it was so limited. Being immobile inside a speeding car at night allows the narrator to make the invisible daylight world "visible" while he talks, while he drives. For me, *Whistlejacket* is an American book, through and through. I think now that the connection between the novel and the film is nebulous. I doubt that anyone having seen that film and having read this book would actually see the connection. My novel does not have, never could achieve, the same sense of mystery that is in the film, partly because of the veiling art of the camera. The film's obscure, I wanted a clear plot. I think of Mike as another version of the artist—he's even more remote, less connected with life, less able to have personal commitments than any such character I've created yet.

MORROW: Does that make him more American to you?

HAWKES: I hadn't thought of it that way, and perhaps his identity as a New York fashion photographer is incidental to his unusual personality. Perhaps not. At any rate, for somebody to whom, as he says, the image is more important than the act, an actual sexual experience is no more personal than taking a photograph—or of no more "value." Women he hardly knows turn up in his bed, yet he doesn't bother to turn on the light. Not a national attitude, I suppose. Yet I like to associate that mind with New York.

MORROW: How did this personality emerge just now in your work?

HAWKES: I'm not sure. But a few years ago I first saw David Salle's paintings and felt an immediate rapport with his "dead passion"—a phrase from *Travesty*. Often he creates a tone of muted eroticism, and I wonder if the tone and even subject matter of *Whistlejacket* mightn't owe at least something to the glimpses I've had of Salle's sexual still lifes, as I like to think of them. I wasn't able to write about a painter, or about the artist in *The Draughtsman's Contract*. But a photographer—at least a fashion photographer like my narrator—is a version of the visual artist. Of course my main interest has always been in the visual imagination and an intensity of language which in itself is erotic....

FRIDAY NIGHT, DINNER

HAWKES: I was just trying to prove that I'm a feminist. I said "erotic," Pilar, not "the rock."

PILAR COOVER: There's little fossils inside the rock.

HAWKES: You know where they come from? They come from a swamp.

PILAR COOVER: I like the swamp in the rock stage.

ROBERT COOVER: That's right, the petrified swamp.

HAWKES: Well, I'll tell you what. I think the tree would have a bloody hard time surviving in a petrified swamp.

SOPHIE HAWKES: But Jack, there are petrified trees as well.

HAWKES: They're rock, they're not alive anymore, they're dead as doornails. Swamps are all rimmed in moss.

PILAR COOVER: But they're full of mosquitoes and typhus.

HAWKES: I tell you what, Pilar. I have never heard a woman, especially a woman who exemplifies—
ROBERT COOVER: The swamp.
HAWKES: Exactly. Like Pilar. How can she talk the way she does? Since in the way she looks, in her cooking, she exemplifies what I'm talking about, which is eroticism. I mean you, Pilar. The woman embodies the swamp, the glorious swamp.
PILAR COOVER: The swamp drinks up rocks.
HAWKES: There's no winning this argument, no sirree.
ROBERT COOVER: You're a bloody tree trying to argue with a swamp and that's what you get.
PILAR COOVER: Yeah, nice try.
HAWKES: A talks to B and B says Z, not a rock but a fossil—no, this is not going to work. Well, you know, if anybody else would try to explain what I mean, people would say, "Oh sure, isn't that interesting that man wants to be identified with a swamp."
SOPHIE HAWKES: Pilar's very convincing, too.
HAWKES: Rocks? I don't want any rocks around me right now, I can tell you that.
MORROW: Where did the trees go? How did we get to rocks? I thought the choice was a tree or a swamp.
ROBERT COOVER: Jack offered a simple choice, but no swamp would ever accept a simple choice.
HAWKES: Pilar, you had to go and introduce a third element, the rock, what can you do with a rock except sit on it? I don't want to sit on a rock, too sharp, too pointed. A rock has nothing to do with anything. A tree grows up. A swamp grows wide and it grows deep.
PILAR COOVER: And a rock stays put.
HAWKES: Exactly, the rock stays put, you can't say it any better. A rock is just a rock, it's dull. You know what we do? We tie rocks around our necks and jump into swamps.
PILAR COOVER: It's my Catholic upbringing, everything's built up around rocks in the Catholic church. The rock is the symbol of growth.
HAWKES: Come on, you're emancipated. You don't believe in that anymore, you don't believe in that stuff.
PILAR COOVER: I took it with the bottle, with my mother's milk, all these rocks.
HAWKES: Yes, yes, you've been drinking from Bob Coover's wine bottles for years.
PILAR COOVER: All the Catholic growth is based on it. The Church is

the pillar, all is rocks, all the virgins are on top of pillars.

HAWKES: Pilar, why did you wreck my little argument?

ROBERT COOVER: In fact, the Virgin of the Pillar which she's named after is on the top of a rock, a piece of stone.

HAWKES: Really. The Virgin and a piece of stone. There we have it. We're not talking about virgins, we're talking about swamps. The pillared Virgin: it doesn't make a bit of difference, she doesn't feel a thing, she has nothing to do with anything, it's a horrifying image, I think of it as the pilloried Virgin. It's a little bit too much like the medieval executions with the pointed stakes.

PILAR COOVER: I thought you wanted to be a tree?

ROBERT COOVER: No, he doesn't, he's a swamp.

HAWKES: Well, I'd rather be the tree that grows through the Virgin than the Virgin who's gotta sit on the tree till it comes out the top of her head, I'll tell you. Any old day. No, but I don't want to be either one.

PILAR COOVER: No tree and no swamp.

HAWKES: No Virgin. No tree, no Virgin, no stake coming out the top of the head. I only want to be a swamp.

PILAR COOVER: Honestly, wouldn't you like right now to be a virgin again? Start it all over—

COOVER: You're not tempting him at all with that.

HAWKES: And she's not tempting you either. Pilar, maybe if you were understanding me more, you'd be more sympathetic, you'd see the glories of the swamp again. Mosquitoes? I tell you what, mosquitoes only buzz around the saddest of swamps, they're old swamps, they're swamps that are drying up. My swamp is fresh, luscious, lovely, full of color, peaceful, yellowish. It's all slime.

PILAR COOVER: Slime?

HAWKES: Slime. Slime. It's a swamp full of slime. The most beautiful word in the English language is *slime*. Think of what it suggests. Saliva. Salacious. Sin.

SOPHIE HAWKES: Sex.

HAWKES: Sly, slippery. Slime, though, is a word different from all the ones we've just said, supreme in its own right—lubricious, it's the ultimate lubrication, it's slime.

MORROW: But did you ever say exactly why you wanted to be the swamp?

HAWKES: Because it's so complicated, never in stasis, always moving, always in movement. And because its definition is always changing. The lips, its perimeter, is there and not there. It has powerful definition, but it's elusive. It changes all the time. The mystery of its depths is unique. What else? The labyrinth. The slime, the sea shell, the vagina are all related to the labyrinth. It doesn't matter that the labyrinth tends to be rather fixed, say in its definition to the swamp. The swamp is a kind of slimy labyrinth or the swamp is a more elusive labyrinth because it is ever-shifting.

MORROW: It's both digestive and reproductive.

HAWKES: Yes, and out of its digestion comes reproduction. It's the colors, it's that I like moisture that's not water. As opposed to solid, as opposed to water, you have what's in between. That moisturized substance is warm of course, in fact hot, body temperature and more.

ROBERT COOVER: How does this relate to putting words on a page?

HAWKES: Well, tangentially. We were talking about—well I don't know what we were talking about that brought up the whole idea of this.

MORROW: We were talking about voyeurism.

ROBERT COOVER: It's a metaphor for fertility and for generating imagery and new ideas.

HAWKES: I think that Brad and I were actually talking about being tremendously isolated. It has to do with voyeurism, tremendous isolation and what happens in isolation. When we were young, if we were really isolated, did we or did we not imagine, try to get beyond where we were, try to conceive of the forbidden sight, the forbidden vision because if you can get there you can get to another one, and beyond and beyond, always trying to escape some horrible limitation, whether it's my puny eight-year-old asthmatic self, or children in Alaska who literally couldn't move beyond certain limitations.

ROBERT COOVER: So the swamp isn't just a bubbly, oozy stuff that suggests eroticism, but also a dark, private, withdrawn space, so it's not like the tree sitting up in the middle of everybody.

MORROW: The model we'd worked out was that the isolation of Jack's childhood stimulated his imagination, and as a reaction the imagination acted as a kind of defense mechanism the organism could rely on. This led to the discovery of voyeurism and eroticism, combining those two as a way of escape.

ROBERT COOVER: I'm trying to link all this to the swamp. How did Jack find the swamp as an image for all that?

HAWKES: I suppose the swamp came years later. Recently, in fact.

ROBERT COOVER: But it does sound to me like a childhood image too, being in this lonely isolated muck.

HAWKES: Well, now wait, don't you know it's pink.

MORROW: This is a very vaginal swamp.

ROBERT COOVER: When you offered me a choice, you didn't say pink tree or a pink swamp.

HAWKES: I'll tell you why. It's a shabby old shorn black tree or a pink swamp. Pinks, pearls, of neutral colors, translucent, transparent and slimy.

ROBERT COOVER: Okay, you've convinced me. I'll take the black tree. Swamps get paved over. That's what parking lots are made out of. They're used mostly for dumping garbage.

MORROW: Don't threaten Jack's swamp. It's a good swamp.

HAWKES: Yeah, Bob, I'm supposed to be the pessimist and you're supposed to be the eternal life-bringer. Will you stop covering my swamp with macadam, for Christ's sake, or garbage? There is no garbage in the swamp we're talking about. We're talking about pure woman. And I don't mean pure. I mean absolute woman, concentrated woman, woman as woman. Uninhibited, real swamp. And I think that the way we've been talking about swamp is essentially *seeing* the swamp. We haven't been swimming in it, we haven't been diving down into it or submerging ourselves in it.

ROBERT COOVER: Though sort of smelling it actually.

HAWKES: That's what you do with photographs, you smell photographs. When you see, all the other senses get activated, all you have to do is see. The flame we begin to smell, the oil that's burning or being consumed, the fire. All the senses become activated. The swamp is a visual image, so we see it. I was talking about seeing as a way of getting myself beyond the prison of a limited town, Juneau, a seven-thousand population town, a thousand miles up into southeastern Alaska, or just locked into ourselves as children with no other children, nobody else, no books, hardly parents at all, nothing, nothing except the dark, the dark and you wheeze and you hear a few horses kicking.

MORROW: And as you were saying in our lost conversation, you would look at your Sears Roebuck catalogue and in it find images that were useful to your imaging.

ROBERT COOVER: Did you make stories out of those catalogues or what? I mean, how did you look at them? Were they purely erotic imaginings? Or did you invent stuff out of them?

HAWKES: No, that's for you, you looked in them and saw stories. I didn't see any stories.

PILAR COOVER: Did you cut out the ladies in their underwear?

HAWKES: I didn't cut them out, I was looking at them. We were just talking about seeing. You don't *do* anything, you just look. Looking is a marvelous experience.

MORROW: What Bob was saying is interesting, though: what's the transition point from just wanting to see to wanting to use a pencil or a pen on paper, begin to scratch, and build?

HAWKES: Probably there is a leap when one is not even aware of seeing at all; simply for one reason or another you're in a situation and you start using the pen, the pencil, the typewriter, whatever it is, and you start using words to hear. But in my case, when you start using words, you do see. Bill Gass argues that he never sees anything when he writes. If he writes about table, he said once, it's all just concept of table. Table to him means essence of table. I don't know what essence is and I don't care. Table is something I can see, more or less. From spindly 17th-century ones to some massive, scarred wooden thing in a country kitchen.

ROBERT COOVER: I'm curious though, Jack, how you moved from your isolation, from a fascination with certain images which may have been erotic and so on—it's difficult for children at any age to look at these things—and how you wanted then to make words express those things, and what it was you were trying to express. Did you feel there was something you wanted to make words describe so that you could hold it? Or was it something you wanted to make move somehow? I'm thinking of the difference between story and lyric. Calvino had a similar experience. He also grew up with a feeling of being isolated. He was born in Cuba because his parents were over there doing scientific research. They had a very secular scientific attitude toward life so he grew up in a home which rejected a lot of traditional stuff. There were no storybooks, for example. And as a little kid, before he was even reading—and he learned to read slowly—he got his stories out of comic strips. He would see these pictures in the comic strips and look at them and try to figure out what might be going on. They were all comic strips borrowed from America with the balloons taken out, replaced by doggerel verse he couldn't read anyhow. His approach then was: a story is there, I've got to see the story of it, see why this leads to that—

HAWKES: Why this leads to that. A child looking at comic strips— and there are no words—has to make up the words, so he makes up the words. He not only makes up the narrative—this happened, that happened—he makes up the cause and effect. He's already in a camp over there, which is the cerebral camp, the conceptual camp. It's fiction dealing totally with ideas. I'm over here. There is no narrative at all. The only thing that's happening is a kind of stunned relationship with an image that one knows nothing about.

ROBERT COOVER: Like a woman in a girdle.

HAWKES: Yes, and you haven't the faintest idea what a girdle is, God knows what a woman is, and all of a sudden you're ten years old in Alaska, the rain's pouring down, the place smells of fish, nothing but fish and pine trees, steep mountains, nothing but water, cold bitter black water, miners coming down from their mountainside with all these horrible candles glowing, the smell of carbon lamps, and here's an image of a woman—no narrative, no conceptualizing, no "what story's involved?" Who cares? I'm not interested in any story. I was only interested in mystery. However I made the leap from poetry to prose is just an accident.

MORROW: What about the leap from youth to poetry?

HAWKES: I don't think there was any. I was writing at a young age and I thought words were something like photographs. And there I was telling stories at ten. I was writing bear stories, or about treasures lost in old gold mines in Alaska. And I think it was an effort at that time to emulate my extraordinary father, my 6'4" father who was a bear hunter, an adventurer and an Alaskan miner, not a miner, a—

ROBERT COOVER: A prospector.

HAWKES: He wasn't a prospector. Those are old shriveled guys who shake their pans in creeks. My father wasn't that. At any rate, I was small, underweight—seventy-six pounds of asthmatic boyhood, isolated in this place, had never read a book, never even saw a comic strip. I was telling Brad I had nothing whatsoever to do with the United States. I hate comic strips because I had nothing to do with them. I heard Jack Armstrong on the radio and I was just baffled. At any rate, trying to make the leap from image to word, the word is the best approximation, it's all I had. I wasn't a photographer, so I would start with images. But when I began to write fiction, I had an idea of sorts, well not an idea, but a set of figures, Sophie's parents in mind, and I made fun of them. That was the first, a highly sophomoric work. Embedded in it are moments of strong visualizing with a lot of sensory experience conveyed through words. Always visual.

ROBERT COOVER: Like stills rather than moving things.

HAWKES: Or slow moving pictures. Always trying to see beyond, see the next figure at the turn of the corner, the next hand that protrudes, the next finger that comes into focus, and that's all. It went on and on. I have never been interested in cause and effect, why or why not, or anything else. I am not interested in concepts or ideas. I see and that's all. But since the age of about fifty-five, I've become more interested in narrative.

ROBERT COOVER: It's what one does usually at age thirteen.

HAWKES: You got interested in narrative at age thirteen. Not me. I was a little more interested in narrative at fifty, because Barth finally took me to task at Buffalo one time. We were with some of his students. "Oh Jack," he said, "You must stop making these awful remarks about plot, character, setting and theme as the true enemies of fiction. Plot is not the enemy of fiction, and you should learn that." Ever since, I've been trying to learn a bit about plot. It's difficult. I'll continue to struggle with it. But we should move to the fire.

SATURDAY MORNING

MORROW: You mentioned yesterday that there were no books in your childhood and that your education was erratic. The life your parents led must have contributed to that since books are heavy and hard to carry around in trunks and boxes. Did your mother teach you how to read?

HAWKES: I think so. I remember my mother reading some Uncle Wiggley stories to me, and a strange fairy tale called "Otto of the Silver Hand," which I used in *The Passion Artist*. Otto is a prince who has an artificial hand of silver, a rather ornate, elegant castration, it seems to me. In Alaska we had five years of permanency and I did finally go to school. My mother had tried to teach me and I resisted every single moment. I argued, I remember, that the sums in arithmetic were arbitrary. I would say, "Why must two and two be four, why can't they add up to five?" I don't know how she stood those afternoons of lessons. At any rate, in Alaska I was unread and innocent, the isolation was overwhelming. Juneau had mountains on three sides, a dark and ugly channel on the fourth, where the ship came in from Seattle. Wiley Post and Will Rogers died in a seaplane that crashed against a piling on a take-off in that channel. Fog, rain at least three hundred days a year, overgrown, dank; we lived on the edge of the woods. Actually I liked the place in some strange way. Long after, I thought it was like growing up in *The Lord of the Rings*. There were marvelous dark secrets to discover in Juneau's mountains.

MORROW: Enclosure and interiority again seem to be the constant defining aspect of setting; in *Virginie* and *Innocence in Extremis* we are in closed estate landscapes. Family and a few friends, perhaps, react to each other within a closed circuit, generally of crisis.

HAWKES: It's true. In *Second Skin* there's the same idea. Donne of course wrote that no man is an island. But I think that every man is an island. We can't get onto each other's shores either.

MORROW: These enclosures either provoke or make possible the dynamic of voyeurism as the only way one can try to communicate in or through these texts.

HAWKES: This developed first in Connecticut when I was eight, when trying to earn fifty cents to take a half-hour riding lesson at the stable behind my grandmother's. I worked in a garden, so I'd be wearing my jodhpurs and kneeling in the dry earth on a hot dusty day trying to plant something, which I hated because only a few yards away was a stable with its dark interior filled with giant, strange, beautiful animals that I would hear at night kicking and snorting, because our house was that close. One day a young woman came trotting by on a gigantic chestnut—that's a reddish-brown horse—and I saw the girl's body in combination with the horse itself, the way her seat rose and fell, and was trim, tight, and how it fit to the saddle every moment or two. She was a remote figure, a momentary illusion, a mythical girl. I'm sure my fiction started there, and I've been pursuing that image ever since, the image of eroticism and aestheticism fused, perfection in a life source.

MORROW: She is probably alive and out there somewhere now, doing her dressage, completely unaware of what she catalyzed all those years ago.

HAWKES: No wonder I'm still taking lessons in basic dressage. But what were we talking about?

MORROW: Your interest in voyeurism.

HAWKES: I remember first the young woman on her chestnut, then a day in Juneau when I happened to see in a shop window a magazine called *Film Fun*—which did have something to do with Hollywood and films, but existed mainly in order to portray women in bathing suits—I was overwhelmed at the sight and managed to make myself go back to the shop and buy the magazine. I smuggled it into my room. We lived high on the third floor of an old house belonging to Judge Wickersham, an illustrious Alaskan, the first to bring law to the Klondike. It pleases me now to think of myself and that magazine in the old judge's attic. Both the photographed women of *Film Fun* and the elegant young woman rider were part of the genesis of my fiction. No image is more arousing than the fleeting image. Blurred travesties of Dante and Beatrice, Petrarch and Laura. Yet just as idealistic.

MORROW: In the lost conversation we talked about the books which were important to you, but mostly about what you didn't read. You went to Harvard something of a virgin in that sense.

HAWKES: The first Harvard courses that meant anything to me were Music I, where I learned the rudiments of music, and a course on Jacobean drama and—to my great good fortune—Chaucer.

MORROW: What kind of music interested you?

HAWKES: I don't remember anything from that course except the Landini cadence. And I don't remember anyone offering a course on Shakespeare, which was the great loss of my life. When I first taught here at Brown I read *Twelfth Night*, *Macbeth*, *Hamlet* and *Othello*. But in 1943 I had read nothing. When I first got to Cambridge I lived in Adams House, near the Grolier Bookshop where I saw a copy of Joyce's *Pomes Pennyeach* and bought it, read it, loved it. I was first influenced, I think, by those few Joyce poems.

MORROW: Joyce was an influence on your first published work, *Fiasco Hall*?

HAWKES: I meant an influence on my early fiction. I wrote the poems in *Fiasco Hall* when I was in high school.

MORROW: How did you know what a poem was?

HAWKES: I've no idea. I hadn't read any that I know of.

MORROW: Never even read the Alaskan poet laureate, Robert Service?

HAWKES: Never heard of him, I didn't know anything about poetry. When I went to Harvard in the summer of 1943, I took my poems to Robert Hillyer. He picked twelve or fourteen from a hundred, I think, and I had them privately printed. That's as far as my poetry went. I took poetry writing classes with Theodore Spencer; John Ashbery was in one of them. But my real moment came when I returned for my last two years to Harvard. Sophie and I had met; and a few months later, in September of 1947, we were married in Montana, where her father was stationed with the Army Engineers at the Fort Peck Dam. That September, back in Cambridge, I met Albert Guerard and got into his fiction writing class. I'd started writing fiction in Fort Peck the summer before; I had athlete's foot and had to sit with my feet in a bucket of potassium permanganate.

Since I couldn't move, Sophie gave me a novel to read. I didn't like it and said I could do better. She gave me a pad and pencil, a child's ruled pad—I've written on them ever since—and began my first short novel *Charivari*. Because of it, Guerard took me into his class. So I had a friend and mentor from then on.

MORROW: Joyce aside, you can't look to any author and say, this work has had an influence on me?

HAWKES: Not that I know of. I was thinking last night, harking back to the idea of not feeling American, of how I went up to Harvard from a rural town that I had nothing to do with, marked for the kind of person I was by my brown-and-white saddle shoes. One of my strongest early Harvard memories is of being ridiculed by a seventeen-year-old Polish count who lived in the adjoining suite and who used to go around in patent leather dancing shoes and an old jacket out at the sleeves. In the American Field Service during the war, I was with a group of Americans who were all outsiders. A midget, an epileptic, a seventy-some-odd-year-old painter, several alcoholics. All of us had problems. Every once in a while we would be near other Americans—mainly flyers—and I remember them stomping around, dancing, and I was simply in awe of them, appalled that young men could have such an American esprit. Certainly I didn't share it. Whereas the English and Irish troops we were with were so alone, shabby, homely, isolated, deracinated, so dead yet admirable that I felt I was more British than American. On the other hand, long ago Bernard Malamud became a friend and on one occasion—it was on the phone—he reacted against those, including myself, who identified my work more as European than American. Bern was angry and said I was the sort of American who belonged with Melville, Hawthorne, Poe. He insisted that my fiction was purely and deeply American.

MORROW: You still don't agree with that, or do you?

HAWKES: Malamud made that remark in connection with *Second Skin*. He couldn't have been more sustaining, and in the sense he meant, yes, I'm American. I finally read *Moby Dick*, *Billy Budd*, *The Confidence Man* and so on, at Harvard—under Guerard I began to read fiction.

MORROW: Who do you look on, among your contemporaries, as having affinities with your work?

HAWKES: I feel close to Barth, Gass, Barthelme, Coover. We know each other, they write what I most admire. Last fall, in the *New York Times Sunday Book Review*, Edmund White, in a review of Robert

John Hawkes

Coover's *A Night at the Movies*, compared those five of us as myth-makers in our various ways. I happen to like grafitti, and a few weeks ago, in the men's room at a local cinema, I saw written above the urinal—it was one of those old vertical urinals that look like wet porcelain mummy cases—this grafitto: Power to Imagination! That's my credo.

MORROW: One of the greatest losses in yesterday's "lost conversation" was about Michael's meditation on buttocks and the word, buttock, in *Whistlejacket*.

HAWKES: I'll get a dictionary. In the opening pages of *Whistlejacket*, Michael is obsessed with the word *corgi*; near the end of the book, suddenly, in connection with one of his photographs, he returns to image and language by thinking of the painter Boucher and the word buttock, which comes, it says here, probably from the Old English, *buttuc*, and means strip of land, ridge, rump, also called nates. Strip of land, ridge. Landscape, the great landscape, the greatest landscape of all. Buttocks. Let's try this dictionary. It says, Middle English, *buttok*, more at butt, the back of a hip that forms one of the fleshy parts on which a person sits, seat of the body, rump. This is the *Webster's New Collegiate Dictionary*, which is a less interesting dictionary than the other one. But we were struggling to discover why that portion of the woman's body is so striking, appealing. Why is it that we are forever looking at the woman's seat, or buttocks? First, there is shape itself. Just as any rounded surface has its appeal, as in the hardboiled egg in its slick and white pristine state. Then there is the concept of the existence of what does not exist, as expressed in Keats' "unheard music" and most succinctly for me, in Georges Braque's "The vase gives shape to space, music to silence." In the case of buttocks, two curves come together, curve into each other, and disappear into a depth that doesn't exist—to the eye at least. The anal area is kissing cousin to the vaginal area, and they keep energizing and adding to the nature of each other.

MORROW: They're diptychal, like your work structures.

HAWKES: A nice thought. Michael complains about the inadequacy of the word buttock, and in so doing tries to lend it euphony. The visual image I want to find is lyrical.

MORROW: You're about to retire after teaching at Brown for thirty years. What do you have in mind to write next?

HAWKES: I'd like to finish the life of Uncle Jake, who is based on my father, of course. We have his childhood in *Innocence in Extremis* and his adult years and death in *Adventures in the Alaskan Skin*

104

Trade. Still to be written is his early manhood in the Great War, which he spent searching for his dead brother, a pilot who had crashed in France. It's alluded to in three pages in *Alaskan Skin Trade,* and I'd like to expand those pages into a novel in which Uncle Jake finally revisits his old grandfather who at ninety years old is still on his horse while troops are bivouacked in his fields around his chateau, and all France is at war. Also, I plan to write a novel called *Monks in Shadow.* Sophie was talking to our daughter on the phone and I heard her say, "Oh, monks in shadow," and she mentioned the exhibition of the Spanish painter Zurbaran, who made some gorgeous paintings of monks in their cowls, high-peaked, some of them quite sinister, guilty, furtive, in shadow. As soon as I heard the phrase, "Monks in shadow," I knew I had to write something about monks. Eroticism and a monastic order—it might be one more way to pursue the kind of innocence I'm drawn to. I'm still trying to write fiction that the reader wants to eat. This is the way a woman writing in the French magazine *Elle* described *Innocence in Extremis.* Another French reviewer compared my work to Watteau's painting. France is my landscape of the imagination.

105

Ilex

Barbara Guest

From the doorway we watched. Alexander
at the basin washing   his face shone
          in bottled water from the green doorway.

———————

Qu'ad Ashir besieged   the iris in bud
blue water with blood   camel shackles
then a comet fell said the astrologer
          castle emptied   yellow bonneted meadow and bone.

The mountain covered with sharp ilex
locally a spiky plant called holm
          Iran heresey like manna
          on the giant winged eagle rock
damascened
                    oasis lily of silk knives   Babylonia.

———————

His passion for abstraction is gripping—

the phalanx in bird leather—
when you parted the copper-eyed leaves the armor
squeaked   sparrows in   modern setting

          looking out from the invisible
          into the past without heads—

          gifted with 'living'—

———————

106

White daphne   Thrace silvered
ghost trained hares in the young snow patches—
    lit by fir cloud   risible Danube
where it widens   blaze of hunted water at horse teeth
                    ode grouping
                    Illyrian sequence—

    apprentice oars.

    Alexander's 'greatness'—a linnet

————————

                    from a floating rock.
three bathing maids   ilex tangled
mauve bassarids—
cavorting   thump
across jealous   sands   the warriors

            Olympias rakes the mirror.

(the noisiness of maternal fame)

————————

        boisterous geographically
                married in tumbled red
        and appropriating mythic comfort
                endlessly Hellenizing
        in a jeweled casket his guarded Iliad
                hero wooing.

————————

            He wears pleasure trousers
                olive bird—
    nomadic filter—the harsh bridals—
            sand eclipse Oxus.....

    "Beyond the limit of our world"

we beg for lustered sleep—Argival—

107

Barbara Guest

———————

psychogenic   they live as if alone
with a shadow thief   Macedonians move in innocent
oil lamp   "esthenia"

Now he is called the God of the East—
        ilex forgeries—elegiac

———————

He comes to a Babylonian garden feverish
beside the pool—"thirty-two years old and
six months"—

        over-stepping Aegean wideness—

We inquire of the night God if we should move
him to the temple....the answer is "no"—

———————

white palms....molded lattice—
Sirius—are his watchers—

        we wait in bronze liquid air
with the pull of soft knots

———————

        we lost him. he disappeared.
rinds of gold   stitched to his aura—
at the entrance armed with blocks—
the stylus blunt—

        mood of helmeted star light

Three Poems
Karin Lessing

NIGHT-ARK, ADRIFT

sea-
rolled, there
where
no blade
propelled, no
whirr, the
sails' —
none of your gulls;

no cry
hooked
land, no
branch, greening,
stepped forward—

night-
ark, adrift...the
water-
divided stars

*   *   *

FORCALQUIER, CANDLEMAS 1986

    stone lips
    that feed
    on stone

their weather-
ing
embrace

final, appeased

for you, water-
addicted
one, breath

our breath
vies
with, stains

the snow
purple

        *   *   *

Bee-orchis,
fluted
up from the root: the

Cyclades
in grass, a
hush
of air, of
sky, as

of flight opening—

in the pale
glow
of those minute,
wind-
drafted idols

TABLET XXVI:
From the Laboratory Teachings Memoirs of the Scholar/Translator

Armand Schwerner

...THE LURE, MIXED LURE, of the beginnings...Five millenia...the particulars and the general Ancient Middle Eastern locus of what is now shards—did the Old Ones experience in a different way? More "total"? What does that mean? As if their past were, well, shallower? That is to say, less dense, less clotted with historical and linguistic embolisms? Less apparently crowded with oppressively insistent repetition? I often feel all that's left for us is pattern, the millenial juices having been subject to so much repetition.

As I age and my eyes weaken I do not read fewer books, but I finish a smaller proportion of the ones I take on. How different from the way I ate books in the greed and ever-new abandonments of adolescence and early manhood. Did the Old Ones, like me in my dawn, live in the revivifying newness of discovery? The history of my mind besieged by 5000 years of written documents is the history by turns of a weary and oppressed animal and that of a repeated and sometimes galling insistence on confronting and mastering the unabsorbable. And their minds? And what about their consciousness, the nature and the growth of their consciousness, they who are perhaps, in the Way of mind, our coevals in one lightning blink of 5000 years....

These speculations lead me to reiterate, but with much stronger intensity, basic haunting concerns which I have alluded to in the course of my editing and translating labors on these *Tablets* as I push back the boundaries of consciousness to earlier and earlier historical—and eventually pre-historical—periods; I have found myself increasingly targeted by adherents of various ethnic, theological, anthropological or psychological points of view. Godfrey Hardy, one of Britain's leading mathematicians, is reported to have made the toast: "Here's to pure mathematics! May it never have any use." As I descend further into the interstices between tablets, between utterances, between graphemes, between pictographs, examining the hollows and the indwelling shadows of their morphemes in the hollows, I too would wish that my studies be, as Leonard Dickson, a University of Chicago mathematician has said of number theory, "unsullied by any applications." This is not to be. What I do *will* be used by persons and groups unknown, in the predictable and sometimes violent efforts to perpetuate their own agendas in the world. I continue my work, but within such penumbras.

Though little credit has been given or recognition tendered to the possible development of a radical self-plumbing before the beginning of the 3rd millenium BCE, recent palaeographic research yields a sense of person as Self-examiner far earlier than any posited up to now. To the almost miraculous and widely recognized period which gave birth among others to the Mosaic teachings—1500 BCE, Socrates and the Buddha—500 BCE, and the Essene Christ, and their outflows, we must now add (ca. 3200 BCE) the excursions in subjectivity hereunder subjoined; most probably non-Semitic, the Mind/ Texture/Determinatives whose recently discovered existence I shall reveal in the course of this laboratory teachings memoir seem ancestral to such true openings into Self as are found in St. Augustine and the desert Fathers— in whom so many historians had previously found the founts, the early openings into self-traveling. Indeed, the perversely refulgent harmonics of the Great Sanhedrin, of the great Inquisitor Torquemada, of the great avenging presences in contemporary Teheran—undoubtedly in most polities of the present world—these harmonics infect my sleep. But work makes freedom.

I would also call attention to the power of the unsullied literary imagination evident in the texts which are the object of my studies, a power generously evident in the work of the so-called scribes, who were of course also redactors, a vector we usually ignore. Thus often the line between redactor and author is hard to draw.

The magnificent and hallowed pictographs which, after Falkenstein and Schmandt-Besserat, I see as only very occasionally translatable into sound values, were certainly the work of our most genial, and probably our only non-Semitic precursors— the *first*, Sumerian, civilization. Deep time. Without them the very scripts of the Akkadians, the Hittites, the Babylonians, the Assyrians, the Ugarits—the scripts of so many Semites, in use for more than 3000 years, amassing an endlessly and immensely unpayable debt to the Sumerians—without them these systematic scripts are inconceivable. But beyond the pictographs, and specially as complexly articulated *with* them, the Mind/Texture/Determinatives recently discovered truly reveal the nascent stages of the history of consciousness. (In the later course of these *Tablets* I shall push back this early notational frontier some 16,000 years and attempt to reveal an articulation. Here I present a few pictographic phrases merely at this phase of our work to acquaint the reader-looker with some of the visual forms and combinations.)

114

Armand Schwerner

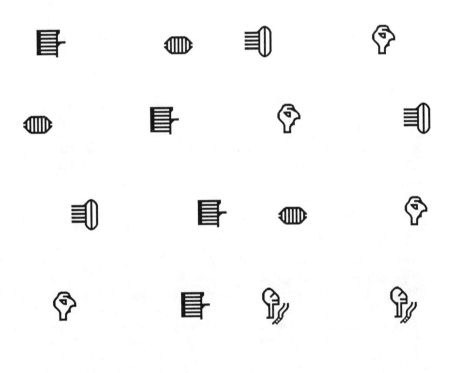

Besides a number of these representative pictographs, essentially Sumerian and pre-cuneiform, Tablet XXVI also includes Mind/Texture/Determinatives, most probably conceived by a blind Tiresias-figure who is, exceptionally for that culture, in touch with mind-texture, differing strata of consciousness, a particular quality of informed subjectivity most surprising for this period in history. I have thought in this connection of Rilke's angel, "in whom space was included, as if he were blind and looking into himself." These contributions, early notations embodying archaic beginnings of human consciousness, appear to be roughly contemporaneous with the earliest systematic human pictographs (although it is not clear whether the artificer is actually such a relatively esoteric occurrence in his cultural climate, whether his contribution is an idiosyncratic conceit, a kind of gnosis, intuitive and undescribed in any available tablet or later papyrus).

Esoteric tradition, as found only in the Tetrahedral Texts, suggests that his blindness was due to schisto-ocularia, or cleft eye, an unusual tropical disease following upon the parasitic infection Bilharziasis. Cleft eye, rarely a serious affliction since the advent of open-eye surgery, causes eventual loss of sight through the slow but inexorable development of a kind of nictitating membrane—a membrane normally present in some birds, which moves from side to side on the surface of the eye. When afflicting human beings this developmentally atavistic membrane extends itself during the slow course of the disability, from the inner corner of each eye nearest the bridge of the nose toward the other side of each of the eyes—a matter requiring generally a duration of some fifteen to seventeen years, during which perception takes on for a while somewhat the mechanism of a stereopticon.

But the object is seen as larger for only a brief while; the damage to the optic nerve has the idiosyncratic effect of doubling and miniaturizing everything in the perceptual field before sight finally fades. It is true of course that the magic lantern, or stereopticon, projects rather than perceives, but the ambiguous relationships between the M/T/Ds and the pictographs puzzle the present translator in ways that often evoke the problem of the distinctions between perception and projection. The blind transformer of his private vision, whom merely for purposes of referential convenience I will name the Ur-Aryan, attempts to embody his remarkable otherness in the Mind/Texture/Determinatives—we will come upon at least 15 different types, all very near each other in kind, but, as we will observe, remarkably subtly differentiated, each, it appears, indicative of a Way of Experiencing. The archetypal form of the M/T/D icon seems a highly stylized graphic whose general design may have been drawn from the traditional 4-part ruminant stomach of various grazing quadrupeds—wisent, urus, ox and so on; existing in another temporal layer it may also represent— a kind of palimpsest—a pictographic determinative incorporating a less detailed stomach as well as the liver and gallbladder, all of course often used in divinatory processes. Any close examination of the spatial configuration involving the liver, stomach and gallbladder of a ruminant quadruped will immediately convince the skeptic of the likely derivation of these icons.

(I reproduce the Ur-form in a font size slightly larger than the graphic pictographs clearly derived from it. Curvilinear forms characterize only a few of the very earliest pictographs. Archaic scribes, yielding to the obdurate characteristics of damp clay, very soon abandoned such forms and attempted stylized duplications of ellipse and arc by means of short lines. Incising went more quickly and with simpler reproducibility. This technological improvement gave up the cursive. Deep time. A loss. We Gutenberg it and we're so hot for the one face of the one writer and the particularizing name):

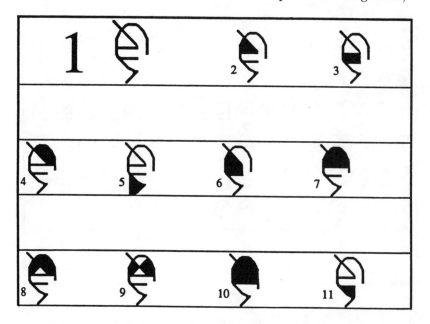

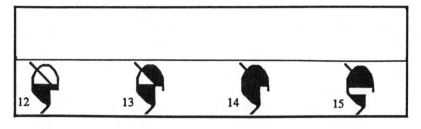

And below, approximately as seen on the one remaining wall in the lowest level at Jemdet Nasr, 162 appearances, the Ur-form again, as a total utterance utterly untranslatable; we know that the 86th icon in this utterance generally represents in later periods the element Mercury and often introduces the variable of ambiguity....

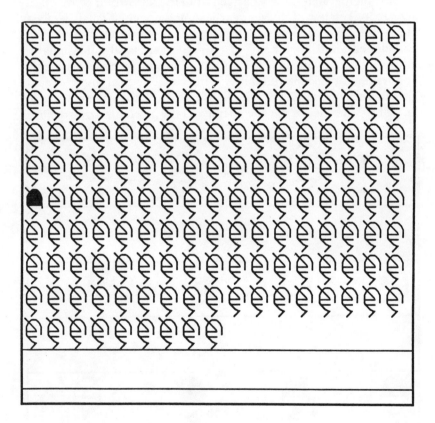

Obviously resulting icons such as these are as I have suggested highly stylized representations— rendered I believe by a sighted scribe doing his best to convey the artificer's inner vision in archaic graphic form. It can probably never be made clear whether the probable originator of the Determinatives had been sighted before succumbing to blindness. What puzzles me, though I am on the track of a possible solution, is the vague resemblance of the icon to a human face. We know that to many archaic peoples the stomach not the heart was the seat of feeling and thought. But—does the face equal the stomach? Or is it conceivably the gallbladder, or a hepatic lobe? The absorption of the profane by the sacred, mythical unification....

Such speculations evoke Octavio Paz's intriguing comments, in one of his magistral disquisitions concerning Tantric Buddhism, about the ineffably close connections between the face and the ass, "...the (repressive) reality principle and the (explosive) reality principle...the metaphor both as it works upward and as it works downward—the ass a face and the face an ass—serves each of these principles alternately.

"At first, the metaphor uncovers a similarity; then, immediately afterward, it covers it up again, either because the first term absorbs the second, or vice versa. In any case the similarity disappears and the opposition between ass and face reappears, in a form that is now even stronger than before. Here, too, the similarity at first seems unbearable to us—and therefore we either laugh or cry; in the second step, the opposition also becomes unbearable—and therefore we either laugh or cry. When we say that the ass is like another face, we deny the soul-body dualism; we laugh because we have resolved the discord that we are. But the victory of the pleasure principle does not last long; at the same time that our laughter celebrates the reconciliation of the soul and the body, it dissolves it and makes it laughable once again." Such Western cautions relating to many contemporary transcendental enthusiasms for imported teachings remind this writer of Jung's salutary 1952 warnings in his "Psychological Commentary" to *The Tibetan Book of the Great Liberation, or the Method of Realizing Nirvana through Knowing the Mind*: "I do not doubt," he says, "that the Eastern liberation from vices, as well as from virtues, is coupled with detachment in every respect, so that the *yogi* is translated beyond this world, and quite inoffensive. *But I suspect every European attempt at detachment of being mere liberation from moral considerations....*" (My italics.)

Tablet XXVI, as well as most of the materials following it, seems to embody the beginnings of early though incomplete and dualistically strained adventures into the nature of Self, the figure of that Self, flawed because in its subjectivity the ego as a dualistically reflective subject does not have access to itself as subject; its access to itself is always unavoidably as an object; the ego is separated and cut off from itself. But the impressive power of insight and the graphic incarnations of states of being, as it were of Hosts, embodied in the M/T/Ds, and variously juxtaposed with different combinations and permutations of pictographs, make essential inroads into the mystery. As instances:

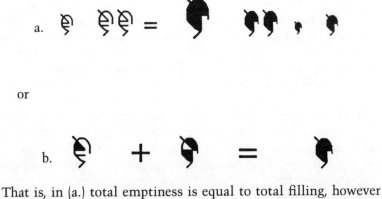

or

That is, in (a.) total emptiness is equal to total filling, however many individual segments are involved, and no matter what their relative sizes. In (b.) we see what seems to be a simple additive process; however further investigation into the nature and function of the first icon in reference (b.),　　　, will reveal its idiosyncratic use as an instrument of transformation in the majority of expressions in which it appears.

The most painful aspect of this editing process consists of the fact that inscriptions, language, forms unroll in time; only a massive graphic large enough to accommodate this entire *Tablet*, a painting obviating Time, could ameliorate my desperate spiritual hiccuping, the physical manifestation of my unappeasable desire to lay it all out at once.

For a more complex example we take the following instance from this *Tablet*, XXVI, drawn from the sequence of pictographic phrases

120

rendered above; Mind/Texture/Determinatives sometimes follow such sequences, sometimes precede them. The phrases under question contain as far as I can discern no transitional, prepositional, conjunctive or subordinating elements, no apparent inflections except maybe those of hope. Imagine the openness of the pre-inflective!

Believing strongly in the moral imperative of sharing the process of cognizing and translation with my readers in the course of presenting archaic gestures, and persisting in that belief in the face of possible misunderstanding and boredom, I now reunite some of the pictographic phrases with their common adjuncts, sometimes general Mind/Texture/Determinatives, sometimes Spharagrams— from the Sanskrit *sphara*, extensive, related to Latin *spatium*, space, and Skt. *sphayati*, increase, grow fat, akin to speed—a neologism I have on appropriate occasion preferred to the somewhat long-winded term Mind/Texture/Determinative.

Before settling on Spharagram to denote an aspect of mind-work I shall soon present, I conceived of the term Sphayatigram, which I abandoned because of a lack of euphony and overhanging tinkles of obesity which would have skewed the true intent of the term as I understand it.

The Spharagram I think of in moments of linguistic and acculturative desperation as a counterpoise to my frustrating efforts to digest the true significance and function of the riverish shiftings of the M/T/Ds, sometimes all mouthings, occasionally fat deltas, not so rarely arising from the source headlands of undescriable thought-mountain sources. A very hell of a natural wonder in fact.

The Mind/Texture/Determinative has complex attributes; occasionally it implies benign, or transformative, or restorative functions; sometimes it represents negative aspects of the general precognitive substratum, which represents the ground within which a specific utterance occurs. Let us take as an instance the

phrase cited above : ⬛ ⬛ ⬛ or earth/*ki*, great/*gal*, fire/*izi*.

When the Mind/Texture/Determinative 🏴 completes the phrase,

as in ⬛ ⬛ ⬛ 🏴, the sequence : midsize earth + midsize great + proportionally large fire usually = oneness, at-homeness, ease-

in-dwelling, large-acceptance, from the usual meaning of ⬛ as fire or sunlight scorching to a final oneness, unity, particularly when the icon, relatively enlarged, is used in terminal position. But when the sequence is completed by the M/T/D 𝕭 , the significance changes radically, given the usual meaning of this determinative: **egocentric demandingness**. What has been called the "behind" quality of mind, inert, heavy, viscous, hot, subject to internalizing fortification and hatred, part of the pervasive texture of experience, is an aspect most characteristic of many M/T/Ds, and rare evidence of archaic iconic representation of complex internal states. In this case the phrase under consideration signifies not ease-in-dwelling or unity but rather profound homelessness, tendency to attack neighbors, irremediable sadness leading to the sort of inner heat that consumes not warms. Certain human attributes—fury; envy; unselective appetite; contempt; unbridled ambition; massive despair; unboundaried self-pity; terror; pleasure at the exercise, however apparently benign, of power; overeating— all carry powerful characteristics of this "behind" quality of mind.

Much has been written recently about the *dépaysement*, the *heimatlos* condition of the present world experience. It is thus of the greatest interest to have discovered in these materials from Jemdet Nasr not merely ancient progenitors of ultimate loss but immediate relatives.

The Spharagrams include Determinatives which particularly emphasize the aspects of openhandedness, freshness, clarity, trusting but not oafish confidence, generosity unaddled by mental soup. (The categorization is instrumental not hard and fast. One scholar's spharagram may be another's M/T/D fumble.) Thus the phrase

𝕭 𝕯 𝕯 𝕯 𝕯 , literally: clarity/opening-out/giving health/recognition of the object, + 4 vulvar pictographs signifying woman, = *garden, world-vulva, heavy-liquid-of-becoming, power*. The Spharagram itself does not *indicate* or itself contain the knowledge of the how of consciousness development, but it opens a vector and opens spaces for one's realization of such knowledge as the looker/reader does his practice through the text. Deep space. Thus the icon is part of a symbolic system not altogether unlike musical notation, which alters and interprets the ground of human performance, in this case not merely linguistic but through and across the bridge of the linguistic and symbolic—fully appreciating and going beyond cognition by means of experience.

Before presenting the first of a number of extant versions of Tablet XXVI, I now consider a few more examples of the ambiguities and amusing perversities which the translation of these materials entails. Take for instance the expression:

What is the nature of the implied relationship between M/T/D terms 1 and 14 in this phrase? We have already seen that 1) *clarity/ opening-out/giving-health* is the Ur-Spharagram. We know from intensive linguistic research, and we have seen, that in

total emptiness, opening-out, seems in a few expressions functionally equal to *totally filled,* however many individual segments are involved, and no matter what their relative sizes. The lack of logic embodied in this lopsided equation seems to me to require further examination, all the more because I am drawn in by some shadow of conviction informing the relationship among the factors, a shadow that seems to me not to deserve serious consideration. Often what can be initially experienced as an entertainment, as in this case, continues as a sadness. I cannot open the inner knot. If I could get into the space between the icons I could know something, say as if living inside Mozart's music, find a fact about the distances, about the nature of the M/T/D reciprocals 1 and 14—converse or supplement.

The boundaried expression presented earlier on,

is in some extant versions the initial, medial or penultimate segment of Tablet XXVI and gives us *earth/great/fire + earth/*

great/fire + earth/great/fire + star/god + mouth. A straightfor-
ward reading might yield the sense,

In the great ease-in-dwelling, in the large acceptance, in the oneness,
In the at-homeness, the constellation (米米米) which is the god
Lives within the boundary, within the voice, separated but near
Separated from the man's house, the woman's great lit house,
Separated + + + + and so near the woman's earth, the man's great fire
Near and separate from the fire/sun scorching into unity
The great land, the house, the great woman and the man, the great
Dwelling in the recognized ease of the great lit earth
In the utterance of the person at the end of the incised clay trail
Which is the wake of the trail of the great lit land & house & the god
And the voice.
          Where is he, mouth of the ear
Great artificer . . . . , perturbed basket of claims
Shoot of shoots & shrinker of [retinues]
Making the mazy watery blue one oozing red
Entreating stutterer in the meaning cave
When they ask Whose, your back curves the answer
In a lion's bending . . . . of a mongoose
Where is he seedling tribulation mixer in the fat ground
Jewel testicle of the mouth & listener, great ear of the mouth
& self-abused leader in the brief low mind mushroom constellations
Quickly unforming to black ooze & rot & stringy filth
Separated and so near the woman's earth, the man's great fire
Near and separate from the fire/sun scorching into unity

The earliest appearance of the extract above excludes determinatives, one of which, in each of four later versions, appears in a
crucial position and of a qualifying size, and, within the focus of a
certain kind of consideration, puts into question the essential direction of this entire text, which seems to concern itself with the figure
we have identified above as the blind transformer, the Ur-Aryan, the
artificer. In these presentations, we persevere in the use of the
following symbols: . . . . for 'untranslatable'; + + + + + + + for
'missing'; [   ] for 'supplied by the scholar-translator'; (?) for 'variant

reading.' Tablet XXVI, we will observe in the course of our work together, includes little hymns of departure, ambiguous lilts of arrival, putative transmogrifications, grievous insult apostrophes, paeans and dirges. We find the variant,

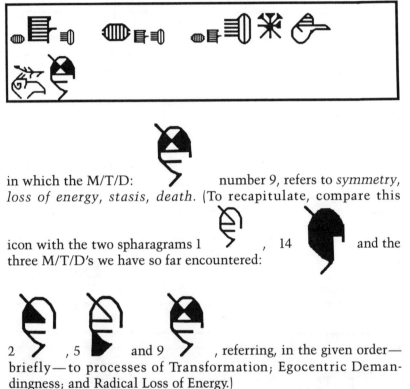

in which the M/T/D: number 9, refers to *symmetry, loss of energy, stasis, death.* (To recapitulate, compare this icon with the two spharagrams 1 , 14 and the three M/T/D's we have so far encountered:

2 , 5 and 9 , referring, in the given order—briefly—to processes of Transformation; Egocentric Demandingness; and Radical Loss of Energy.)

Most remarkably, the variant phrase given above contains a singular instance of an M/T/D-blocker; that is, when any Mind/Texture/Determinative is preceded by the following untranslatable

pictograph: , apparently a face looking up at a branchlet of some sort, that Determinative is totally neutralized, as if a charge in an electrical field had been electrochemically held to absolute balance within all particles. Of course all analogies break down, and I do not mean to press this one too far. It will serve as suggestion of force field activity. Thus, to return to the variant phrase,

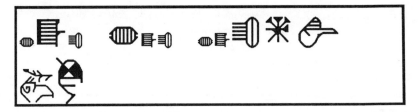

no change occurs in its meaning. Why in this case was the Determinative not simply left out? Many languages manifest unreason-
able conservative fixations, the *gh* for the sound *F* in English, the *spr*
for the sound *T* in Tibetan and so forth, *sprulku* sounded *tulku* for
instance. This may be a somewhat similar persistence. However, it
may be that an unknown redactor of Tablet XXVI intended to void a
significant semantic alteration of the text, potentially encumbered
by whatever eventual socio-religious repercussions he might have
envisaged, and feared. Unfortunately, we do not know the circumstances or the provenance of even the first change in the phrase,
which itself originally presented the Determinative.

We have however recovered the four following sub-variants,

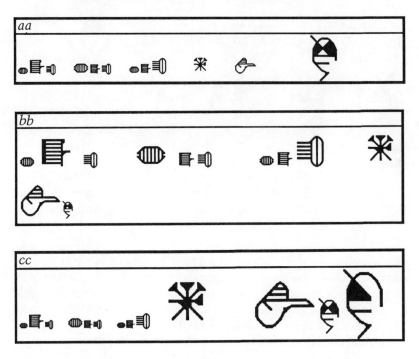

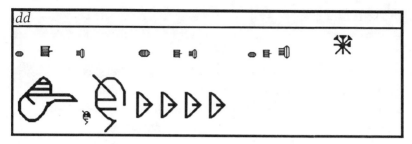

what are we to make of these instances?

In the first sub-variant, *aa*, all pictographs have withered, being barely recognizable:

Ironically, given the down cast of this version, these pictographs are among the most finely incised examples of any surviving work on clay. Little ambiguity attends *aa*. Cognate inscriptions and the logic of the linguistic and historical circumstance lead me to believe that we have in *aa*. the following, completed by the succeeding lines, already presented:

He is already dead. He has died. The ease-in-dwelling atrophies + + + + + +
Separated, small, risible, voiceless . . . . ridiculous, filiform, dry,
The blackened fire & the whitened earth swallowed like the stupid greatness
Of the helpless constellation, the house and the memories of water,
The chastened mouth, the dismembered voice + + + + + + + + + + + +
The boundaries are lost in the . . . ., the sepulcher of the no-memory
Of the moles & saliva & lost fingernail-parings & the dried eyeballs
Stare not even seeing the nothing of everything, they are absent
To themselves, juiceless, blind staring mad. Husk. Rabid in death.
                    Where is he, mouth of the ear
Great artificer, perturbed basket of claims
Shoot of shoots & shrinker of [retinues]
Making the mazy watery blue one oozing red
Entreating stutterer in the meaning cave . . . . + + + + + + +
When they ask Whose, his back curves the answer, proud execution

Of a lion's back dancing .... of a mongoose bending a snake
"As if in my stomach," he would say, right hand by his mouth & voice
No mere picture making on the cave wall
     Where is he seedling tribulation mixer in the fat ground
Jewel testicle of the mouth & listener, great ear of the mouth
& self-abused leader in the brief low mind [mushroom] constellations
Quickly unforming to black ooze & rot & stringy filth
Separated and so near the woman's earth, the man's great fire in
+ + + + + + + + + + ... + + + + + + + + + +
So near and separate and far from the fire/sun scorching into unity.

To avoid unnecessary and possibly tiring duplication and repetition I shall present all three translations of the three remaining sub-variant segments in succession; I shall dispense with an overly detailed analysis of my translation process in this case; the attentive reader-looker may at his leisure work out the correspondences. And I remind him that I do not indicate lost or partly obliterated passages in these representative pictographic sketches, although I may include them in my translations, indicated as usual by the following symbols: .... for *untranslatable*; + + + + + + + for *missing section*; (   ) for *variant reading*; [   ] for *supplied by the scholar/translator*. (Variants *cc* and *dd*, incised separately upon the last remaining wall at Jemdet Nasr, are directly followed by the untranslatable 162-unit spharagram-constellation reproduced above.)

Briefly, the burdens of the sub-variants *bb, cc, dd* indicate the following:

bb. He is not quite dead (pictograph f, *mouth*, increases a bit in size at the expense of M/T/D #9, *symmetry/loss of energy/death/stasis*).

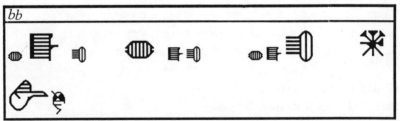

bb

cc. He is someone else, perhaps an animal (M/T/D #2, Spharagram of Transformation, overcoming the somewhat shrunken M/T/D of symmetry and death and loss of energy, completes the phrase here).

dd. He will surely never die (the pictographic molecule, *heavy-liquid-of-becoming; power; world-vulva,* is added to complete the phrase; in addition we now find between the pictographs *star/god* and *mouth,* pictographs *i* and *u* representing *sun/early morning,* , in conjunction with the pictograph *childbirth,* , a very powerful intensive, also understandable as *great-eye-of-light* and *birth-bird,* both extant in a joint presentation in one other appearance at Ras Shamra, with the signification *birth-giving-eye-which-fuses-opposites-through-holy-scorching-and-which-blinds-for-seeing*).

129

Armand Schwerner

He is not quite dead. Between the star and mouth
The abyss sucks the tiny winging desert flies to dry death and also
Between the great fire
And star in the forlorn symmetry of the beautiful.
        The blind artificer said:

> *When I was young they would praise*
> *just about all I'd say, as if I breathed*
> *with them; my times are bad, the past is a joke,*
> *former admirers hound me, alone and treed*
>
> *what's left of my ties with them who*
> *praised anything out of my mouth—my voice*
> *now that life floors me and they cut*
> *my best song, seeing what, lies?*
>
> *what we had together is lost; they praised me once*
> *for any language at all ; I'm now to fall,*
> *now in my troubles; my merit is my seeing,*
> *their hate infects my days*
>
> *I was acclaimed: whatever came*
> *deserved their praise; now hostage to my life*
> *I encounter their contempt for my dearest*
> *song; I live in loss and strife.*
>
> *they laugh at the breath I love—*
> *once, whatever I voiced, they'd give me*
> *praises; my life now in a painful*
> *fall, what do they see?*
>
> *is nothing left? my friends and my time*
> *have turned on me who once*
> *was the target for praise: the oracle*
> *turns dunce.*
>
> *what we had I was*
> *acclaimed what I love has turned dearest hostage*
> *any words at all*
> *out of my liver; what I gave I gave*

with my mouth from the inside
of my eyes now that life floors
I encounter anything their need for the fall grain
is nothing young? they praised as I breathed
my times are with them the past is treed, alone I said
which dunce was the target for which oracle?
admirer's a joke bitterness
a dunce the hound of the empty is the full,

        was what we lost
what we had?
now my best lies in the cut of my trouble every target
deserves work   beauty
is the purgation
of superfluities

In this stony ground of the great artificer,
In the holes, between mountains . . . . hot . . . .
Wild bulls compose themselves in his breath which is the hot wind
Of the desert of his words but also in his bitter word-trap he is
Inhospitable to lost cows and goats, brutal to the lost. Where
Is the room in him for the tame, the life of milk and riverrun fields,
Overcome as he totters over the cave of his stomach holding his words,
Great carpenter of the insides.
          The sweet language waters grow
From his stomach, ... his + + + + + + + + + + +, his . . . .
From his testicles, and in his heart the semen grows
Into the fetus-form of his [verbs]. That will kill him in a great fire
Separated from a house. That will sicken him in a vast house
Cut away from the life of flames and scorching. He goes. May he die.
He leaves. May he die. We will continue + + + + + + + + + + + +
In the bleached world. He dies.
We will store what even his greed can not curb. Still riddles pierce us.
He is who? A she. Giving out. Leaping in. Cut away and thinning out. Deep
Song. Great shaken word-stuff + + + + + + missing + + + + + + ...
Leaving a change. The abyss is a hope
Yawning between mouth and star.

131

Armand Schwerner

The barley of his words
Swells in the wrong ground of his liver, the child of his verbs puffs up
In the wrong field of his sickening heart, he is wrong in body
For this bearing, he is shaken . . . . + + + + + + + + +
As in the pitiless beak of a gliding
Vulture over his own stony ground, the rock-words of his hot tenancy
Themselves overcome in the trial, he falls + + + + + + + + +
Mushroom dark [spider]
In the filiform sadness of his heart's thin remaining afterbirth language
After his perverse gift, his rain,
In the near-death and the blind rise of his word-fall happiness.

He is someone else, perhaps an animal. He lives inside plant names.
He races inside his messages of fleet means. He is the calling voice
Of the names inside the wheat and the barley. He can't say them
Forever. He tells them +
Through the inside of his eyes, he sees
The inside of his eyes and describes the animal names of plants.
He looks and he tells. He lives inside the scorching sun, he also leans
+ + + + + + upwards + + + + + + + downwards + + + + ...
In his long trial toward the sun
. . . . the name of the water falling, the voice
In the water slithering and trekking underneath the soil calling
To receive the good names, to say the good names, and to receive
And to receive . . . . like the king of the hurricane who draws
Lightning and + + + + + + + + + + + + the sound, the proper
Voice for the saying, the murmuring, the uttering, the chant

132

Of wheat and barley changed by murmur into animal liveliness,
By uttering, by striking the stomach and opening the ....

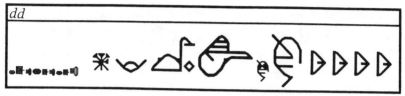

He will surely never die. The world is made of his voice.

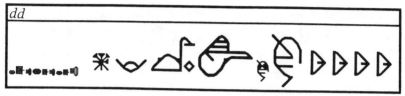

Armand Schwerner

                    Where is he, mouth of the ear
Great artificer, perturbed basket of claims
Shoot of shoots & shrinker of [retinues]
Making the mazy watery blue one oozing red
Entreating stutterer in the meaning cave . . . . + + + + + + +
When they ask Whose, his back curves the answer, proud execution
Of a lion's back dancing . . . . of a mongoose bending a snake
"As if in my stomach," he would say, right hand by his mouth & voice
No mere picture making on the cave wall
                    Where is he seedling tribulation mixer in the fat ground
Jewel testicle of the mouth & listener, great ear of the mouth
& self-abused leader in the brief low mind [mushroom] constellations
Quickly unforming to black ooze & rot & stringy filth
Separated and so near the woman's earth, the man's great fire in
+ + + + + + + + + + + + + ... + + + + + + + + + + + + +
So near and separate and far from the fire/sun scorching into unity.

To the degree that I am involved in the process of formation of the canon of this sacred material, and to the degree that I will be responsible for the slamming of the gates to any future inclusions, I have experienced a certain resistance against the placement of the segment **"Where is he, mouth of the ear..."** after the affecting brevity of variant *dd* and the monumental presence of the 162 Jemdet Nasr cave wall graphics. I tend to think that in the interest of their teachings earlier redactors might very possibly have omitted the rhetorically diffusing movement following such an inspirational apotheosis. But palaeography is not propaganda.

Three Quintets
Iliassa Sequin

self-circumvented
perhaps it was—the only child of an effeminate
juggler
receding in amusement

      with the avarice of stringent crimson, without
      a clown's imprints on her suckling face

perhaps she has deceived th' encrusted plot

*

against luscious arbiters of fear, incest drew on me
           with darkness

counterfeiting ...... sisterly in self-betrayal
to reconcile 'unbridled-blood's forborne streaks'
'upreared brotherly by lust'

      you loved me

*

(heretical) self-veered in her white moon-squadrons, somebody
      unlaced the weapons, the tambourines
      bulging

Iliassa Sequin

(among contorted angels)

melodious-self-mimicking......his life......
              in pastoral relapses of a novel boredom

                                   *

captives of hawked words, rebuffing-mouthed—if they spoke
or pried—

              on groveled tongues' shortest defeats
              'hindered by alchemies' assaulted trophies'

if they will succor with expiring lips
              scarewafers of eloquence, triumphant

                                   *

              what forfeit of light on shifted inspirations,
              due to unmake solstitial excuses
              strove

              in a crystal indolence   'curdy or viscid, forgiven
                                                      redder'
betraying, pitying – – – – under his slanted firmament's
unpainted eclipses

                         *   *   *

while wallowing famine relished its own—gray, unriddled
feathers
(emaciated seagulls have ravished)

while
quietly following me
'engrossed by charity's enfeebled counterparts of viscera
 forgiven'

....

*

though you have cudgeled their lessened bequests—
with white farrows

vanity's peerage.....
(self-delivered in a sleuth-pelvis)   straddle in resolution

                'over an' over, heredity of vengeance'

—adhering on gluten awards

*

—condensed in nude perjuries—   growing asunder ,,,
    his voice echoed ...... 'the nuptials of the deer-stalking'
      male, benumbed

                   so long ago a cry

'the lips that leaped over cadence' to virgin
mimicks

*

137

Iliassa Sequin

uneven to their lust-deficient owners
recount ,,,,
   —seduced by prayers for having received and convulsed
,,,,,,, flitting expansions
   'carried on jaundiced images of lacerated tokens'

  preposterously
  among my fingers' oars on oars, drowning

       *

    'let me inter these margins by you,
    under swollen unicorns, unfeignedly ridged'

slandered with weakness—
to rebel
      'out of mercenary visions,
      hornless within a festered sky'

    * * *

chance
  having relinquished 'shuttles of dreams' , , , , , ,
 —devolved to nothing, counterpoised away
        in offal-hearts
        until tomorrow

  it might warrant in oblivion 'mourning-wefts for their
           treason'
(portending backwards another masquerader)

       *

decrepit hands, unfurling his caresses
'I have scorned and dispossessed
    thoroughly (their) fate

never so conjured by the reels of (my) fortune, shivering . . . .
on a last, inclement line
        with fishmongers
                drawn to (my) womb

*

with a drunken leer, they abjured to converse ....
of thickened urchins   'hawkers of temperance'

slyly daggled in rickety embraces (like untried partners
with loutish disavowal,
like guileless dwarfs
distending their melancholy)

*

being solicited to its procurers of scarlet interims,
     orange, the oracle of lust   'ripened in infirmity'
     abstained , , , , , , ,

 'threshed from his injuries
  below'
invulnerable under your masculine-breasted
    fissures , , , , , , , , ,

*

Iliassa Sequin

sulphurous hounds' bilious revenues
of death

    —were given in crumpled detention – –– – smeared
    over a bias for lickerish, callow butterflies
    against prudent vigils

so contritely—infectious by rescuing a surfeited mongrel – ––

Paul West

An Interview by Bradford Morrow

WE BEGAN with a telephone conversation around Veteran's Day last year, continued through correspondence over the next four months, concluded on St. Patrick's Day with a tape recorder running during lunch in New York. Like the Hawkes, this dialogue has taken on its own form—the letters sorted themselves out into three autobiographical essays as my written questions and promptings dwindled away very naturally into a silence. Questions I asked at lunch were meant purposely to fit like mortise to the tenon of the letters, and so that is how the transcriptions have been placed.

1.

In the Derbyshire village I grew up in, the word "book" denoted a magazine or an illustrated supplement. I have no idea why one of the noblest words we have fell thus in status, even pronounced to rhyme with one of the ignoblest ("gook"), but I developed early on a quiet obsession that only a book deserved to be called a book. A book was holy, solid, and secret, worthy of hushed tones and the best brown wrapping; you didn't get it wet, didn't—if you could help it—lend it out, certainly not to somebody who thought a book was a floppy, outsize, glossy thing. You might get them to recognize what a real book was, but somehow the returned book would seem the worse for its stay among the heathen.

I was surrounded by book lovers, most vividly at the house of my paternal grandmother, where an entire big family, excepting only my father, moved in and out of jobs as if treading upon magma. Roguish, dramatic-eyed sister and equally roguish but more sedate brothers could be found almost any day of the week fast asleep at four o'clock in the afternoon snoring happily after a long night with John Buchan, Rider Haggard, or Edgar Rice Burroughs. Shiftless Irish people I heard them called, but I never thought of them like that. Rather, they were the priests or maintainers of a pleasurable cult;

141

they didn't want to work, talk, or get married, they wanted to read, and they shut out the daylight lest it interfere with the assimilated magic of black words on white paper. This was the cult I aspired to, although I worried about what I found under the beds while those chronic readers no doubt dreamed of Richard Hannay, Prester John, and Tarzan of the Apes. Big chamberpots brimming with urine became inextricably linked with the act of sustained reading, and I envisioned my aunts and uncles crouching to relieve themselves without for a second taking their eyes off the book, which is hard to do if you have to walk a while or open a door, or take aim. My grandmother slept when they slept, all eight of them, but not from the exertions of all-night reading. No, she was weary, I told myself, from emptying chamberpots, and from slicing enormous roasts of beef to make the delicious salted sandwiches that kept the readers going from dusk until dawn. Around four o'clock, if you were lucky, though you wouldn't get a cup of tea you could help yourself to several half-eaten sandwiches, the meat dried out, the bread curly and brittle, but edible fodder for an eight-year-old adventurer.

An adventure it was when I peeked at the books, while Annie and Mable and Norah and Ivy and Colin and Bert and Raymond and Frank snored on, or, more venturesome, peered into the triangular cupboards that filled the corners, bearing out of the bedroom a small stack of faded volumes. There were lots of love stories. Not so many adventure ones. The good books were always out, on the beds or the floor, never in the musty-smelling cupboards. Downstairs I would go, to settle in and have a good read in the mood of the house until Mother came to collect me and return me to the world of every day. This was how I came upon Bram Stoker's *Dracula*, hair-raising (and difficult) for a kid as young as I, yet indelibly poignant as I remember it: a tale of horror shot through with matters quite other, the last of which struck me even when I was a little booklover: "This boy will some day know what a brave and gallant woman his mother is. Already he knows her sweetness and loving care." Much earlier in the book I had come upon references to the "Arabian Nights" and "the ghost of Hamlet's father," both of which puzzled me until I asked my mother, who told me that there was another kind of literature, *hers*, in which the Haggards and the Burroughses, maybe even the Buchans, didn't rate at all, but for which I was not ready.

I was never ready, nor was I in a hurry. I was worming my way, confident for reasons still unknown that all I needed would reveal itself in time. All I had to do was keep on reading, like my aunts and uncles, like my father, who stayed up nights, reading, as if he had never left his parents' house, and then I would soon be like my mother, who kept normal hours and had read everything already. When I went to my paternal grandparents' house, I was delving into a morass of popular literature, getting a foretaste of the lurid and the melodramatic, but in the house where my mother grew up the books were quite different: ponderous works on metallurgy and chemistry, thinner ones on grammar and harmony, several bound collections of the unillustrated story "comics" called *Chums* and *Boys of the Empire*, in which clean-cut boys of almost culpable loyalty learned how to sacrifice themselves for the colors. I saw that my father and his siblings read for fun, in heedless hedonism, lost in a vicarious trance, and did not want to become better readers, whereas my mother and her siblings thought of reading as catalysis in a life enterprise leading to improvement, service, and leadership. Going from the one house to the other was like going from the underworld to the daylight, it was an ascent from decadence to uplift. If there was a choice to be made, I never made it, wanting the best of both worlds. At Grandmother West's the books were upstairs among the semi-clad people, and there was something illicit about both, something barbarous. Upstairs, there was a hopper of boundless natural vitality. Upstairs at Grandmother Noden's there was a sitting-up-straight room designed for you to read books in, almost as if you were in church, present for something tonic to be done to you, so you braced yourself, got ready for it, and only then would Dickens or Mrs. Gaskell began to address you. You had to be in the right state of mind: stiffly at ease, aware of your responsibilities as a book-reading soul. In this way I became acquainted with Kipling's *Kim* and A.E.W. Mason's *The Four Feathers* and—since there was a piano in the room—the way music looked when written down. Yet, reading through those big heavy sail-like pages, I learned more Italian than I did music, being word-obsessed; musical notation was no more to me than a constant parade of tiny golf clubs linked together, whereas *presto* and *andante* meant volumes.

My mother and father had removed their own books from their parents' homes, so on *our* shelves the two realms of reading collided: the atavistic and the righteous, although it was noteworthy that they each had their own favorite dictionary, my mother's an Ogden's, my father's a John Bull. Even then, at ten years old, I thought it natural to have parents to whom a separate dictionary was as imperative as a separate towel, even if having one interfered with the art of communication. My mother taught me grammar, on her knee, next to the shelf on which sat her Tennyson. My father taught me geography and military history as I squatted on the rug, head level with the lowest shelf, on which there sat his copy of Jeffrey Farnol's *The Amateur Gentleman* and works of Alexander Dumas. Whereas my mother had George Eliot and Lamb's *Tales from Shakespeare*, my father had several racing novels by Nat Gould and *Covenants with Death*, a book I was warned not to open—it was a collection of atrocity photographs, there to remind my father of the war in which he lost an eye. I thus saw my first pyramid of human heads, Armenian ones, presided over by two grinning Turks.

Gradually my own books found their way onto my parents' shelves, and for the first time I seemed mentally real to my parents. In situating my own books among theirs, I began to find other books not theirs at all, such as the copy of Alphonse Daudet's *Mes Bêtes* that belonged to my mother's youngest brother (dead in South Africa at twenty) and a treatise on bell-ringing that had belonged to my father's father, who once showed me how to firm up a mended bellrope with my naked foot. After a while I realized that book-shelves are there not to keep the books quiet, but to offer them up, not to make the books turn their backs on people, but to invite readers to browse, and that included strangers too, even those who, without asking permission, at once headed for what you had thought was the most private thing in the house and made free with it: "Oh, *Barnaby Rudge*, fancy having that." Then they'd ask to borrow it, *to take a book away*, and I would flinch. Well, they could have *Barnaby Rudge* but not *Aircraft of the Fighting Powers* (accurate plans with photographs and heaps of data: a tiro's *Jane's*). It was only much later that I discovered the possessiveness of Oxford's Bodleian was equal to mine, and when I had to swear never to light matches or light fires in that august ancient library I knew only too well what they were getting at. Of course they wouldn't lend, and they would only let you read if you had the magic green card, the very thing I'd have asked my parents to insist on if I'd been able to think ten years forward.

When on September 3, 1939, I heard the radio say that we were at war with Germany, I walked down Church Street, past Church Row, through Gashouse Lane, to the Old Mill, to buy a bag of apples, in case food became short (my parents were looking ahead). But, before I picked up the apples, I scouted the nearby wood for a place in which to hide my books, or my favorite ones anyway, and made mental note of an old coke oven shaped like an igloo: I could dig a deep enough hole, wrap the books in a waterproof groundsheet or even a cyclist's oilskin cape, then bury them. The brickwork of the coke oven would keep shell fragments and rain away, although, to be sure, it would invite animals in.

This part of the woods was uncanny to me, not so much frightening as out-of-this-world. Only a year before, I and some friends had gone wandering through there in search of young ash trees from which to make bows for our arrows. We found ash wands all right, but also, dangling inert and pale-green-faced from a high bough, a young man, who must have been there at least a couple of days. He was wet. This apparition was so far beyond our range of experience that the only thing we thought to do with him was to swing him gently to and fro, with gingerly fingertip shoves. Like something out of *Dracula* he did gentle pendulum in the afternoon, within reach yet beyond it too, not so much a dead man as a man we did not understand. It never occurred to us to cut him down or to check him out. He was a given: monstrous, maybe, but as final as an oak tree. After a quarter of an hour we crept away, having given him a last shove, easily enough momentum to keep him on the move long after we had left the wood. We never told. And I never heard any more about him. He certainly had disappeared a week later, but only into my reading. An anti-Tarzan, he had swung into a mythic realm that was mine alone, in which the spectacle of a small boy swinging a corpse about, even if with an almost pianistic touch, was far from bizarre.

Carrying the bag of apples home, I pondered boltholes and hiding places. What if you wished to hide yourself along with your books? What was the good of going into hiding without something to read? The best, yet most impossible, place to conceal a book, I found, was the cockpit of a Messerschmidt 109 fighter plane shot down over Sheffield and put on show to have us be of good heart: a pale blue, tattered flake of a thing with bloodstains on the instrument panel, from which the dials had been removed. Behind *that*, I thought, you could hide a couple of precious volumes, except from the hands of enterprising schoolboys such as I. In the end, the solution I came up with was quite different; my mind had matured, and so had my ways of loving books.

I had, I recognized, to take possession of my books in a subtler way, linking their ideas seamlessly into a daydream that was mine alone: unbombable, uncapturable. In the presence of a little, vivid mind, the books uncurled like vines, tangling up with one another, no holds barred. In no time, my head became a thicket of weird segues. I discovered the impulsions of the made-up. The siren song of fiction found me out as a willing accomplice, and I have been unable to say it nay ever since. Not only that: some years later, browsing in one of our two dictionaries, I discovered etymology: not just the bricks the books were made from, but the mud and straw, and the way in which kindred words float far apart, like *quartz* and *siren*, to be reunited only by juvenile pedants such as me.

So when the browser-borrowers came, my books had vanished into fictive fusion and etymological dispersal, both blurred and dismantled. I was off into a new realm whose first version had been what we called comics, except that these had few pictures and lots of small print. Boys whose parents could afford it could buy one each day, each having four or five stories (there were none for girls, so my sister read mine). Monday you got *Adventure*, the name of the comic. Tuesday nothing (a bleak day indeed). Until the next blank of Sunday, you got *The Wizard*, *The Rover*, *The Skipper*, and *The Champion*. Each comic had a different emphasis, with *The Skipper* and *The Champion* offering too much uplift and not enough thrills. In the others I rediscovered the exotic melodrama of Grandma West's underworld: watered-down Sax Rohmer and Edgar Wallace, until the same kind of material began to appear in large-octavo paperback form, its print small and smudged, its jackets lurid and never quite dry, its interior a swamp of ink's aromas. I remember inhaling and inhaling the smell as I carried the book home. It was really more a magazine in format, but it was book length. Later on came smaller formats, books so tightly bound you couldn't open them (they would have worked well as mousetraps), and a few of these found their way among the books on the shelves, much to my mother's disapproval. To compromise, I agreed to put them to the right of *Mrs. Beeton's Cookbook*, where I had already agreed to put my *Boy's Book of Magic Tricks* and the Stanley Gibbons catalogue of postage stamps. I now realize that to the right of Mrs. Beeton were only the resident psychopaths of our times, Hitler, Mussolini, et al. Tyrannical and stodgy, her recipes required a vampire's tooth, and I thought it would be nice to seal her up entire, going from page to page, sticking 1 to 2 with moist dumpling, 2 to 3 with thickened Windsor Soup (very brown and gritty), and so on, until I had converted the entire tome to something approaching mummification.

On the shelves below the books we set gramophone records ranging only from waltz to foxtrot to quickstep, and on these we arranged the successive weekly issues of the periodical succinctly called *War* and another one, almost *Life*-like, called *Picture Post*, both of which we bought in order to see what kind of mess the country was in (it would be about 1942). Spurning the binders offered for these, we preferred to keep the weeks loosely assembled, like mourners, hardly daring to bind up with wires and clamps fifty-two install-ments of horror into a new *Covenants with Death.*

Eventually books sat flat on top of other books. Intruders all, Kinglake's *Eothen*, Rousseau's *Reveries of a Solitary Walker*, and Molière's *Le Misanthrope* balanced like tiles ready to fall as my younger sister and I addressed ourselves to the corrida of university entrance scholarship examinations and such appalling questions, answerable from within no book, as "Do you find the categorical imperative stylish?" or "To what extent are the last lines of Shake-speare's tragi-comedies, so-called, palinodes of the first lines of the Books in *The Old Testament*?" Other questions were even worse. It was as if the calm, serene, contained world of knowledge had been irradiated overnight and had given itself over to horrendous muta-tions designed to leave you speechless. Somehow what you learned from books had to be adapted to this regime of the pyrotechnical perverse—but only in the scholarship exams. The routine exams, intended for steady readers with good memories, were no touble at all, whereas these others, mainly cooked up at Oxford or Cambridge, were there to separate not merely the sheep from the goats but the unicorns from the elands. No one could pass.

Books piled up on books, almost like a desecration of such a pleasant habit as family leisure reading. We crammed. We boned up. We learned to skim, to survive, even to win, but we missed the casual attitude to books of our earlier years and envied our parents when, with tender indifference, they weekly lifted away the termi-nal moraine of our school books and chose one of the old stand-bys: *The Mill on the Floss* or *The Count of Monte Cristo*. You spend the rest of your days making a list of all the books you'll read or reread "when you have time," as if time were something whose back you could bend, like a book's, or whose hold on you you could sleep away.

2.

BRADFORD MORROW: How do you account for your reaction to this remarkable moment in the forest and your response to it?—that is, because of the family's almost blind obsession with books, and the separate worlds in them, and your own constant immersion in the world of the word, do you think that you'd begun to blend an internal with external in your imagination and response to life?

PAUL WEST: We were a gang of kids, Our Gang, and not one of us had any overt response. We were each keeping our cool in the presence of the others. We didn't quite realize what we'd found at first, and then we tumbled to it and somehow went into anesthesia. We weren't old enough to recognize it in a serious way. We were initiated enough to see dead animals, and kids pretending to be dead. This was out of our experience. As I recall, nobody used the word dead. It was a simple transit from the final recognition of what this was to the next step, which was to shove him around a bit. I think it was adolescence, and not a literary experience. I knew it was not a book that was hanging on the rope.

MORROW: When did that moment come when external and internal became blended for you—because I know from talking with you in the past that moment did come; then it would have been a book hanging on the rope, wouldn't it?

WEST: The blurring of voices, or whatever they are, came when I was fourteen or fifteen. Suddenly I became aware of a buzzing in the head, and it's never gone away. Occasionally I wish it had, but I'm kind of glad of it. A lot of those voices yield novels. I've learned to listen to them. I was a spellbound child, but that spellbound child had also gotten an idea of what World War Two was like when dead people were not unfamiliar. I link with that the fact that my mother's father was a butcher, and had a small abattoir around the corner. I used to go and watch them kill sheep, pigs, cows, with a humane killer. I was more disturbed by watching the killing of a beast than watching the guy dangling from a rope. Thirty years later I'm much more disturbed thinking about the suicide in the woods than the animals killed for food. At one point I took my three-foot teddy bear around to the clamming house and humane killed it. It was full of straw, so it was all right, but somehow I had initiated my teddy bear into this realm of death. All those kids who saw the hanged man were traumatized not only by the death itself but by the War, which was explicit. We got bombed and saw pictures of people blown apart. This went on for five years. I'd always known that death existed, though. In the bath at night, hearing the wind stutter beyond the river and make that sucking sound in the drain while some night freight chattered along the tracks north I would get this freezing sense of desolation, of body's frailty and mind's vulnerability. It was out there, I knew, looming and hovering, poking around, looking for someone to nail. Atmospherics, yes; it was like being smothered in *Macbeth.*

MORROW: When did that shift take place that moved you from reacting to the violence of the world by killing your teddy bear to writing about it?

WEST: I was writing stories when I was twelve about epic heroes who flew planes and dealt with death. It was consistent with the imaginative life I was leading.

MORROW: It's consistent with what Jack Hawkes was telling me not even two weeks ago—the child-artist operating as best it can within the world of the imagination, then pushing forward into a more visceral response to that world by beginning to compose adventure stories.

WEST: I didn't know I wanted to write novels, but I certainly had this itch to make up stories like the stories in the comics I got every day. The weren't pictorial, simply columns and columns of prose, all adventure stories. *I, Said the Sparrow*—which I wrote at speed, it sort of fell out, in a week—looked to me like a wholesome, rather well-adjusted book. Several people who read it carefully said that on the contrary it's a morbid book, full of death, so I reread it, and they're absolutely right. It is loaded with death imagery. To some extent it was like Monsieur Jourdain speaking the language of death at age eleven.

MORROW: The title is steeped in death.

WEST: *The Fall of the Sparrow.*

MORROW: And Catullus' poem.

WEST: The original title was *The Earthenware Embryo*, which I got rid of.

MORROW: As in poetry there's a bodily response to rhythm, music— Pound pointed out that poetry can never successfully move too far away from dance—in prose fiction is there a bodily response? With a long work of fiction the reader must relinquish to the text a significant chunk of time. The body is forgotten, to some extent, but still remains with the reader.

WEST: I've had to deal with my own body too much. When I'm working I don't move. I can sit for five, six hours like something made of stone. Only my fingers and wrists move. This gift for immobility is useful but at the same time I'm very much aware of the rhythm of what I'm writing, and often I know the rhythm of the twenty-third sentence down the pike: I don't know what the hell's going to go into it but the rhythms in between are there and the rhythm of the sentence that's way down there is there too. I can't explain that. It is true that this binds with the body and a sense of dance.

MORROW: There is a projective intuition at play, too, I'd think.

WEST: Projective intuition, an extrapolation from the sentence I am working on—I can't explain it, I don't hear words, I do hear curves and loops and repetitions. This is reassuring. I find it a great, flexible banister to hold to, but never mind, it's a rope ladder. I know that I'm not going to have trouble writing the third page from now because I can already hear the rhythms going on, which are not the rhythms of the sentence or paragraph coming into being now.

MORROW: Do you pin this projective intuition or extrapolation on a preconceived series of reference points that you work out before you begin a book, or do you just shoot like a ray?

WEST: I just go. I have planned books in enormous detail, with fanatical precision, and then rarely taken notice of what I've planned. It's good to have meticulous plans but I rarely go back to them. The energy takes the thing along. I suppose it's Dionysian. The planning, the details of outline, are Apollonian—but they're a kind of insurance policy. With *I, Said the Sparrow* I simply sat on a balcony with a pile of writing pads and ball-point and didn't plan anything. In fact, when the book was finished it was one long splurge of 180 handwritten pages and I went back over it and divided it up into sections and chapters. It was spurious, because it was a big pop and to subdivide a pop is spurious. Ted Hughes pointed out when he reviewed it that this was a higgledy-piggledy book, like the contents of a small boy's pocket being tumbled out, and he was right. If I ever reissue that book, I will take out the chapter divisions and let it be one splurge. It was fun to do. I had no idea all that stuff was there. That was written to a large extent on the rhythmic principle, too, if it is a principle.

MORROW: Do you think that comes out of your muscial experience with your mother?

WEST: Probably. I'm writing to the sounds of my childhood, of being uncritically loved for having been born. It gets me back into a totally defenseless condition, anything can come into my head, there are no taboos. It's also enormous security. I don't listen to music while writing book reviews, because that's a more awkward discipline than writing fiction.

MORROW: That you can work so swiftly and create such density at the same time seems unusual to me—does the density come through rewriting?

WEST: I rewrite very slowly which often makes things longer than they were. In the old days I used to revise quickly or not at all. Now I write quickly but revise slowly. I don't embellish, but inflate, check things out to see what extra potential they have. I'm not sure how much that increases the size of the text.

MORROW: Do you have a sense when you begin a book of how large the structure will be, in terms of quantity?

WEST: I did not plan the Hopi novel to be as long as it is—it was intended to be three or four hundred pages and turned out to be two and a half times that, because I got interested. I thought I could handle it economically, but that was impossible. The Stauffenberg novel was a thousand pages long, and I cut five hundred pages out of it—none of which I could use, though it's the size of an alternative novel; those pages are mere scaffolding, interesting detritus, that's all. The novel fell away from them, the scaffolding fell away from the novel. It's a flexible process, I suspect, I never quite know where it is I'm going, and I'm not sure I want to. I don't want to see the green light at the end of the novel!

MORROW: Again, thinking of the body and now not the reader but the writer: in composing fiction there is necessarily a "body" of experience which is quote unquote *drawn on* and the body must go through experience and then work, as non-body really, when writing. In *Out of My Depths* you reformulate Descartes's maxim as "If there's thinking, there is a thinker." What's the relationship between thinker, i.e. body, and thought, i.e. noncorporeal?

WEST: My awareness of the body, which is to say my own body, increases daily. In the early works it's always bodies of other people. My body doesn't figure largely in them. They're the writings of a brain. From *Stauffenberg* onwards the body comes much more into my writing. The bodies that are being hanged, which relates to that childhood experience. When I learned to swim finally I was delighted enough to write a whole book about the feat. I remember I did collages, and constructions with cardboard and paint of swimming pools and pictures of immersion. And illness, too, has had a tremendous impact. You can't suffer from illness without becoming aware of the body you've always had and how it's been going wrong from an early age, having rheumatic fever which does something to the electrical system of the heart, so that you're like a flashlight that doesn't work. Forty years later you have to take chemicals to brush up the electricity you need. I was never aware of these things. Since being ill I've taken a relentless interest in medicine. It's fascinating to use Doppler Echo on yourself and look through a window in yourself and see your body, behaving, misbehaving, in beautiful colors, like looking at a stormscope on a plane where you can see thunderstorms in yellow, green, and red. It's like looking at a Dufy of yourself—picturesque and not at all frightening. All of my personages are going to have something wrong with them from now on. Coleridge has a coinage, he calls it Isness—sounds like fake Heidegger; the Isness of my body has become very present. I had not recognized what a wonderful machine it was, and that has helped a great deal to balance out some of the wordplay in the writing.

MORROW: Barth has written that novelists must become experts in any field which interests them and use this expertise, then throw out the expertise—or simply forget it—once they've finished their book. Residues remain, but no authority in the field, and the serious interest may have decayed once the subject is gone.

WEST: One subject a year, I tell my students. The history of chocolate one year, the heart the next.

MORROW: You all but become a chocolatier. It's not an approach from a distance.

WEST: It's a deep shaft into the world, and the world is not a vague place. A lot of inferior writing is vague. If you go out and pick a blade of grass or hold a rock in your hand, their measurements, caliber, and nature are precise. There is no way you could come up with a vague measurement of either. If we applied to our writing that kind of specificity, we would live in a very different literary world. Vague, generic, allusive writing puts the burden of identification on the reader. Nabokov used to hide behind the trees at Cornell and leap out upon unsuspecting students and say "Do you know what kind of tree this is?" They never knew and he would chide them out there in the cold, saying, "You should know what the trees are. How can you live in a world you know nothing about?" I think he was right. Inattention to the world, inattention to basic competition: you are surrounded by the works of a Creator who publishes relentlessly and in enormous detail, too. Many people write as if there were nothing out there. They don't look at what surrounds them, they have no context. By the same token, they don't realize that when they write they have to supplant that world, have to manufacture from words a world that is more interesting, more arresting, perhaps, than the world of nature. It's difficult to do. You have to bounce the reader out of the one and into the other. But you learn how to do this only by looking at the one that already exists. There's no such thing as a one hundred percent imagined entity. Everything is derivative. Your derivations can't be of any use to you unless you have studied their matrix.

MORROW: In *Gala*, in the Alley Jaggers trilogy, there is an arresting link between body and imagination—you are in the basement creating the Milky Way, you are in the attic building seaplanes. The body is there, working, making things in the physical world, very manual, yet its fabrications fly far beyond what is tangible to Deulius and Michaela, or Alley. You cannot voyage the universe in your basement and yet you can. In here somewhere, and I don't know whether I can articulate where, is one of your most individual obsessions as a writer—

WEST: It has to do with surreptitious inward operations of the spirit. In the attic, up the chimney, I had my super plans for World War Three wrapped in oilskin, and when I had my chemistry set I brewed various as I thought unknown chemicals, put them in bottles, and stashed them up the chimney, too. It's an image of hiding what is most precious, not exposing it to the world, but knowing you have this wonderful thing—in case of emergency you can always go and find it and use it to save yourself or your people.

MORROW: Is there an impulse to build words around yourself as a barrier?

WEST: I don't think so.

MORROW: It's an act of exposure, making novels?

WEST: The writing of the novels is in each case an opening of the secret door. There is a secret compartment and it has in it indefinable, unmentionable *treasures*. Each time I write a book I have raided my supply—not necessarily the same kinds of images. But the act of opening the thing up, pushing it out into the world, then closing the door again, saying I still have something left: It's profoundly mythic and I'm not sure I understand it. Go through my checkered autobiography you will find places where things are hidden, secreted— it's secreting things, taking a piece of the world and making it absolutely mine, maybe for further use, maybe never to use it again, but I know I have it. A hunter with his trophy, perhaps?

MORROW: There is a secrecy in the reading experience, too, isn't there.

WEST: There certainly was. Some of my books were very private

153

even though they were in public. *Gala*'s a private book, *Caliban* is.

MORROW: *Words for A Deaf Daughter.*

WEST: For sure, very private and very public. My books are less private now, more accessible.

MORROW: I wonder if they're not more imagined, too, less autobiographical. The Hopi book doesn't come from the same autobiographical vein as *Gala* or even *Alley Jaggers.*

WEST: They're much more imagined although they look more historical, more tied to ascertainable facts. The amount of imagining that goes on now is much greater, there's little transcription and the whole thing is mutating as I handle it.

MORROW: Also, you seem to have moved from *Tenement of Clay, Gala, Deaf Daughter, Rat Man of Paris*—from sequestering settings, cellars, alleys, urban landscapes—to mesas and big skies in the Hopi book. You're moving toward your beloved universe maybe.

WEST: I am, but don't forget that the mesas are full of kivas and they are as secret as you can get.

MORROW: So you never get too far from the notion of secreting.

WEST: The idea appeals to me very much.

MORROW: Poulsifer hiding the rat in his coat and suddenly revealing it to strangers is a way of appropriating attention, of making an impact. There's an idea in here somewhere, though it may come out like bouillabaisse.

WEST: It may come out like sausages. If you want to dig and dig, you will find a secretive child at the root of this who knew that he had some side to his nature that didn't quite fit, didn't belong anywhere.

3.

I've always hungered after, insisted on, *detail* in any writing, otherwise it's just a vacant trope unmoored, but I wonder when I first recognized the everywhereness of everything: perhaps after I started taking astronomy seriously and rid my thinking of dichotomies. The universe wasn't *out* there, or *up* there, it was all over. This was "heaven," I was in it. I've always had a keen sense of the structure of things. Even as a kid I was drawing cross-sections of airplane engines as an extra to the kind of machine drawing I had to do in grammar school. They used to think I was off my rocker, doing extra drawings, but I cared a great deal about what went on inside. If you think about the atoms in things, you know that you are made of star-stuff. I never had that much sense of being my own thing, my own person; I was always the universe's possession, on loan to myself at a high rate of interest, but at any moment combinable back into a form I wouldn't have recognized myself in. When I really got to grips and studied maps of the Milky Way, the local cluster of galaxies and other clusters adorned with the names of men such as Maffei and Stephan, I got excited. I remember Donald Menzel's book *Astronomy*, which had in the back some exquisitely chiaroscuro maps of the universe. I would plan little trips for myself, murmuring the names aloud and averaging a light year a second as I went down the great Cygnus Rift and places like that, going up the long estuary leftward, with Altair on my left, then Sagitta and Vulpecula, on my right, after which it was plain sailing down to Deneb. I was astounded to find so many bays, inlets, gulfs, and offshore stars such as Procyon, like lighthouses not quite in the Milky Way. It was the supreme form of journeying.

We were a mappish as well as bookish and blue-printish family. I'd always had fun on geographical maps, dipping my thumb into Hudson's Bay and Lake Victoria. I have always suffered from a severe case of the sense of wonder. I am amazed to be here, to be alive, able to think about my thinking. Isness, that's what staggers me. It should. Yet it doesn't stagger many of those middlebrow, parochial, mercantile writers who churn out the sad music of banality about the price of cucumbers without once figuring out how extraordinary a thing a cucumber is. My head is always abroad, faring far, which accounts for my constant look of truculent self-absorption. I love words and names because they are so arbitrary: categories of a kind, imposed on the flux of phenomena. I live in my head, a confusing place to be, which is why I like to have things around me tidy. The commotion within is daunting. All I have to do is look out at the back yard and I know that evidence is backed up: we are in a universe, a galaxy, a solar system, absolutely pumped cramful of marvels, and to be alive in such a context is a blessed membership. Even as I work, my body alters the signal my little nine-band radio picks up. The waves are pouring through me all the time, and I feel both perforated and repeatedly made whole: very much on the receiving end.

My craving for the vision beyond everyday vision has something to do with my frustration in England, my eagerness to get away from a country where, if a thing had already been done, then it was okay to do again, whereas, if it hadn't been done before, it was taboo. In the United States, a country to which I came with all the zeal of

Frederick Delius hitting Florida back in 1884, if a thing hadn't been done before, that recommended it. Emigrating, I was entering the universe. I could have tuned in to the bigger-all back in Derbyshire or Oxford or Canada, but the United States, as I saw after my formative year at Columbia, was a social universe, an anthropology on wheels. I came from acute claustrophobia to something like agoraphilia. You have only to look at the no-nonsense suburbanism of the contemporary English novel to see how much a misfit I was there; by the same token, you have only to look at that dryrot's American equivalent to see how wary I have had to be here. In a democracy the passion for mediocrity is constitutionally sanctioned; in a monarchy, such as England, that passion reveals literature not getting above its station, and not being too foreign, too arty, too narcissistic.

Anyway, as an undergraduate supposed to be reading Sir Walter Scott, Thackeray, and Goldsmith (all those tinsel British oldies), I was into Ernst Jünger, Georges Bernanos, St.-Exupéry, André Gide, and André Malraux, who all seemed to have a much more urgent, dare I say Shakespearean, sense of life. Like Marlowe, and sometimes Byron, and T. E. Lawrence. In the end I found an English-speaking Europe in America and made do with that, although my secretmost yearnings have always been with the Latin Americans and the least demure Europeans. But Melville and Faulkner were reason enough to take American literature seriously. Hart Crane and John Berryman. Wallace Stevens and Djuna Barnes. This was a country in which *some* people shared my yearning for literature that didn't give a hoot about being well-behaved, polite, genteel, reassuring, and so on, but about being vital, dynamic, visionary, Elizabethan, cosmic.

I'm not sure I know how my novels begin. Often as short stories getting fast out of hand. Perhaps they have been whizzing around inside my head and, every now and then, coming into the open for scrutiny and testing. There's a creative fantastic continuum I seem always to be able to milk; an ongoing supply that smelts things down after first hoarding them up. *Tenement of Clay* came from hearing about Casper Hauser, but my head had always been full of deformed guys lurking in cellars, elephant men, werewolves, vampires. The raw material was there to begin with. Politer books should have been tops, but they weren't. I wanted strong meat. The Jaggers trilogy came out of my native village, based on recent events: a local plasterer really did bump off his wife and Cask-of-Amontillado her in a wall. One of his relatives used to come to my mother for music lessons, another was a girl I dated in grammar school. The fabric wasn't far to reach. I was among it all. *Colonel Mint* came from my casual, serendipitous reading of a book about angels. I saw an angel cameo and that was that. *Caliban's Filibuster* came from much peering at the spectrum. *Gala* really did come from peering at Donald Menzel's maps of the heavens, the northern Milky Way especially, of which I drew and/or built many versions, some hand-sized, some ten feet in length.

I got into a habit with my Stauffenberg novel of fixing on a *donnée* from the press or from gossip, and then taking it over through imagination. That was how *Rat Man of Paris* began: friends coming back from Paris with this tale of a man on the boulevards, his rat in his raincoat. I at once saw scores of images, almost like an untidy movie going off unbidden in the head. My Hopi novel, *The Place in Flowers Where Pollen Rests*, came from being out in Arizona, meeting some Hopi, reading about them, and then discovering their kachina dolls: it was a way in, and once in I was hooked. The Hopi sense of the world beneath and beyond seemed close to mine, not that I'm a theist. I just marvel at the latticework of Creation, musing on the ingenuity of matter. I go out on a clear night and, instead of looking through my telescope, stare at the fuzz-balls. They seem so close, trapped in a visual murmuring, and I think how we live inside a goldfish bowl whose walls are loaded with this stuff. Even in the daylight I think of it. I felt vindicated when 1987's supernova erupted on my birthday; henceforth, Sanduleak, the star that blew up, would always be a little bit mine. The sequel to *Rat Man of Paris* came from a photograph in the newspaper of a young man who'd lived in various treehouses in Central Park for years. I cut it out and glued it to a piece of cardboard and stared at it for months, making notes in the margins, then, as I often do, attaching pieces of paper to extend the margins, until the whole thing begins to look like an ill-proportioned paper flower, flopping about. Once I get to that stage, I know I'm on to something good. In some ways it's the most exciting phase of the creative process, when I have no idea which way I'm going to go, if I'm going to go at all. After the first enthusiasm, I get quite deliberate about things, making charts and curves, of themes and colors and motifs, also of word-numbers per chapter, and then the less-than-aleatory side of my head takes over, making patterns and schemes. *Gala* is the most fanatically planned novel, written strictly to the pattern of the genetic alphabet. Whenever I see the movie *The Double Helix*, I see Crick and Co. planning my novel for me.

There is a carpenter-craftsperson deep inside me who wants to make something much harder and faster than the spew of words. Hence all the models of the Milky Way; the cardboard models of Count von Stauffenberg, with hinged arms and legs all painted in lurid colors; the thirty or so collages I made from pages of *Paris Match* for *Rat Man of Paris*, with various shots of Klaus Barbie combined with other shots of jails, gibbets, cafés, riots, dinner parties, and so forth. I had meant to include them in the novel proper (almost as a kind of flick-book), after Breton's *Nadja*, but eventually decided the words should stand alone. I was right, but the collages helped me to focus and keep the book visually in tune with itself. For my nonfiction book, *Out of My Depths*, about learning to swim late in life, I did make many models of pools, undersea chambers, and turned them into collages too. I began as a painter, you know. I find the final novel not much of an *objet* to handle, not like a model plane, say, or a bronze sculpture. The final feel isn't much. Books look more like other books than they don't. At the end I want to have a fresco I can look at, something I can open up and fling over myself as an Indian blanket: not those rows on rows of monotonously defaced white.

I hope I have learned something from Genet, as from Beckett, neither of whom in their mature work have the faintest notion of the well-made novel, the short story *comme il faut*, as dreamed of by dinosauric editors who keep asking about plot and character and, what's that old length of dental floss floating in the sewer, *story line*. So many insist on homage to the shaduf in the age of the turbine that one ought not be surprised; but this one is, all the time, as people fifty years out of date go on running things and waving the big stick of tradition at an otherwise adventurous reading public. On the page one should be free to let the rhythm or the prose take one places undreamed of. Fiction is always an adventure: plastic, osmotic, Arabian of course. I suppose all those lapdogs who have finally arrived at Mozart after a lifetime of wondering have their counterparts in the reading or editing public. Those who see fiction as some kind of air conditioning or laxatively deliquescent margarine. It's weird to see those who let the book clubs do their choosing for them, people who have no idea that the arts actually mutate and evolve. On their deathbeds, they may discover that *failure* rhymes with *dahlia* (any similar astounding verbal felicity poised between nonsense and mind-melting epiphany) and they wonder to their last living engram what they missed, what the regimental mores of the publishing trade told them they had to miss. *Literary*, I'm afraid, is still among publishers a term of apologetic abuse, and articulate will probably be next.

The reactionary in esthetics isn't just esthetic, it's political and societal. Most people don't want life to be an adventure, but merely something to be got through with minimum thought. The trouble now that publishers are merging with almost sexual ardor is that the number of editors left who really care about the *art of writing* gets smaller every day. What the public wants is what the bigtime publishers have taught it to want, the circle is complete. And nobody out there is educating anybody any more. Every year, the caliber of those who enter college gets lower, their command of English vaguer and more feral, and many of those doing the teaching are incompetent too. If I had children to educate, I'd teach them at home, I'd let them do what they still say at Oxford and Cambridge: *read* for their degree. A noble idea, that, and palpably seditious. Education, after all, should *unfit* you for society, that big engine all ready to steamroll you into assent.

Our myth is whatever we make of things we'd hoped all along to do better. Point is I don't ride a camel to work; I don't get messages by drums or smokesignal; I don't lather with a brush, cook in a coal oven, chew raw foxglove for my heart, or have lunch with Arnold Bennett, whose heirs rebuild ever anew. I don't use a word processor either (I always thought a brain was a word processor), but those little tapping sounds are all around me, and the sound of the *Zeitgeist* is that of fluttering plastic keys. Respect Henry James and Emerson as we may, and I respect them both a lot, we have to heed what we work among, and we have to be careful not to cite modernity, science, technology, or growing illiteracy as reasons for doing things with minimal energy, minimal inventiveness. We have to work twice as hard as Virginia Woolf did when she was writing amid all that scientific and mental ferment in the first decade of the century. The same old cosmic matrix encloses us, it's just our tools that have changed; and what we have learned, or have failed to learn, from Proust and Joyce and Faulkner, won't go away. This means that anybody who thinks art is five thousand simple declarative sentences all beginning with He, She, They, It, I, The, Then, And, *et cetera*, is immitigably benighted.

4.

MORROW: If you were going to teach the ideal course on the contemporary novel, what would the curriculum be?

WEST: A rotating list of maybe fifty books. The two constants are Genet's *Miracle of the Rose* and Beckett's *Texts for Nothing*, because they are inexhaustible. One is a maximal book, the other is a minimal book. Other constant presences on the syllabus would include Robbe-Grillet, Blanchot, Garcia Márquez' *The Autumn of the Patriarch*, either Günter Grass or Arno Schmidt, *Correction* by Thomas Bernhard, Clarisse Lispector's *The Apple in the Dark*, Djuna Barnes's *Nightwood*, Hawkes, Gass, Fuentes, Goytisolo, Vargas Llosa, Osman Lins, Juan Benet, Claude Simon, Virginia Woolf, Nabokov, Proust, Gide, Colette, Salvador Elizondo, Julien Gracq, McElroy, Guy Davenport, Beryl Bainbridge, Kenneth Gangemi, Eva Figes, B. S. Johnson, Lawrence Durrell, Georg Konrád, Peter Weiss, Claude Ollier, Augusto Roa Bastos, Robert Coover, Alejo Carpentier, José Lezama Lima, Borges, Marie-Claire Blais, Julio Cortázar of course, Witold Gombrowicz, Primo Levi, Anna Maria Ortese, Nathalie Sarraute, and anything translated by Richard Howard, Helen Lane, or Gregory Rabassa. Either my mind or my memory is giving out. If you teach Comparative Literature, as I often do, you develop a justified pejorative sense of the home-grown product. You see how pampered and narrow it has become, mainly because bookstore chains direct the publishing trade in America and England. Those people, and they are legion, who pretend that both the century and the world don't exist, have only another dozen years to sustain the illusion through, and then they will be able to sit back, lifting their heads from the sand and their asses from the fronts of their padded chairs and say the twentieth century never was. A dream.

MORROW: There are a few American authors, post-World War Two, whom you haven't commented on at any particular length in print for one reason or another. For example, Barth.

WEST: The house or mansion that Barth built has not tumbled down, although the light has gone out in some of the windows. I prefer Arabian Barth to Barth the Augustan pasticheur. After all, the Arabs invented algebra, whereas the British seventeenth-century and eighteenth-century mind came up with arithmetical prose.

MORROW: William Burroughs.

WEST: Burroughs I admire. The split-screen texts I find very interesting as well as the cut-up method developed with Brion Gysin. *Naked Lunch* is the most Dante-like American novel of all.

MORROW: Gaddis.

WEST: One of my defects as a reader, I suppose, is that I do not much care to listen to people talking to one another, so I have to work at my Gaddis, becoming something of a resolute overhearer, going against my nature. That said, that *accomplished*, and set aside, I turn to the side of him I am competent to register. He has tremendous rhythm; indeed, he's one of the few Americans with a long sense of rhythm over a paragraph, over a page, you can hear it coming, very musical—

MORROW: There's a connection to that projected intuition of yours we talked about.

WEST: Yes, I feel close to him when he's doing loops and you know that he knows if he's writing page one what it's going to sound like on page three. There is a long paragraph in his entry in *World Authors* in which you are invited to describe yourself and your experience and his is one of the best written self-portraits. It's wonderful because it's all of a piece, seamless prose, with cadences, climaxes, implosions, reversals, a very musical performance. Superior writing on perhaps an inferior occasion, but it stands out from the other entries: not just ectoplasmed-out. Autobiography as work of art.

MORROW: Hawkes.

WEST: A contemporary master. He gets better and better. His imagination is always mobilizing more and more of itself, more and more of it's coming into play. He's the most French, the most European writer of all of us.

MORROW: Which books of his would you recommend for your curriculum?

WEST: The new one, *Whistlejacket*, certainly. *The Cannibal*, *The Blood Oranges*. *The Passion Artist* is one of my favorite books. There's a lot to be said about it. It's intense and, to some, unsavory.

MORROW: That would make him happy. Susan Sontag.

WEST: I'm just rereading *Death Kit*, to teach it. She doesn't write that much fiction. The most recent thing of hers was a wonderful story in *The New Yorker*, a story about the plague, AIDS, which was an incredible combination of French New Novel and fluent apocalyptic witness, one of the finest things she's ever written. In *Death Kit* she's a nimble, adroit narrator; she rings the changes of narratorial tone with almost levitating ingenuity. I wish she'd written

161

more fiction. *Against Interpretation* is a book that all students of literature should read every year. Then, she's in the straight line from people like De Quincey. She makes a lot of sense about literary enigmas. Literature is full of enigmas and she understands this, probably better than anybody, and can make students understand what she's talking about, too. As a fiction writer, she's underestimated.

MORROW: James Purdy.

WEST: I've read him and enjoyed his wonderfully hectic, Sitwellian imagination. There's a whole circus going on in there. It all comes out in the same kind of prose, and perhaps that prose is sometimes not quite as violently charged as I would like it to be if it were my own.

MORROW: Have you read Coleman Dowell?

WEST: *Island People.* I couldn't understand why he didn't do better. He was a sumptuous, rich-textured writer, with a lot of luscious visions. He wrote about things that few Americans write about. He had a real sense of the absurd. Not the societal but the cosmic and ontological absurd. He was a good writer, had a real style, a real presence on the page. I was very sad when I heard about his killing himself. We can't afford it.

MORROW: We can't, no. You know Walter Abish's work.

WEST: One of the subtlest spring-steel stylists we have. Again, a European mind, but not restricted by that. He's a fastidious worker and looks like a minimalist, but he ain't. He can make the minimum resound a hell of a lot. And he has a wonderful, wacky, off-the-wall side. He can produce an experimental piece out of very little material and make the sense of experiment large. He reminds me of Varèse, who said, I don't write experimentally. I experiment *before* I compose. I don't see Walter experimenting from word to word, ever. He's done it all beforehand in his head and there's a state of mind he gets into which is experimental, but comes out formally, rather ingratiatingly. No shocks. The shock is in the early phase.

MORROW: In the conception.

WEST: In the conception, which is probably not true of me. I probably do more shocks en route, as the thing comes out. Walter should write more about himself. He would do distinguished autobiographical stuff.

MORROW: You've worked with nearly every possible literary form— poetry, *The Snow Leopard*; scholarly criticism, the book on Byron and *The Modern Novel*; autobiography, *Words for A Deaf Daughter*,

Out of my Depths. You've written the trilogy about the Jaggers family, with mad Alley being one of the most extraordinary creative-mad-minds of postwar fiction. You've written autobiographical fiction, such as *Gala. Rat Man* and the new Hopi novel seem to be imaginative travels outside your personal experience. *The Very Rich Hours of Count Von Stauffenberg* is an "historical" novel. With the amount and sheer range of work you have done, what amounts to a monumental achievement, do you "write for yourself"?

WEST: It's a compulsion, it's not even for me. It's something built into the mechanism. I'm not a book-writing machine, but it seems to me a natural way to live is to write books about what it feels like being alive, whether they are nonfiction, fiction, poetry, or whatever.

MORROW: Which of those forms do you like working with best?

WEST: Fiction, fiction. I love to write essays, but I've written enough essays by now and I think naturally as a novelist and I always did. I need scope and space. I was never until now a miniaturist in any shape or form—all my short stories were novels that never made it. I use the past because, since a rather well-regarded shortie of mine called *Captain Ahab: A Novel by the White Whale,* I've been doing a series of tiny things, one-pagers, about people who interest me, mainly dead: Count Basie, Amy Johnson, Nixon, Madame Mao, Pelé, Gershwin, Borges, Delius, Frank Whittle. I'm going to read aloud from them, having always envied poets their option of reading a dozen short things whereas novelists often have to read one long thing or two. Just think of all the breaks, and the patter possible within them. What a relief. Reading novels aloud is a Spartan pensum.

MORROW: I have a friend who read the Vietnam piece—"A Feather on the Breath of God"—and didn't know anything about you biographically and still doesn't believe you weren't a Vietnam Vet. You're comfortable working in strictly imaginative form, not historical or autobiographical forms. Sheer imagining is one of your fortes.

WEST: I'm a free imaginer, inasmuch as any imaginer is free. I imagine the facts. It's always intrigued me that there are certain facts. But if those facts didn't exist, you should really be able to imagine them into being. The trouble is you wouldn't know what the facts would have been. But you should be able to imagine into being facts that are every bit as cogent as the facts that you can get from text books. It's a good exercise for people, for students to take the assassination at Sarajevo or somewhere like that and then try to write something comparable in a different country with different

163

leads.

MORROW: An act of making fact. How would you define a fact?

WEST: A fact is a socially arrived-at myth, a socially sanctioned myth. There's a difference between fact and truth. Truth is a platonic thing, fact is empirical. Myth has an empirical basis, too. Myth is taking advantage of the facts and extrapolating them or amplifying them, giving them an almost divine force. That's not very different from imagining things into being. You can't invent from scratch. You can't invent from nothing. Even the most far-out invention is tethered to the empirical world. That means that the person who is the free imaginer, or thinks he is, is not that different from the person who takes a blatant stand on history and imagines from then on. We're related. It's not an either/or thing. It's a matter of emphasis and shading. The historical novelist is the sibling of the free imaginer, because, essentially, you can't imagine ex nihilo. You're both doing the same thing with different emphasis. That whole thing has been distorted and has caused a lot of rather stupid criticism of work that is fairly free-imagined. Not just speculative science fiction, but stuff that looks as if it were 99.9 percent freely imagined. It's all historical in the long run. You're writing out of history, you can't escape history and your ideas can't fall out of the universe. My essays always go to the brink of fiction. The temptation is to imagine freely in the act of writing the essay and this can frighten a lot of people.

MORROW: Gass is the only other person I can think of who pushes it that far.

WEST: He does it. I think he agrees with me that this act is not two acts, it's one act, all the same. No matter what the premises or pretexts are, imagining is imagining and we shouldn't be frightened of it. I don't write that many essays anymore, because I feel that I should be writing fiction straight. But sometimes the essay has become an introduction to a piece of fiction, has become a warming-up exercise, and probably more than that. So you may find a lot of essays taking shape inside the novels. I have an essayistic cast of mind, anyway. I'm happy when one character or another gets it into his head to meditate or brood on things and formulate ideas. It never struck me that a fiction writer had to avoid ideas. The Novel of Ideas to me is not a contradiction in terms. It's a wonderful notion. I like to write about thoughtful people.

MORROW: A little aside, how do you think that contradiction between a character and an author takes place?

WEST: Characters have their own worlds. I've had characters who have filled my head with their voices and their minds, who really have taken on an autonomous existence even after the book's finished.

MORROW: *They're* working on *you* the way you're describing.

WEST: Some are, mostly women. I can still hear the voice of Alley Jaggers and the voice of his wife. Maybe they were part of my childhood. I still hear Dot.

MORROW: You talked about compulsion, I veered into responsibility, but what I want to move to is this: do you have any ambition for your work as a whole entity?

WEST: Probably not. If it comes out looking like a patchwork quilt, or a Joseph's coat, that's fine. What I want to do is write another long novel, some fusion of essay and novel, something Proustian. The Hopi novel is long but in a way not the long novel I want to do now, which might be about the human body vis-à-vis the human brain. I have in a steel drawer an unfinished novel that is a journey through the brain. There are 600 pages of it, a planned novel moving from *amygdala* to *pons*, from *fornix* to *hippocampus*, all of them places in the brain, as Altoona is in Pennsylvania. I may go back to it. It would be hard to produce an intellectual pattern for my total output—I'm not sure I could or would want to. I don't think one should try to stage-manage one's output over twenty-five years. The ultimate stack of books must have an impromptu, serendipitous feel.

MORROW: You trust your intuition with the individual work; as a collective that principle might serve you well also.

WEST: This never worries composers of music, or painters of paintings. It worries people who write books.

MORROW: If someone were presented the entire Paul West shelf where would you send them as a teacher to begin reading, how would you have them approach it?

WEST: I would do what I've heard they do at the University of Kent, Canterbury. Literature is taught by beginning at the end, so in the first year they read in the 20th century, in the second the 19th, and so on back to Beowulf. Maybe they stay on campus for ever. I'd start the reader with the most recent book and work backwards, omitting a couple.

MORROW: Which?

WEST: *Colonel Mint* and *A Quality of Mercy.* I don't feel behind them anymore. *A Quality of Mercy* was a sighting shot, a warm-up exercise, an alternation of Faulkner and Hemingway, and it got wonderful reviews but didn't deserve them. *Colonel Mint* is a little superficial, fun to write and a number of people enjoyed reading it apparently, but it's flip for me.

MORROW: You have said somewhere that *Gala* is your favorite, or one of them.

WEST: It is, for personal reasons, because I'm an astronomy nut, and have this strong sense of walking around in the Milky Way, always did, it's weird. You look up, there it is, quiet, oppressive in a way, there, above you, around you, and you're made of the same stuff it is, and you're walking around in it. This is an epiphany. I have often wanted to speak, write, as a galaxy, much as I have wanted to sound like a piano, somewhat as an Indian widow committing suttee wants to behave like a fire. I imagine the sound as not at all Christmasy: no tinkles, no chimes, but snuffling like someone with a cold, and creaking icily like a grandfather clock with arthritis; Catherine wheel of spun glass with a spermy bouquet.

MORROW: Think of all the remarkable things going on in the dark interstices, too—

WEST: That you can't see—

MORROW: That's where all the life is—

WEST: There's only dust in the way.

MORROW: Were one to ask the really impossible question of how does this tree of so many different branches add up, how work, how unify into perhaps a few simple, single ideas that might indicate who Paul West is, what he intended, what would the answer be?

WEST: He's a sometimes exuberant witness. Nobody asked him to do it. He volunteered, or indeed he was volunteered, it was an automatic thing, he began volunteering to witness. It's important to people who read books to have people who look at what happens to them. If you have somebody who imagines, not wildly, but at large, then in a way you want to tether them down to the circumstances of his life from day to day. If you want to have a fantasy you must also have a diary. My output is fifty-fifty, ten nonfiction books, eleven fiction books, and there's some need in me to balance the one against the other, maybe because I don't know the damn difference between fiction and autobiography. Fiction could well be the supreme form of autobiography, the most far-ranging form. I think it is.

MORROW: You don't see fiction as the vehicle for expression of preconceived political or philosophical ideas, it's not an act of ideation, in other words.

WEST: *Philosophical*, of course. Politics? I think one writes about the things that really matter and if politics is one of them, okay.

MORROW: What matters to you?

WEST: Having a body, having emotions, knowing a galaxy, having myths to live by. What interests me is that life has no narration and every time you write a fiction you are giving people something that life essentially doesn't give them. This is deeply significant to those we call readers.

MORROW: It sounds like a secular religious action.

WEST: It is a mediation, a coming between the unmediated universe and the willing reader. Imagine a fiction that came into being but had no supervisor, or driver. Sartre said it would be like a toboggan going over the crest of a hill and whizzing down the other side, apparently out of control. I would like to know how to write that—the fiction sans coach, sans overseer. The phantom stagecoach with just horses. But it impresses me that life has no plot, no narrator. Much has been said of the apparent fraudulence of narrators and our getting accustomed to reading novels which nurture in us the desire to understand people, to lift the top of their heads off and see what goes on inside, whereas perhaps it's closer to the facts of life not to do that, not to show people as fathomable, but to show them as indeed opaque and impenetrable. Just think of what has vanished when a person dies: all that onrush of hardly used interior conversation, all those second or third thoughts just as much them as what they actually said and set down. I think it's just as dense to insist on this relentlessly—the "bogusness" of art—as relentlessly to ignore it—the headlong suspension of disbelief. It's *all* music.

When Mother is a pianist who also teaches music, you are likely to hear sonatas through your homework, maybe in your sleep as well, and even while leaping around on the football field or flying gliders of tissue paper and balsawood. I did. And I hear the aftertones as if the music room's hum entered my head forever.

I was brainwashed by music, and I link it with joy or rapture because my childhood was more or less happy, and because classical music has a peculiar effect on me that experts will no doubt find banal: it induces in me a peace sustainable for hours, long after those dear and near to me have fled in percussed horror. I glut myself thus because the continuum of music matches a continuum already in my head: of ideas and phrases forming themselves into sentences that sometimes feel ready-made. If this sounds like possession, mnemonic or other, I thank the fates for it.

There is another role for music in my creative life, though, and I

167

mention it well aware that for some novelists (Nabokov, for example) music is anathema. It stimulates the subdominant hemisphere and saps the power of reason. Nowadays more than ever I write to its accompaniment, mostly piano music, not for "inspiration" but to go back to some golden plateau of cornball boyhood when, to the sound of Chopin or Satie, I smoothed out the cream, laid pages of my exercise book and contemplated the paradise of paper onto which I could write anything I wanted to while the fire churred and my mind roamed, filling up with ideas faster than I could set them down. Writing while listening, with perhaps only half my mind on what I was doing, I came free. Unknown, undreamed-of dimensions rushed into view, and I turned into a callow mystic obsessed with some architectonic of rhythm to which I had to find the words.

Over the past three years, working on my eleventh novel, set among the Hopi tribe of Arizona, I found myself turning to piano music more than ever. I had not been in Arizona long before the spell of the Hopis managed to make itself felt; I began studying kachina dolls — made by Hopis to teach their children about the immanent spirits in nature — not least because these dolls were commercially available and devoutly collected, and I could actually buy some for myself. I liked them because they were the small-scale version of what happened at the Hopi dances up on the mesas, when, dressed up just like the dolls, the Hopi enacted their ancient rituals. Fire, steam, wind, hard substances, became more real than electric light bulbs and money; and it was this transcendent, otherworldly vision of the Hopi that lured me. Not only that: I had heard about a master carver up there, almost blind, whose carving was unlike the commercial sort — his dolls were plump, hefty, and it was this figure and this figure's figurines that haunted me long after I left Arizona. My novel is in no sense a documentary, but I did at least acquire two of the dolls he'd carved before I left, and one of these, of Sotuqnangu, god of the heavens, rarely carved and never impersonated in the dances, pleases me more than I can say, having, I am sure, seen me through the disastrous illness that struck me soon after I left Arizona for the east. Lying in intensive care, I thought about the feisty egolessness of the Hopis in their extraordinary bleak, vivid, other-directed world, and about the god with the lightning bolt in his fist, and achieved a certain amount of calm; after all, part of me was as inert, as numb, as a Hopi doll, including my face and mouth to begin with. I didn't have Sotuqnangu in there with me, but I would have if they'd allowed it. I see something in witchdoctors, especially of one's own making. Much of this novel has to do with illness and death, dying and the non-self; but I had little glimmering way back when of how my interest in the Hopi would interact with the texture of my life. One example: in the Hopi language, the verb forms inflect according to the done-to, not the doer, which I find fascinating. It so happens that my way into the recesses of Hopi mysticism took the form of music, mainly Busoni-Bach, yet not Busoni-Bach at its most clanging, triumphant, and truculent, or the music that Busoni composed after Hopi Songs. Alas, or happily, I knew of neither while doing most of the writing; so the credit if any goes to Paul Jacobs and the *Sonatinas.* Sadly, Mr. Jacobs died not long ago.

The book is a *Künstlerroman*, a novel about the maturation and death of an artist, although I realize that Indians don't take the kachina dolls half as seriously as we do. To them the serious things are the humans dressed up as kachina spirits, and that is how the novel comes out, with Oswald actually becoming the Mastop kachina. His new-found religion is still art, though. To put it another way: the Hopi teach their children about kachinas by giving them dolls to play with. In my novel, Oswald goes through this process as an adult and actually at one point manufactures a life-size doll of his own from several corpses. The novel itself is the reader's, and author's, doll; it is, after all, a homage of sorts to the master carver who was also the master teacher, needing no dolls himself but some close contact with the spirits evoked and impersonated in the dances. The novel is about impersonation and how impersonal an inspired human can be. We, at the consumer end of the process, where the dolls get bought and sold in trading posts, are like those people in Plato's cave taken in by appearances, whereas the Georges have been the real thing, the flame, or *they think they have.* It might be worth adding that Hopi children shoved into white schools, and humans shoved into uniform, and illegitimate children, are all dolls of a kind.

Busoni's *Outline of a New Esthetics of Music* (1907) always appealed to me because he tried, as both critic and composer, to create a future, to take music where it had never been, and I had his aloof, slightly belligerent face in my mind all along while his wry delicacies marched forth from under Mr. Jacobs's nimble hands, sometimes like perversely tilted echoes of old piano favorites I'd dreamed I'd heard, sometimes as bravura runs of faintly tainted chiming. I had never heard piano music so scalpeled yet so hummable and whistleable, and sometimes my mouth picked up his tune above the whirr of the electric typewriter. I should, no doubt, have been listening to Steve Reich's *The Desert Music* or Olivier Messiaen's homage to Utah, *From the Canyons to the Stars*, both of these thematically pertinent; but Busoni, strict purveyor of the muted and the incomplete, was giving me my main assist, and I kept wondering why. I sensed an aridity, a wholly unapologetic otherworldliness, in this music. The six sonatinas merged before I could tell them apart, a random suite for piano and novelist, and I actually gave Busoni's face to one of my Indians.

Yet this wasn't "program" music. Here I was, getting something almost ineffable but useful from those stately and forlorn single notes of his—he who hated what he called "motivic" composition— eerily alone, I along with the notes leading me into what sounded like a *Kindertotenlied* played on an out-of-tune piano. Some of the music sounded almost like scales, or difficult exercises with sudden changes of tempo, some of it as if the piano had gone hoarse or its voice had broken, or the composer had almost lost heart. Or even the pianist himself. The music limped yet kept on going forward. It seemed to be thinking about itself, tastefully doodling, then it would erupt into glacial chiming, then into a parody of how children thump out certain standard pieces. And some notes seemed sustained for too long as if the tape were dragging or the music (all of a sudden a deliciously slewed version of Bizet's *Carmen*, all smears and drones) were coming through an old water pipe. The yearning got moribund, the lilt went stale.

It may sound as if I didn't enjoy this music very much, but I came to dote on it; and, without quite going so far as to call it mesa music, I began to intuit from it some of the attitudes I was using in my prose: not just otherworldliness and obliviousness, but asceticism, defiance, sprightly introversion, wan hauteur, tart ennui, a whole range of things. After several dozen hearings, Mr. Busoni and Mr. Jacobs had become part of my workroom, and I remembered how Carl Ruggles, overheard by Henry Cowell as he hit one chord again and again, said he was giving it the test of time. In my backhanded way I had discovered in the music the ghostly uninterruptedness of mesa life, but also, through constant replayings, the essence of eternity. It worked. I did some fifteen hundred playings of the tape for some twelve hundred pages, and the music now evokes a place of extraordinary privacy in which Busoni, the Hopi, and I worked some spells as I came out of (I hope) my comfy place in technological civilization. Yet there is nothing in the novel that matches anything actually in the music, although I will never forget the fee-fi-fo-fum or bom-ti-bom-bom-bom passages, or the elated runs that collapse because like leopards their hearts are too small for what they want to do. Nor do I link Busoni's Fellini-like accelerations with any sudden increase in typing speed or my speed of thought. No, what I got from the music was myself denatured, stripped, wearing a stranger's glasses.

Busoni was my tent, my layette, my *doppelgänger*, not so much an oiler of emotion as an athlete of tonal control along for the ride. As was I. But his variations do remind me of the closely related verbal alternatives that presented themselves while I worked at dull red heat. The music occupied parts of me I didn't need, and at the same time tuned up some I didn't know I had.

All this must sound opportunistic in the most heathen way, like using an angel as an ashtray, and I wish I could say that I have now gone forward to learn the musical notation my mother always urged me to learn when I was little. All the same, the deliberate abstractness of that music taught me something about the abstractedness of the Hopi way. One language I couldn't read taught me about another, in which you find a word for something we think we don't need *one* word for. *Políkwaptiwa* means "a butterfly sitting on a flower" and *kuwányamtiwa* means "beautiful badger going over the hill." We use so many words for what, to the Hopi, is a byword, as well as for the impact of an abstract art, music, that is far beyond words altogether.

The White Knights
William T. Vollmann

Photographs by Ken Miller

Though you suffered disgrace
and sorrow grieved me,
though I was outlawed and you dishonored,
joyful revenge will now proclaim us happy.
Wagner, *Die Walküre* (1856), I.3

ELLIS STREET

GREY SKULLS AND GREY SHIRTS, blue eyes and blue shirts; and a
cigarette in every hand. The skinheads yelled and fought beneath
the midnight stillness of the kitchen ceiling.

"Boy, what're we gonna do tonight?"

"I dunno, it's only ten-thirty."

"When I first met you, Dickie, and you got drunk, you used to get
so obstreperous, man."

"I got *loud* and *rude!*"

"Then you would push me and I'd push you back. The next
morning I knew I'd jumped on you. I was like anti-subconscious,
man."

"That's right. That was when we had our skinhead harem. We had
a squat in the city. It was wall to wall pussy."

"I don't want to hear it," said Dickie's bootwoman, Dan-L.

"WALL TO WALL PUSSY!" the skinheads yelled. "WALL TO
WALL PUSSY!"

Dan-L left, slamming the kitchen door.

"Well, we can talk about the harem some other time," Dickie said.
"Anyhow, you got so drunk and mad, you kicked me in the balls.
Then Warren got mad and kicked me, too. But I fought you and
Warren."

"And got your ass kicked!" Dagger roared. "Just kidding."

"We used to fight all the time, you goddamned bully."

"Hey, dude, don't call me no fucking bully," Dagger said. "I got
fucked with by bullies when I was growing up, man."

"Suck my dick, Massah!"

"Stick it up me, Massah!"

172

"I remember it all," said Dickie wisely. "If you gotta fight somebody, you gotta fight 'em. Never back down."

"You gotta have principles, though," said Dagger. "You can't just fight like a nigger. For instance, I believe every man should have respect for a man's house. I won't whip your ass inside your house. I'll always give you a choice; you can come out and get whipped, or you can stay inside and I'll tear the place up. I remember when I was scrapping with my foster father, he said, 'Step outside.' He fought me outside, treated me like a man. When I whipped his ass, he went in and got his gun and chased me off the place. And I *respect* him for it, man."

Anthony, whom they'd been calling the Wop all night, because that was funny, was polishing his boots, black boots with red laces. He was stropping them one at a time between his thighs.

"Well, you do all the fighting, but I don't have no record, Dagger," said Dickie. "I always said I was the smarter."

"Hey," said Dagger, "I may not be the smartest, but I know when to back up and when to jump 'em."

"Yessir," said Dickie dreamily. "I was the original organizer."

"*You* were the organizer, uh?" cried Dagger, injured. "I was the organizer, man! In your day everyone wore fucking Mohawk haircuts!"

This was a stunning rejoinder, bringing only silence. Dagger pressed his advantage. "Anyhow, we didn't have no leaders," he said. "We was sayin' skinhead things long before *you* came along. We was sayin', 'We got to take care of all the Cholos and niggers.'"

"Aw," said Dickie. "People been saying that for two hundred years."

The generic beers were piled up in towers on the table, with George Thoroughgood tapes beside the player, and an ashtray for every man. The skinheads stroked their black shiny boots and bluejeans. Their shaven heads made them seem particularly thoughtful, with all the profundity of skulls. Dagger picked at the checks in his shirt, and Dickie relaxed, attended by his girl in her camouflage cap, her bangs down to her eyes, this girl who was in love with him. Even when she slammed out she could not stay away.

THE LAST BALD EAGLE

When Dickie put his arm around her, and she around him, they both looked at the world unflinchingly, but without her Dickie

found things to concentrate on, like the cassette player, like fights, like lighting his bong, while Dan-L sat in the corner by the window, staring into heaven with clasped hands. Dickie sat crooning inwardly to the cassette player with his eyes closed, the clean shadow of his head and neck doubling in outline a soldier's helmet upon the kitchen door. Other shadows connected him to the tape player, the two round eyes of its speakers rolling dolefully, like those of an old dog; and Dickie tilted his head back farther, rigidifying the black helmet that he dreamed so freely in; and the shadow of his sleeve flared like one of those venomous elbow-spines sported by insects; and it was impossible to understand what he was thinking, his soul resting in a lone grave beneath the leafless tree of some Civil War battlefield, or wandering through the dugouts of Verdun, stepping from timber to slimy timber with the smell of mud all around him, and looking in the pockets of his dead comrades for extra cartridges, holding his breath when he reached into the swirling little pools of chlorine gas where the others had fallen, leaving him alone to await and admit the attack; for it is a lonely thing to be a skinhead, so lonely that only other doomed soldiers can imagine it. Let us get killed, then, in order to see the new mobilizations of

Dickie's soul, helmeted by his skin-padded skull (padding out, hard side in) to protect him from Japanese attack in the Solomon Islands in '43 as he waded through the blood-warm water on his knees and flung himself behind the palms with his assault rifle blazing the way and cocked KER-snap!, Dickie (who was an Order of the Arrow Eagle Scout) being in action at last, soon to be killed in action, meanwhile sole survivor of his platoon, which lay in sodden, bloated khaki-covered pieces on the beach beside shattered wood and bamboo, the corpses' eyes transformed into mouths of pink rolled tissue—and then it's WHUMP! WHUMP! WHUMP! WHUMP! WHUMP! at Wesel and at Bremen and at Hannover, the eternal present tense of a German conflict, American shells turning blocks of apartments into grey plains stamped almost evenly by close-clustered craters; and the First Battalion strides down narrow, high-walled streets in Bensheim, blowing away the last pale, sweating Krauts hiding in doorways—but whose side could Dickie be on? He's American; he's a Nazi; and as the close-shaved, cropped-headed boys from Tennessee and Virginia march past splintered trees, splintered houses, sometimes Dickie is with them and sometimes he must be against this force that struck down the ole Reich whose emblems skinheads bear in their flesh—how many swastika tattoos have I lost count of?* (Of course the inmates of Buchenwald were the ultimate skinheads:—stubble-crowned, tattooed, naked and angular.)—At least both parties agreed on hating the Soviet Union.

THE BUTCHER BOYS

"I'll tell you a story," Dickie said. "This is an early skinhead story. Long time ago, I don't know how many years ago it was, we had this house out by the river in West Virginia, a big house, and we were living together for about six months (we was even living with this nigger fella then, a guy with hair abnormally long, down to his butt), when these people started coming to town. I met this first skinhead; his name was Butch; he was driving a Chevy truck. Right away we made this rule that anybody that came in had to shave his head.

---

*The question, "What is German? What is American?" is still not solved among the skins, *Pfeffer* going through the High Consonant Shift to become *pepper*, *Rasse* becoming *race*, and *Nazi* becoming *Republican*, hardly to the detriment of skinhead self-esteem.

"We needed food, so we started the Butcher Boys; that was what we called ourselves. We went out killing all kinds of animals. We hung the meat on a line, and the way we got it was, we had this deaf pit bull named Blockhead, who barked funny on account of he couldn't hear himself, and he had a big square head and white spots on his shoulders; the girls used to draw circles in black magic marker around his eyes, so he'd look like Petey of the Little Rascals. Once that dog nearly got us arrested. We were in a McDonald's waiting for somebody to get off work, and Blockhead started barking real funny, like this, *Oooooh, oooooh, oooooh*; and somebody called the cops and said, 'Those skinheads are abusing their dog,' and the cops showed up and started giving us shit until some nigger woman went by, and of course Blockhead barked at that, and the cops said, 'Holy shit, you're right, he does bark that way natural,' so they let us go.

"Bein' the Butcher Boys and all, we'd send Blockhead into a chicken coop; he'd go in one end and the chickens would come squawking out the other, and we'd go *bam, bam* with a board— *haw!*—take us home a mess of chickens! We killed lotsa pigs, too, but most of what we killed was billy-goat. Those billy-goats were tough, which was why we usually sold the meat instead of eating it ourselves. We got like ten or eleven goats one night. They were in a pen. We just walked in there with our knives, *pop, pop!* (That was how I got this scar on my hand, gutting a goat.) We'd wrap the meat and sell it at this shopping center; all kinds of niggers bought it. They didn't know what they were buying.

"Now, this is how I got the bestiality charges: There was two of us, and we went and got this sheep. So, we went across this fence, and this sheep had two little lambs—really sad, heh, heh! So, anyway, here's this fucking sheep with bells on it, so I go *blap, blap!* with a sledgehammer, then again for health, and we put it in the pickup and started driving home. I remember that we picked up this hitchhiker, and we were horsing around with her and she started freaking out. All the sudden we hear this noise in the back—that sheep was only knocked out! We started going for it with a two-pronged spade, and Blockhead and the other dogs were ripping at its neck, and guts and blood was spurting all over the truck, and that hitcher goes, 'Oh, my God, let me *go!*' so we let her go, and went home with the sheep and did the usual, right, 'cause we was the Butcher Boys.

"The next day, we see on page one of the paper that somebody's goddamned sheep got stolen. It was somebody's fucking *pet!* That was why it had the bells on it. It was in the papers, Snowy the

Dancing Sheep; can you fucking believe it? — They had a five-thou-
sand-dollar reward on it for two weeks. — Well, right then, just about
the time we finished serving up Snowy, the girls took Blockhead
with them to the shopping center to sell goat meat to the niggers, and
he didn't come back. The girls said he ran off. People said, 'So,
where's the dog?' We joked and said, 'Well, we ate it. Then we had a
good time fucking the sheep!' — Just kidding, but this new cop heard
about it, and it was like bestiality and thirty counts of rustling."

"So what'd you do with all the bones?" said the Wop. "Feed 'em to
Blockhead?"

"Hell, no," grinned Dickie. "We had a *big* barbecue pit."

"Hey, dude," said Dagger, tapping his middle finger on the table.
"Flip the tape."

"We didn't listen to 'Dixie Fry'," said Dickie.

"Fuck *you*, man, I don't give a *fuck*!" yelled Dagger.

"I flipped it over," Dickie said.

"You're a *fucking* liar, man!"

The skinheads got into an argument over what to play, knocking
each other around with their tattooed muscular construction arms
bursting with veins, glaring, showing teeth, yelling, "*Suck my
dick!*" until they drowned out the music, the police sirens outside,
the terrible life of the Tenderloin streets.

MARK DAGGER

Dagger's head had two narrow bars of shadow in which his eyes
were set. Whereas on Chuckles's shoulder was tattooed a sneering
skull resting on a basket of spidery skeleton-fingers poised over a
heap of little white skulls above the words EXTREME HATE upon a
skull in a bullet-pierced Nazi helmet, like one of those aboriginal
myths about how the world rests on the back of a giant tortoise that
balances itself upon another tortoise that seesaws upon still another
blackish-green shell as the creature splays its wrinkled legs out and
voids its turgid white reptile-piss on the ten million tortoises below
it, except that instead of tortoises it was all skulls, and surmounting
this totem pole of defiance was Chuckles's head, a smooth intelligent head that was usually smiling faintly; whereas, in short,
Chuckles had a lot of tattoos on his arm, Dagger wore only one
blotchy green skull on a bicep and below that his identifying message, THE FUCKUPS, with a backwards "C" and an upside-down

question mark. The skull had very intelligent eyeholes, though, and a chittering uneasy smile as if it were ready to come rolling out of a graveyard to bite you. "You know those zombies, with no eyelids and no lips?" said Dagger. "I'm gonna get one tattoo full of tombstones, and a hand reaching out of a grave, grabbin' for a dagger; it'll be one of them zombie hands, and the dagger will be right over it, and above that it's gonna say DAGGER." —Dagger was heavily built with big arms and big legs and a wide chest, and his face was a skinhead block, a stolid casting on a barrel neck, seamed only by a scar above his youngish dinosaur brow where he'd been knocked out in a fight by a two-by-four because one night at the club this little kid was bothering Dagger and Dagger knocked the kid's head down and the kid fell and started crying, and all these people started to shit with Dagger then so he threw his beer on them and *bahh-whamm!* some dude came up with a two-by-four and cracked his head. Dagger was dead out for awhile. "That was a good hit you put on me," he said sarcastically to the dude. "I never hit a motherfucker with a two-by-four; I only hit with my fist." —The dude didn't say anything.— "You shake my hand," Dagger said, "or I'm your enemy for life." The dude said, "Get away, man." Dagger said, "Okay, that's cool." The dude jumped bail to move to Texas the next week. And he was *smart* to do it, too, because if he'd shaken Dagger's hand Dagger's plan would've been to climb onto him and drag him out back and beat the shit out of him.

Dagger's eyelids drooped when he was at rest; his bullet-head hung forward. He had a way of holding his cigarette between two fingers, his thumb cocked behind it as if resting on a trigger-hammer, but he also liked to just let his cigarette hang out of his mouth and drop ashes on his dirty T-shirt, with another cigarette waiting on yellow alert behind his ear. He had the naked muscles of skinhead youth. He could sit straight and still, but when he walked down the street he stepped toes-out in his boots, cocking his head and looking at people, and people in the know or sometimes out of it didn't give Dagger any shit because he'd just gotten out of San Bruno. The reason he'd been stuck there in the first place was that he'd been on this TV talk show "People Are Talking," explaining how much better skinheads were than punks, and a month later he was up on Skinhead Hill where it was sunny and you could play football or frisbee with the other Skinz or whomever happened by, enjoying the good weather and keeping an eye on Haight Street at the same time, because Skinhead Hill was what the hairheads called Buena Vista Park, a long narrow block of trees and grass that sloped up Central toward Sutro Tower, and at the bottom of it was Haight Street, with golden cement stairs in a golden cement wall, and you could run up the hill having war games and yelling and lobbing bottles in the bushes and getting drunk and as if you were a dragon-kite swooping in the clean San

Francisco sky, far beyond the world, your string dipped in glue and glass to saw every other kite outta the sky, just a Skin among Skinz; when all the sudden this punk rock chick came up to Dagger and started talking *shit* about him, and Dagger wasn't gonna let this insignificant cunt bug him with her punky stink; she was all fucked up on wine and stuff, so he told her to chill out, and she said, "Mark Dagger's a fucking pussy!", and Dagger told her, "Hey, bitch, you'd better stop or you'll get hurt," and she swung at him, and Dagger blocked it, and then she kicked him in the balls, so he kicked her in the jaw. He only kicked her once. He broke one side of her jaw and two of her wisdom teeth. —Even though *she'd* started it, *he* got convicted of assault. The trial took place in the courthouse on Bryant Street, Dagger sneering at the other so-called toughs who failed inside when placed at the bar and pissed in their pants and croaked diffidently, "I was not aware that the car above me was double-parked," or, "In both cases I was never outta the vehicle for more than two minutes, and I didn't have anyplace else to park, Your Honor," but then it came *Dagger's turn*...and they led him in hand-cuffed, and he was wearing an orange jumpsuit, and the back of his head was shaved bone-clean so that all the spectators sitting behind him in the courtroom saw the monster-skull tattooed there, and the monster-skull glared at them, and Dagger just stood there during the trial and nodded as the indictments were read, and he turned around slowly and bowed to the other skinheads, and the judge said, "Mark J----, you are a menace to society; I'm going to throw the book at you; I'm going to give you the stiffest sentence I'm allowed to give," and at that, Dagger turned around one more time and bowed to the skinheads again, and the skinheads rose to their feet and filed to the door and then they clicked their heels and saluted and said, "*SIEG HEIL!*" —Dagger was in San Bruno for a year.

Several of this pureblood statesman's letters survive. They are written on the stationery of the exiled, namely lined yellow paper. Here is one of them:

> well well what's up yea I got your pictures and
> Man there cool as fuck thanks alot well I only got
> 108 days and a wakeup and Ill be back on the Haight
> raisen hell but this time I have to move carefull well
> Ime not much of a writer but Ill try if you have any
> more pictures please please send them the ones with
> the Hitler signs arnt that cool to send but fuck it

send em anyway fuck these niggers my buissness is
my buissness write? I get alone pretty good in here
and nobodys fucked with me but Im ready if they do
Ill killem Ha Ha. well I can't think of anything to
say exept send me some pictures of so wimen out
there ok. be cool write back.

friends

MARK DAGGER

He was up on the fifth floor for three-and-a-half months. He got
jumped by eight niggers. They tried to take his tray. Dagger said,
"You don't disrespect me." He started kicking the first guy's black
ass. He grabbed him and took him down. He whacked his head on
the bottom of a table and split his skull *wide* open. Those niggers
broke two of Dagger's ribs, but the other guy went to the hospital,
not Dagger! After that, he got moved down to 2N with Yama. Yama
had just come in then for assault, so they got to do some time
together. Dagger did his best to help Yama, because he'd be out soon
himself but Yama had a stretch ahead of him, so Dagger gave Yama
the *Playboy*s, the *She*s and all the rest, though he kept the *Hustler*s
for himself. That was all that he and Yama could do to keep sane in
there, looking at photos of nice pink girls with closed eyes and open
mouths who squatted in a corner with their boots on and pulled their
underwear down and spread their pussy-lips apart with their red-
nailed hands, or got down on all fours on the sofa, wearing nothing
but black lace stockings, and waggled their asses in your face so you
could see their twats sticking out under their butt-cheeks. —Each
prisoner was allowed to have up to three visitors per visitation day in
the absence of bad conduct. You and your visitors had to keep both
hands on the interview table at all times. You'd get your bootwoman
to visit wearing a miniskirt and crotchless panties so afterward you
could go into the shower and beat off until your thumb was cal-
loused.

DAN-L

Dan-L went to the refrigerator and got beers for everyone.
"That Dan-L, she's really nice."
"She's the best person," Dickie said. "She's the best in the whole

world. She does everybody favors. It's funny. It *is* funny. Me and her were born beside each other. Our birthdays are only a week apart."

As for Dan-L herself, who always sat so modestly at the table, whose large dark eyes stared at her beer can as if they were embarrassed to be in her oval face, Dan-L with her parted brown hair, Dan-L with her jeans jacket, you could tell she really loved Dickie and would stick with him just the way that when Yama went to jail once his black hound Rebel took one of his dirty socks in his mouth and would not let go of it all day, just crouched in the corner, whimpering. And Dickie would stick with her, too, and had stuck with her, his arm always around her as she walked down the streets beside him in her black jacket that said SHIT HOWDY, which she still wore coming home from work at the cafe where she was about to be made into a manager but she was going to tell them to chill out if they didn't raise her to five dollars an hour; and when she got home she sat down in the kitchen and waited for Dickie and took off her jacket and let her cat pounce on it, and Dan-L remembered how Dickie had helped her when she and the other Shit Howdy Girls got into this terrible fight in New York, back in the days when they were all hanging out getting drunk on the streets and spare changing together and running down alleys where the buildings leaned together marrying each other's corroded fire escapes and in every direction, around every corner, were other buildings rising brick after grimy brick, their windows smashed, their windows barred; and the Shit Howdy Girls pounded their boots in the black slush, and when sleet came down to sting them they went to the liquor store and got the cheapest beers they could and hung out drinking at somebody's house and talked about the meaning of being Shit Howdy Girls. The Shit Howdy Girls were Dan-L, Sadie, Switch and Roxy (they wanted to make Betty Bones a Shit Howdy Girl, but Dan-L said no way, she's not dedicated enough). Dan-L was more or less living at home then. Her Mom was pretty cool. All three times Dan-L broke her camera her Mom took it to the store and told them the camera had been broken when she bought it, so Dan-L got another one free. Her Mom was the greatest Mom in the world. But Dan-L got into fights with her sister, like the time Dan-L was out and Dickie and some of his friends came over and Dan-L's sister had to entertain them, and Dan-L's sister got mad and called Dan-L a slut and threw beer in her face, so Dan-L had to beat her ass. It was certainly her own fault since Dan-L had always told her she was gonna hit her but she just didn't believe it. —The reason the camera had gotten broken that first time was because Dan-L was over at Dutch's and Dutch kept this nasty white-face slobbery pit bull named Judas,* a monster with a white-bleached head, almost salt-bleached, with bones sticking out of fat and muscle and tough rumpled skin, and Judas stared at Dan-L out of his dirty black glazed eyes; and there were dirty black hairs all down his chest and forelegs as he lay on Dutch's dirty rugs ready to bite her; and Dutch sometimes made Judas bite a rawhide rope and then Dutch cranked the rope into the air so that Judas was hanging on by his teeth; and this understandably soured Judas, so that he bit Dan-L's leg and she dropped her camera. It took about half an hour for Dutch to get Judas to open up his jaws so Dan-L could take her leg out. The second time her camera got broken was the fight, one of the most bloodiest fights of her life (though by no means the most violent, she explained; Dan-L liked to make distinctions), when she and Sadie and Switch and Dickie were in a bar and this guy Thor was busting Dan-L's chops just saying all this shit, and Dan-L said, "Switch, should I pour my beer over his head?", and Switch said go ahead and Dan-L did, and Thor knocked it out of the way and it hit this black dude, and the nigger said fuck you and Switch said don't yell at my friend and the nigger punched Switch so Dan-L punched him in the face and kicked him in the nuts, so he smashed a mug over Dan-L's head—that was the first bloody thing—and then he pushed Switch and she fell over the broken mug and got cut and that was the second bloody thing, and Dan-L said to Dickie to come on and do something. Dickie had thought until then that the girls were handling it, but when Dan-L called him he just climbed over the shoulders of the crowd to help her, climbing whether they liked it or not, with so much strength showing in his pink face; and the nigger's friends tried to stop Dickie but Dickie just kept coming, walking on their shoulders and on their heads, which was something that Dan-L would never forget all her life; and some poor guy with glasses got in the way and Dickie smashed his glasses into his eyes without really meaning to (that was the third bloody thing); and finally Dickie reached the nigger and chopped him in the head! (That was the fourth bloody thing.) The nigger was escorted out, and they all took off before the police came. Around then the American Front was started in San Francisco by Chuckles, Albert, Blue and Johnny Beast. Dan-L didn't sit there and go I'm part of the American Front and

---

*I don't know why every dog in every skinhead story was a pit bull.

shit, but she sure said right on.

Dan-L liked New York better because she could get drunker there; there was just something about New York with its cement parks and grey skies and brickfronts and mesh fences and drunks sitting down on the sidewalk pissing that made her able to drink more; she was sick of San Francisco. She and Dickie wanted to go back East for good (*"South*east!" yelled Dickie, drinking a beer), because too many dull crummy things happened here, like the time she was with the other Skinz at the Vats and there was supposed to be a show, but there wasn't, so they went to the Safeway nearby and kept ripping off booze and got thoroughly drunk, and they went to the Walgreen's at Sixth and Mission and tried to shoplift, and plainclothes people were watching so Dan-L didn't take anything but the others did. When they went out, the plainclothes people came running after them down the street and got the others, and Dan-L wasn't about to leave them so she ran back to the Walgreen's and went in and there was this guy standing at the door with his arms folded, and he said you can't go in there and Dan-L pushed by him just the same and saw the Skinz were tied up in the back, and they arrested her with the others but didn't tie her up because when they checked her I.D. they saw that she was a college girl, so the cops just escorted her by the elbow while the others had to wear cuffs; and they told Dan-L to appear in court to get the charges dropped, but she couldn't go to court right then because she had to go back to New York for awhile, so they probably had a bench warrant on her.

MOTHERS OF SKINHEADS

Dan-L loved her Mom. Most of the other Skinz did, too (Boot-woman Marisa being an exception).

"I was adopted when I was three," Dagger said. "For a long time I blamed my real parents for breaking up and giving me away, but just recently I found out my Dad was a fag. Can you believe it? It makes me want to puke. So now I love my Mom even more for breaking up with him. Someday I swear I'm gonna go back down there with a .44 and find that fag bastard and blow his head off, *blam!*"

"You gotta think what's good for you," Dickie said.

"I almost forgot my Mom," Dagger said, "I went to a lot of psychiatrists, and they *made* me remember; maybe I remembered those things in *dreams*, man, but I didn't know what they meant."

"Yeah," said Dickie, "it's that kind that gets you." He sometimes had needle dreams.

"Hey, this is a bad scene," said Dagger, jerking open the refrigerator door to look for more beer. "I ain't seen my Mom in eighteen years."

When Dickie and his Mom had a fight she said, "I shoulda aborted you! You shoulda been a goddamned abortion! You're too much like your goddamned father."

Anthony was still polishing his boots.

THE NEW BOY

When he finished polishing, he started over. "I want these boots to be like *mirrors*!" he cried. "I'm gonna polish 'em up real good. People are gonna see their reflection right before I kick them in the face. It's gonna be the last thing they ever see!"

Nobody paid any attention.

Anthony was eighteen. He'd met up with the Skinz on Haight Street. *Shit*, he *still* hasn't met cooler people! — Hardly had it begun to force itself upon him that he was a skinhead when he looked the part. His skull, newly naked, looked upon the world with a haughty pride in belonging, in defending, in showing itself in its trueness of whiteness, like a splendid moon which had at last broken free of a thicket of kinky nigger-hair nettles and now rose high into the night. Then he got his tattoos. Once that was accomplished, everything began to happen for Anthony just as he had dreamed it would, like the time that he and skinhead Albert from Germany were staying at this girl's house, and Anthony had her down on hands and knees sucking his cock, and Albert stuck a cold cucumber from the fridge up her ass. How she did scream! Later Anthony stuck the cuke in the microwave and warmed it up and rolled her on her belly so she couldn't see and fucked her with the cucumber, and when she saw it she freaked and grabbed it and broke it so a piece stuck in her cunt. Another time he and Albert fucked a girl with a carrot rubbed with vaseline, and she was *loving* it, and then they ran around shoving the carrot in people's faces going, "SMELL THIS!" — Of course life was not always so romantic as that, since being a skinhead Anthony had to always guard himself against the assaults of the world, an example being the time that Anthony was in the drunk tank and this fag came after him when he was pissing and Anthony grabbed his shoulder and slammed his head on the steel partition and cut a

185

triangular gash from his cheek all the way up to his eye. It made him feel good to think about as he sat in Dickie's kitchen now, repolishing his boots. The whitish-yellow walls gleamed in the night like a bone cavern.

DAGGER AND SPIKE

Dagger's pregnant bootwoman, Spike, came in from the living room looking tired. She felt cranky because the doctor had told her not to smoke or drink much, which was hard for her because she needed to be Dagger's bootwoman in full, the way she'd been before when she'd done half of every hit of every drug that Dagger took. — She and Dagger now got into a fight over who should carry the photo album back to the bookshelf. "You tell me to put it back, I'm just gonna throw it on the floor!" Spike yelled.

"Hey," said Dagger. "Why did you stick in those pictures of me with the black eye? I don't like those pictures."

"You can just fucking put it away yourself!" Spike screamed.

"Awright," chuckled Dickie. "You tell 'im."

"Stay the *fuck* out of my business!" yelled Dagger.

Dickie went for him with the scissors. They scuffled in their black Nazi-eagle T-shirts, punching the air and yelling, "I'm losing my faith in mankind!"

"No comments from the peanut gallery!" Dagger said. "You give me some comments, someone's likely to get stabbed. And not by me! Spike takes that stuff real serious."

"I'm not gonna stab her; I'm gonna stab *you*," said Dickie.

"Oh, forget it," said Dagger. "I've known Spike one year and a half, two years and a half before you ever *thought* of meeting her."

"Come on, Dagger, I remember your anniversary."

"You do? Remember Tequila Ed?"

"Sure I remember Tequila Ed."

"Oh," said Dagger, suddenly aged and beaten. "All the good old boys have left San Francisco. Only ones left are me, Dickie, and a couple others. Yama's in jail, Blue and Chuckles split; I tell you, you can jerk off all you like."

THE OLD DAYS

They used to go into bars and pick fights, punch people in the face when they didn't like the way they looked (being Nazis, they were conscious that appearance is everything). At least that was what some people said about them. But the Skinz said they didn't start anything. It was the others who started things, who talked rude to them and then didn't get out of the way. One time Lorelei and Blue were walking down Market Street and this nigger poked Lorelei in the ass with a stick and followed the two of them on the bus. Blue was hooded, like a viper. When he and Lorelei got off the bus, the nigger got off behind them, so Blue hit the nigger in the face a few times and said, "Now you'll remember the skinheads." —They sat on Skinhead Hill, crooning to each other and yelling; they muscled in on women walking down Haight Street with their boyfriends, and if the boyfriends didn't walk away pretty fast they got it in the face. It is not my aim to describe these old times of violent freedom, for this record was made in the decline of their movement, when most of the bars had bounced them out for good; and they sat around in their middle twenties muttering about how it used to be.

At that time, it seemed to me, death was their watchword, death being not a threat, not a reward, but simply a placement. They had no thought for any future day in which they might be gypsies and sing on stairs, their faces soot-darkened for security.

Haight Street

Dickie lived, as indicated, in the Tenderloin, where poor men walk at night, where the windows of parking garages glow yellow and black where stones have smashed them, where whores greet you licking big ice cream cones at midnight as you come out of the 188 Club after a shot and a round of liars' dice, and other whores ease up to your car if you honk and roll down the window, and it doesn't matter that somebody shot out the streetlights or something because those orange whore-eyes *shine* and make you HARD; but most of the other Skinz (and by "Skinz" I am referring in particular to the gang known as the S.F. Nazi Skinz) enjoyed the delights of violence and idleness on Haight Street, which wakes up at 8:30 in the morning when the sad clerks who think themselves artists go off to work; and the patrol cars coast slowly through Golden Gate Park like Soviet tanks mopping up after the Hungarian uprising (the bums who sleep in the Park have now been arrested or gotten away); and then Haight Street dreams again beneath the blue morning, clouds securing Cole Street and Shrader Street from the wind; and the dreams of Haight Street are like dreams of driving through Nebraska or Arizona, which roll by all day on a cross-country drive without anything accomplished; and the sidewalk is held by sleepy panhandlers and bewildered tramps with big backpacks ("So this is Haight Street; now what do I do?"), and just west of the Holy Smoke Barbeque hangs the American flag from the terrace of the skinhead flat, as wrinkled as a fugitive's clothes; and then again between 10:30 and 11:00 the street wakes up again, comes into its real life, the thrift stores and secondhand bookstores and liquor stores and clothing stores and ice cream stores opening; and the cafes leach full of people reading newspapers and sipping espresso and smoking, and people walk along the sidewalks, and Brandi the whore goes yawning to her corner by the liquor store to beg change ("You know what we call nigger bitches?" says Yama, "We call 'em mud dogs!"), and the first skinhead comes out grey-skulled in a grey jumpsuit, and other Skinz groan on the moldy carpet of the skinhead flat, that is to say Hunter and Dee and Nova's flat, and they scratch carpet-fuzz off their shirts and roll dead beer cans away from their eyeballs, wondering whether to take valium and sleep till dark or whether to watch TV or whether they might as well saunter out into the sunlight, as another two or three now do, the first hornets from the nest, already looking hard, looking angry, on the jump for some ass to beat. Later they'll be walking Yama's dog Rebel. For so long now we've seen them loitering in the sun, eyeing the last hippie girls surviving in storefront niches, watching other girls go clopping resolutely by in high heels while the skinheads roar, "She's just another skinhead slut! Roll 'er on 'er ass and stick it up 'er butt!", and the girls clop on a little faster, pretending that they didn't hear, their dwindling asses moving their New Wave trousers out of sight.

Whether it is a happy life or a sad one the Skinz live is of course unknowable to anyone watching them stride by, turning their bulging skulls greedily upon their bulging necks, trying to be pitiless, exclusive; not listening much to one another; but we can consider the question. The lone ones lean up against the restaurant windows, hunching their heads in like turtles at the same time they swivel their gaze in what might be anxiety or might be automatic street wisdom. They spend too much time waiting, but on the whole they are arguably happy, having their fights to look forward to. What more, after all, could anyone yearn for in his guts than the chance to hurt somebody else, jawkicking a soul to screaming subhumanness

in order to reiterate that *I live*? —"Politics," I once heard a conservative say, "is the exercise of power. Power is the ability to inflict pain." By this criterion the skinheads are among our most spontaneous politicians. Let us assume, then, that being spontaneous they are light of heart.

William T. Vollmann

Afternoon at the Command Post

Up in the skinhead house, behind red curtains, a man kept looking out the street window, as if he were on sentry duty. He drank beer and wore camouflage trousers.

"Hey, get off the sidewalk!" he yelled. "You heard me! Get off or I'll give you some beer to drink!" He poured a Bud out the window.

The other Skinz crowded to look. — "Lookit that nigger," said Dee. "He's so scungy."

"They all look that way," said Nazi Dick solemnly, and at that they all laughed.

Powell Street, Emeryville

If you are white then I suppose it was your great-great-great-great-grandfather who started it with his runs for the Triangle Trade, assaulting the walled towns of Negroes by land and by sea, utilizing fire with all diligence for this end; and thereby obtained prisoners, for which he got good prices; and so on to the plantations, the lynchings and all the rest of it, until a jumbo crop of hatred had been painstakingly sown; but by now the wrong lies on both sides, as the tale of how Bootwoman Marisa lost her front tooth will show; so there are times when we hate them as much as they hate us; and it is hard to know or care where in this circle the S.F. Nazi Skinz came in; the Skinz did not care, and out by the Emeryville Marina no one in the workforce cared about anything but beauty, of which there was a productive yield given the way that the purple translucent plastic paper trays glittered in the sun. You could look through them sideways and see through their ribs, through the grilles at the back and out the window across the smog to the windows of other buildings where the bank clerks and software jerks learned the lessons of life from their Tandem mainframes: TAL ERROR 70: ONLY ITEMS SUBORDINATE TO A STRUCTURE MAY BE QUALIFIED. (I wonder if our country was better when Indians lived on it by themselves, fishing, hunting, and weaving blue blankets, or whether it was just as dreary, wastes of bog and forests then corresponding to wastes of buildings now.) Every firm was in convenient reach of the Denny's ("Always Open"), and from the Denny's it was an easy walk to the tunnel under the freeway overpass, a dark cold tunnel through which big trucks went by so loud that your bones hurt. The exhaust

smelled like old waffles. This tunnel was the bus stop for the 57M or
57C, and there were sometimes black boys coming up to surround
you if you were white and grinning at you and telling you to hand
over your money, "or else I'll do *you* a favor you might not appreci-
ate!" because they would be quite happy to hurt you for being white,
just as the skinheads would be happy to hurt them for being black.*

AFTERNOON AT THE COMMAND POST (CONTINUED)

"I got stuck in jail again last Tuesday," said Ice to Dickie in the
back room.

"Oh yeah? What for?"

"Assaulting an officer and drinking in public. Or maybe it was the
other way around."

"Fuck," said Dickie. "They caught up with me, too. Two hundred
and fifty dollars bail that I won't see for who knows how many
months, plus twenty-five dollars court cost. Bitch said I had a gun
and was gonna kill her boyfriend. All I said to him was, 'Buzz off or
I'll kill ya.'"

"And did you have a gun?" said Ice.

"Hell, no. They took my leather jacket, too. Said it was a dangerous weapon." He chuckled. "And it *was*. See, I got this license
plate and cut it in half, then I wrapped it around the sleeve of my
jacket so there was this razor edge. Ripped up a couple tin cans and
did the same thing. That jacket weighed twenty or thirty pounds. All
I had to do was sweep out my arm and I could just gut any old fish,
fuff!"

So the Skinz hacked their way through the buttery blue idleness of
the afternoon, progressing toward the evening, when wicked things
come alive.

A little after three, Dee's husband Hunter came back from work
with other skinhead men. — "You're not a man unless you bust your
ass," Dagger liked to say. "I don't call it working, sitting in an office
eight hours a day with soft hands." The skinheads were doomed to
carry lumber and cement around in open pits, never trusted enough

---

* "We're a very racial people," Dee explained to me once. "We're not prejudiced; we're
racial. There's a difference. We have *pride* in being white. I have *pride* in having a
family. I've adopted a lot of kids, like Nova, but I wouldn't bring a black kid into the
family because it wouldn't fit in. It would get verbally abused."

for the class jobs of hanging sheetrock in warm middle-income bedrooms, never getting to use the bathtub tap to fill their buckets, never swishing that bathtub-issue water into the mudding tray, adding the Fix-All just right to make grey-white dough, spreading it good in the mudding tray, the first layer going smooth over the bare ceiling boards so that they still textured the mud like ribs in flesh. No, for the skinheads work was a stretch of curses in grey fogged-in excavations, office workers leaning over the street railings to spit and comment interestedly while the Skinz sank in mud up to the knees of their jeans, hauling dusty white sacks of cement on their shoulders, having nothing but their strength to glory in, never getting to peek through the back windows on the job or prancing up the fire escape, snapping the downstairs women's lacy lingerie on the line, or opening up spankin' new sacks of Durabond. They worked in the building pits when they got work, those skinheads, and rain dribbled inside their leather jackets; then they came home, their faces, arms and jeans whitened by cement dust. They sat scowling and talking about how much they hated the job. Their supervisors were always assholes. One super lived on the site so they could never get away from him. — "It was all I could do not to put a shovel through his melon," Hunter said. — A man scratched his skull for awhile, swishing his beer. "My dream," he said, "is to build a cabinet

192

in my room and get me a badass gun collection, one for every skinhead. And one day, we'll all just go to the window and open up." — Dickie laughed, "Naw, leave the door *wide* open, and wait till somebody comes in, and *then* open up and *waste* him."

At the window, the skinhead in the camo trousers never took his eyes off the street.

A SUNSET

Outside, the afternoon dwindled in the strange way that it does in Haight Street, the sun baking the almost illegible graffitti on the cracked wall of the deserted technical high school: AMERICAN FRONT—FOR A STRONG AMERICA; then, as the afternoon died, the far sidewalks and buildings turned gold in the slanted sunlight, the pavement underfoot already blue-grey and shadowed. The flat roofs of the Victorian houses brightened to beauty beneath the sky, which pretended to be as luminous as it had been at noon, but wasn't anymore. As clouds came in from the Bay, the first pair of evening police came walking down Stanyan to the head of the Haight, their uniforms already almost twilight-black. Hornets quickened in the night-hive. Skinheads sat in front of their house, scuffing their toes on the sidewalk, smoking, eating bagels, looking grimly from side to side. The first bookstores and antique boutiques were being locked, the steel shutters drawn. New Skinz came walking by very fast, nodding to nobody, wearing ski caps, looking daggers at the new generation of black-dressed Death Ladies whose faces were white and cruel as porcelain; perhaps it was they, whoever they were, who wrote in the doorways FUCK SF SKINZ THERE A BUNCH OF FAGS, or maybe they were responsible for the poem on the front wall of the anarchist bookstore:

> i've got a bullet in my head,
> where there once was a brain, now there's lead,
> but that's ok, fine with me,
> since that's all it takes to be a NAZI

and more and more Skinz now came swarming into the street, staring hard-eyed at all the aliens on the streets whose hair grew thick and bushy on their heads like coonskin caps. A few Skinz went down with Dickie to his place in the Tenderloin, the T.L. Yama called it, down the paved valleys of streets where red car-lights between twin lines of yellow lights lured them deeper into project housing with curtains drawn and past silhouettes sitting in the dark on park benches; then the Chinese restaurants came into view, the yellow-lit tunnels of hotel garages, the Peacock Club, the massage parlors, the old men in decaying footgear taking little wooden-legged steps across the street; and in Dickie and Dan-L's place Dan-L sat waiting in the kitchen with its *1984* posters, wandering into her bedroom, looking at her clothes neatly filed in boxes, her black pirate flag, the forty-eight-star American flag from the Marin county fleamarket, the hooded skull done in pastels by Spike on speed, the drawing of the skinhead saying I HATE THE WORLD (also done by Spike, I think); and Dan-L yawned and went back to her dirty kitchen table with a bottle of Windex on it, sitting around alone, playing with her cat Rambo, munching on Burger King takeout, her breath fogging up the cold black kitchen window, and the refrigerator humming in pulses, like a heart. Her lower eyelids were made up in black, as if she'd rubbed them with charcoal. She was dead tired; she worked counters and her boss wouldn't leave her be; tonight he'd called her up yelling because she'd paid the VCR repairman without his permission, and Dan-L said sorry to him because she couldn't afford to lose the job. She went back to the window, seeing the homosexuals peeking at her from the upstairs window. She hated and feared them because she'd heard a lot of stories; she saw their heads outlined through the yellowness, and when they caught her looking at them they ducked back behind their window plant. She wished that Dickie and Dagger were here, that it was summer and afternoon and Dickie would tell again all about how he met Dagger with Mick the Prick that day on Haight Street when they were tweaking, and Dagger would get a grin and yell "*Suck my dick, Massah!*" and Dan-L would laugh in her soft hoarse way and they'd go up and laze around on the roof the way they used to do, having rock fights; once Dan-L clocked Dagger on the forehead with a big rock and he freaked out, started throwing rocks at everybody so hard they had to run; but now Dagger and Spike had gone up north for legal-fiscal reasons and nothing was happening; the phone rang; it was Yama; he needed someone to meet him when he got out of jail tomorrow; and Dan-L said okay and promised herself to give him a lecture about using speed; and she ate up the last of her cold Burger King, yawning there in the Tenderloin a few blocks east of the War Memorial Opera House where rich people had gone to observe

Verdi's Falstaff sing out, "Aiee! Aiee! Aiee! Aiee!" whenever Mistress Page and Mistress Quickly and the other torturers spanked him with ferns and sang, "Piccatta! Piccatta! Piccatta! Piccatta!", while meanwhile the rich people's cars were being towed by mistake, so that the rich people folded their gold opera glasses shut with a snap and stormed off to the police station on Ellis to demand their rights and called the Channel Eleven News on the phone and scolded the meek night officers some more and made the officers give them rides to the tow company, and the officers did their best to jolly the rich people, saying joshing things like, "Well, at least you get the nice new patrol car, ladies and gentlemen; you see, the other one is used for *criminals* and the back is full of *fleas!*" (this being the patrol car that Dagger and the other Skinz were used to); but the rich people were not mollified and informed each other that this was an OUT-RAGE; and they condemned the officers for being symbols of a hateful bureaucracy, not that it was their fault of course; and that Mayor Feinstein was going to hear of this; and they formed exalted on-the-spot charities and mutual defense leagues to pay the towing costs, and they exchanged business cards to keep in touch for the protest hearing, standing on a parking lot in the Potrero in their black suits and black gowns, with triple strings of pearls dangling down to the matrons' fluid-filled artificial bosoms; and at the end of it the oldest, crossest, sternest lady (who had called Channel Eleven three times already, saying "We have thirty-five VERY INDIG-NANT citizens here and we need your help!") tapped on the driver's window of each departing automobile; and when the driver rolled the window down, *vreeEEE*, recognizing a fellow member of his or her class, the old lady said, "How did you pay? VISA? Mastercard? Good. Stop payment in the morning." —Meanwhile Dickie finally came in with his friends.

After Dinner

"What're we gonna eat, Dan-L?" he said.

"I already ate," she said. "Didn't think you were coming home, so I said fuck it."

"Hey, Bootwoman," teased the Skinz, "when are you gonna shave your head?"

"I've got like this feeling inside," she told them. "I'm a boot-woman, and I don't need to shave any part of my head to show it."

195

"You know," says grey-haired metaphysical Joe, who just blew in from Massachusetts, not a skinhead or nothing, just a would-be sheetrocker and friend of a friend dreaming about a bottle of Thunderbird, which they call a short dog (and to better fill you in I had better tell you that he was almost deaf, like the Butcher Boys' dog, but genuinely was metaphysical, had once been Brother Joe at a monastery back east but he was a *deaf* Brother Joe as you understand by now and worked and prayed and meditated happily inside his cloud of sacred deafness until a new Abbot came to the monastery, at which point Brother Joe's tribulations began, for since he was under a vow of silence he could not explain to the new Abbot that he was deaf, and the Abbot didn't know much about Brother Joe because Brother Joe kept to himself and worked chopping wood and repairing stone walls in the forest, and when the Abbot greeted him Brother Joe never heard and therefore never answered; so the Abbot, concluding that Brother Joe was anti-social, decreed that he had to become a hermit, and Brother Joe wouldn't do that, so he was expelled), "You know," said metaphysical Joe, not having caught too much of the tabletalk or really hearing what the Skinz were all about, because he had his own cross to bear, but gathering that Dan-L was saying something about shaving or not shaving her head, "You know," goes old Joe, "I tried to get rid of my dandruff once by shaving my head."

"Did it work?"

"No."

Joe's attempt at a contribution having sunk into the conversation like a stone into deep water, the skinheads went about their own business.

"You didn't ask me how my foot is," said Dan-L. "I got another acid treatment."

The stale cigarette butts lay very still in the ashtray. Dickie loaded a bowl of hash. "This high makes me feel so nice, kicked back," he said. "When I'm on pot I get paranoid, walking down the street thinking people are looking at me funny."

Dan-L played with the tablecloth, lifting up corners of it. Underneath, the entire table top was covered with black-markered slogans like WHITE POWER and KILL.

"Getting to be hunting season," Dickie said. "Boy, it's been three years. Last time I was out with your father, Dan-L. Remember when we went down to his land in Alabama and he threw tin cans off a cliff and we shot them with his .357 magnum? That was cool."

"The land wasn't much, though," said Dan-L. "And the people were stupid."

"You calling people from The South hicks?" Warren the mover said, leaning forward very slowly.

"No," said Dan-L. "I was talking about my own people."

"Shake it, girl," Warren said. "Just shake it."

Nobody said anything.

"Down south the mountains are so beautiful, man," Warren said. "Out in Chattanooga you can see nine states, ten states with the nekkid eye."

"Knoxville's the place," said Dickie. "Lots of nice places, though. I remember one time when we were in Orchard Hill, one of the last great white neighborhoods. Then some niggers topped our car. So Chuckles's grandfather got a shotgun and said, 'Hey, King Coons! Get the fuck out of Our Neighborhood!' He liked to sit on the porch and rock with his shotgun."

"That's Chuckles's grandfather, all right," Warren said. "My grandfather died couldn't read nor write. But you couldn't forge his X, boy; he knew his X."

Just outside, in the dead glow of Ellis Street, Anthony saw a punk panhandling. The punk's Mohawk made Anthony feel sick. Nothing was worse than a punk, except for maybe a punk and a nigger. He told the punk to head out, beat it for Powell Street where the punks congregated (the way that chewing gum, for instance, congregates in stale hardened lumps under desks and tables), or beat it anywhere else but just get the fuck out of Anthony's sight. The punk whipped out a zapper gun and fired, *phhhh-bzzzzt*! but it didn't work like it was supposed to, just burned Anthony's chest, so that Anthony, rather than falling down screaming and crying onto the hard cold sidewalk as the punk had hoped, shook off the pain as a dog shakes off water, and beat the punk's ass *righteously*! The cops came running. But when they saw it was just a punk, and the punk had started it anyway, they grinned to Anthony's bootwoman, "Your boyfriend got lucky this time. He got a freebie." (According to the F.B.I., one violent crime occurs every thirty-one seconds.) And Anthony ran down the sidewalk laughing, his boots shining, the night worth living through again, and people jumped out of his way.

While other losers, the lame, the blind spinning down the street in firestorms of hallucinations, made their way through life over the stepping stones of others' pity, the skinheads derived power from their isolation and magnified themselves to themselves until the things they could do seemed to them all there was to do. This was but the rhetoric of unavoidable decay, their taut bodies knowing their own decrease, knowing the wane of the city, and desperately the Skinz wrote SF SKINZ in the Sunset, in the Haight, at Church and Duboce, in North Beach; and that was nice but it didn't do any good. Their politics excluded, they were hardly different from the trapped commuters on the Muni, who, dressed in their business best, stared down at their own tapping feet, or read, or rested their chins in their hands, waiting, waiting, waiting.

LEFT-WING UTOPIANISM: AN INFANTILE DISORDER

Back on Frederick Street, Chuckles stamped roaring down the sidewalk, looking for a fight. He saw a black man leaning against a wall. Chuckles slam-butted the nearest NO PARKING sign, yelling, "I'm gonna toughen up my head; I'm gonna use my head for a *weapon*!"* —Whereas some toughs skipped side by side and leaned

---

* Chuckles's favorite song was "If I Could Talk To The Animals."

weightlessly against lit storefronts, watching one of their number do little ironical ballets for them, the Skinz just strode down the sidewalk, swiveling their domes to give both sides of the street equal views of their contemptuous eyes, dying to leave us soon for their own Promised Land. Three Skinz (say the anarchists) went to the anarchist bookstore and kicked in the front window. They hated that place because it was left wing. Whenever they had a free minute, which was often, they went over there and painted swastikas on the door. The anarchists tried to classify them in the reflexive pseudo-biological way of all ideologues, writing: *"The males have shaved heads, high boots, rolled up or tucked in jeans, often with bleach marks, suspenders, and T-shirts or bare chest, often with a black leather jacket..."* — the reiterated "often with" further betraying the anarchists' melancholy lust for typology, as if things would be O.K. if they could just definitely establish the Skinz as a product of late capitalism, the way Franz Neumann had done for the Adolf regime in his treatise *Behemoth* (1941); then the Skinz would stop tormenting them, beating them up, sending them letters like the one they got that fall, with the eagle on it, scowling, the eagle's claws out ready to seize and slice, its wings stubby and wide, like those of an Air Force bomber, and on its chest the "A"-inscribed circle of the American Front; and the letter said (and the eagle screamed):

ATTENTION!

PUNKS, COMMUNISTS, ANARCHISTS, HIPPIES,
AND HOMOSEXUALS:

YOU ARE ENEMIES OF AMERICA AND THE AMERICAN WAY OF LIFE. WE THE SKINHEADS WILL NOT TOLERATE YOUR SPREADING OF UNWANTED DISEASES BOTH MENTAL AND PHYSICAL.

WE ARE JAILED BECAUSE WE USE EVERY METHOD AT OUR DISPOSAL TO PROTECT THE DECENT PEOPLE OF THIS COUNTRY FROM YOUR UNAMERICAN, SUBVERSIVE, LEFT WING MIND POISON.

WE ARE THE GUARDIANS OF FREEDOM AND LIBERTY FOR ALL GOOD AMERICANS. SO BEWARE ENEMYS OF THE FLAG.

YOUR DAYS ARE
NUMBERED.

© AMERICAN FRONT 1985

Upon receipt of this missive the anarchists were seriously kro-potkined, like medieval German churchgoers finding Luther's the-ses on the door, but the Skinz themselves just drank up their beers and forgot about it. Dan-L said that _____ did it and what was the big deal. "He was going around on the street laughing about it and boasting about it for days," she said. "But I don't know that much about it. I heard about it and I didn't give a shit." As for Dickie, he just looked solemn. *"And the South will rise again,"* he proclaimed, *"Stars, Bars and Skinz!"*

KEEPING IT ON

"You know," said Dagger, finishing off his third beer, "that little kid you brought today, he's setting up that guy, Brock, he's been stealing. We're gonna lure him up at the show and kick his ass."

"What about the owner?" Dickie said.

"The owner don't care, man. He's just a fucking nigger. He just cares about money."

"You gonna beat up the kid?"

"Hell, no," said Dagger, "He's a *skinhead* kid. Someday he'll grow up and make a fine skinhead, a leader, maybe. The person to do that is someone who's raised up in it and knows our law by heart. We started it. It's up to our kids to keep it on."

"I'm gonna play that song again," said Dickie.

"Flip the damned tape!" Dagger commanded.

Their big hands started pounding at the cassette player, at each other, grip-wrestling in midair.

"Don't fuck with me, man!"

Dickie leaped up and grabbed at Dagger's neck. Dagger snarled and bit. He sank his teeth into Dickie's cheek. — "But you can also take a motherfucker by the ears," Dickie said thoughtfully, "and you can just *rip* their *ears* off." — "Yeah," said Dagger, "but I bite hunks of skin off, and facial skin, *that* ain't never gonna heal. Hey, you remember, Dickie, when I used to hate your guts and want to kick your ass?"

"You never could!"

"I could rip that lardass nose right off you."

"Now we get along, so what's the *diff*?"

WHAT BRANDI THOUGHT

The skinheads hated Brandi because she was black. "She's a walking stinkbag," said Bootwoman Marisa, "she's a sleazebag. I wish that bitch was rotting under the ground instead of on top of it." Brandi was a slender smallish dark-eyed whore who looked you in the eye when she found you on the street and promised you everything and made you believe in the freedom of her nogood ways and her hair felt like cotton candy and she hugged you and kissed you with the housefronts watching behind so that you thought you were the only one she loved, and she always tried to get money from you because she always needed it. She needed it so much that if you opened your wallet to give her something she'd stand on tiptoe to watch, and say, "There's another dime in there. Let me see if there's a penny in there." —If you gave her money once, she never forgot you. She'd pick you out on the sidewalk and be suddenly in front of you and she'd put her hand on her hip and smile at you with her pretty fuzzy hair done up, and she'd try to get more money out of you, but if she couldn't then you were still her friend. When she stood in her doorway looking at you she was all business, hooking her thumb in her jeans and leaning, like an urchin who might run away or hit you. She spare changed until late at night, sometimes holding her little son by the hand, and the boy, who barely came up to her waist, held his palm out and stared up at you like some sad curious little frog; then when it got dark Brandi took him home and came back more lively and tried to sell nonexistent drugs and once the night was firmly established she started selling herself. There was a dress that she wore with three buttons down the front, and you could tell how late it was or how high she was by how low the buttons were undone. She might look straight at you, so earnest and loving, or she might grin at you with her teeth showing and her eyes wary and old. At two or three in the morning she'd be asking men coming out of bars if they wanted to make a little bit of *love*; or if she were desperate she'd begin flagging down the cars.

"What do you think of those skinheads, Brandi?" I said.

"I don' like 'em," she said.

When I left she stood up tall and kissed me. "I see you," she said.

I once had a dream that Brandi was running because someone was after her, and she held two little black children by the hand as she ran, and she was afraid, and she ran down narrow cement stairs that took her deeper and deeper inside a concrete wall, and the children kept up as best as they could but sometimes Brandi had to slow up for them and they held tight to her hands and rested their heads against her waist and while they rested she looked behind her, and then she pulled the children farther down the damp stairs; and finally she came to a door, and water was dripping from the keyhole, and the door was bulging outwards; and I realized that Brandi must be directly under some large reservoir, and I tried to tell her not to open the door, but she couldn't hear me, and she turned the door-knob, and tons of green water poured in and crushed her and the two children.

MARISA'S FRONT TOOTH

Bootwoman Marisa, hater of Brandi, her sixteenth birthday more recently behind her than her conviction for assault with a deadly weapon, got a ride to North Beach to have her fourth tattoo done, waiting coolly in Bronson's living room where meanwhile a pleasant time was had by others watching videos of Mark Pauline piercing dead dogs' heads with remote-controlled drills, burning dead cats with a flamethrower, firing cardboard missiles full of gunpowder, throwing switches to make dead rabbits walk backwards. — "This is *weird!*" Marisa said, meaning the opposite, sitting on the couch with her felt hat beaked over her forehead, her thick black lines of eyebrows poised above a dinosaur romance. She had a very pretty oval head—I say head, not face, because hairlessness makes the boundary between head and face vanish so that there is only head, the cheeks and temples curving with inevitable naturalness around to the ears and back to the grey stubble (something other than hair) growing out from the bone. It was a finely colored head that Marisa had, clean and marbled like the freckled stone stairs fronting San Francisco houses. The lighting in Bronson's living room caused a delicate shadow to deepen the tone of the right side, bisecting her perfect nose, which must have been crafted of special pink mollusk ceramic, like her lips. She leaned back in Bronson's couch, knees up, blinking her dark eyes and rubbing her dirty black sneakers on the cushions. There was a bunch of safety pins stuck in her earlobes. Her black leather jacket, stuck full of badass buttons and a Hitler iron cross, glittered with galaxies of zippers. — "Man, I hate your dog," she said. "If she bugs me again I'm gonna kick her jaw off." —Her boyfriend was a Nazi skin in Chicago called James who blew up cars

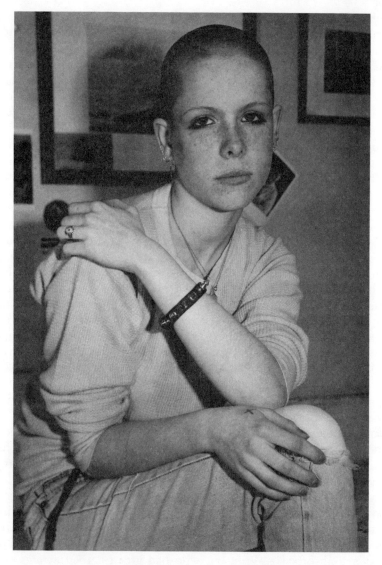

by dropping pingpong balls full of Drano into the gas tank. — Six D-cell batteries in the same place will accomplish the same object, Marisa explained, although in that case the car-bomber had to be patient for the two weeks that it took for the casings to dissolve. — She bought acid in sheets and mailed them to James, who sold them at a considerable profit in Chicago, where skinheads were cool, where skinheads were organized, said Marisa, where it was all for one and one for all. He did not share these profits with her.

The tatt was going to be a dragon, on the right upper thigh. Marisa really needed it, just as Yama needed to get more tatts on his arms (he was gonna get a Joker with an evil-ass face, like a red and black Checkered Demon). Marisa undid her suspenders and slipped her trousers off, grinning. Although she still had her shirt on, her naked thighs and her naked head made her as naked as a hairhead wearing no clothes at all; and this equivalence made her more ordinary, especially since most of her other tatts, such as the red, white and blue boot on her upper arm, were hidden by her shirt; and so, most of her Aryan props gone, she was just another naked girl. No one takes special account of Nazis when they are naked.* Marisa sensed this and became tentatively, submissively young. —"My legs are so fat," she said. —Beginning to outline the dragon on her thigh (he was not ready for his needles yet), Bronson bent over her in his studio of rainbow skulls, while she half-sat, half-lay on the tattooing couch, which was actually an old trunk with a sleeping bag folded on top. Marisa stared into the yellow oval of brightness around the filament of the light bulb, Bronson's music going "*Ooooooh, bunga-bunga bunga-bunga,*" and Bronson pen-sketched, holding in his other hand a fat phallus of deodorant which he applied now and then to keep the ink from rubbing off. Marisa, leaning back on her elbows, looked down at him and lay back, her head overhanging the couch, gazing now at a solar corona on canvas on the ceiling; and she played with the loose strap of her underpants. She had plump pink thighs. —"I can't stand pain," she said, but she wore a Nazi shirt. —"Oh, God," she said, "it's gonna be such a beautiful dragon; I've been waiting for this for such a long time now that I know I really need it on my body." Her pubic curls were the reddish brown of dead roses. —This sixteen-year-old looked hardly like a bootwoman at all now as she lay there, all her prized difference receding to her mouth. This mouth, a hallmark of her narcissism, pouted downward, toward herself, so that one couldn't readily tell whether she was sullen or just self-absorbed. —Bronson, who had green barbed arrows tattooed into the back of his neck, like lizard vertebrae, now began seriously to work. At the rattle of the tattoo gun, Marisa's eyelashes

---

* Could a sorting algorithm be devised to differentiate naked nuns from naked Nazis? (But this is only a wise-ass question, having no place in this definite treatise on naked brains.)

suddenly fluttered, the shadows beneath them somehow darker now, bluer than they had been. I will pass over her cries, and the sweat that burst out on that smooth, round skull, like that of a furry muskrat; while Bronson drilled slowly under her skin, wiping up her blood with a wad of tissue, and the sticky flesh of her thighs clung to the swab as it moved. From behind, Bronson's ear was red and distinct against her white flesh. Her thigh was as pale and soft as a flounder. The needle went in. Sometimes Bronson set the gun down to yawn and scratch at the callus on the middle joint of his second finger, known to those in his trade as the Eye of the Octopus. Marisa recovered herself better with each pause, as the needle lengthened the irrevocable lines already pierced into her thigh; biting her lip bravely at these required mutilations, she smiled wider and wider, smiled wet-lipped until the dragon was outlined on her thigh in ink and blood. Now she was even more essentially and unarguably a bootwoman. — "Are you done?" she said, "are you done? I want to see! If anybody comes up, maim, kill, destroy!", as she buckled her dirty jeans. She put her leather skinhead jacket back on, regaining more and more of herself with each button. When she'd first bought it, she'd broken it in by getting fucked on it. In the righthand pocket was her street knife. "Oh, kill, maim, and destroy!" she screamed, making fists in the air. "I want to sucker-punch somebody!"

She worked as a cook at Bouncer's down in China Basin, making breakfasts from six to ten, lunches from six to three, Bouncer's being a tall yellow building from before the earthquake of 1906, in sight of the water, warehouses on every hand; and inside the half-boarded-up door was Bouncer's Bar where it was always dark, and left of that the Bouncer's Cafe area, illuminated by incandescent bulbs on the high yellow ceiling (one burned out), and there were square plastic-wood tables with yellow chairs, and behind those was the faded yellow countertop, and Marisa worked between that and the faded yellow backboard planks that went up to the ceiling. There was a little dark hatchway where the countertop joined the wall, so that Marisa could slide plates of food directly into the bar, which also opened at six. Whenever I came to visit her she was so happy to see me, hugging me, rubbing her stubbly head against me like a puppy. Trustingly she pulled down her pants to show off Bronson's new work on her tattoo whenever I asked. She was my friend. Once I brought one of my pistols holstered under my coat, and when I brought her hand to it she stared at me and she squeezed it through my coat to be sure of it and her face lit up and she said, "Ooh, dude!", and old Darleen, who worked beside her frying up bacon and egg sandwiches and came from a ranch and wanted to have her own roadhouse in Oregon, teased Marisa and said, "That's right, dude!", and Marisa laughed and said, "Fuck, fuck, fuck! Now I have to have a nice day whether I want to or not, since you came to see me," and told how she was going to dress as a beatnik for Halloween, with hair and everything; and Darleen was gonna be a cowgirl; and there was a sign at the counter saying SEX IS THE ANSWER—NOW WHAT WAS THE QUESTION?, and Marisa seemed happy. (Poor Marisa! —In the Chatanuga Cafe up on Haight Street, a wavy-combed redhead out on a date smoothed her dress and said, "Marisa used to be really nice. We used to be great friends, and then —" "Then she got tough," her boyfriend supplied. —"Yeah, she shaved her head," the redhead said. "Then she lost all her friends.")

"I'd like an egg sandwich to travel," said an old hoss.

Marisa cooked it up. "Eggs with legs!" she screamed through the hatch.

Marisa worked slicing mushrooms and frying up the cutest little pork chops. "I do everything myself!" she cried, dancing to the radio. All the customers watched Marisa's earnest bald head at the corner of the range. She had a way of biting her lower lip as she worked that made her look as if she were trying not to cry.

"Hey, 'Risa, these hush puppies are hard through and through."

"*Fuck* you! Tells me it's raw! It's potatoes; what do you want?"

You could see her bent over the range, her snowy head, her green eyes looking up and around as she ladled oil on the potatoes. For four dollars or less she fixed the best breakfast around. And the customers sat scratching their greasy shirts and reading the paper and laboring over their food. As the months passed, Marisa came to rest her hand on her hip while she worked over the range, in the time-honored fashion of cooks everywhere. The blackboard said: MARISA'S FOOD FOR SALE. And whenever I asked her she took me to the back room, smiling a little nervously with her tongue between her teeth; and then she pulled down her pants and knelt, one hand on her naked hip, to show off her proud dragon. Sometimes the regulars came around to the doorway to peek. "Another dollar for the Dragon Lady!" they cried, putting a buck in her tips jar.

"How's James?"

"James is fine," she said smiling, and you could tell she loved him because she looked so happy just being able to say the word James. "He really liked that little knife you gave me. In fact," she said

206

proudly, "when I showed it to him he took it and wouldn't give it back." — "I guess that's a compliment," I said. — "Oh, yes," she said. "I was really really glad he liked it."

"What's your mother doing, Marisa?"

"My mother? Just being a Jew."

I will never forget the time I brought Marisa a white rose, and she grinned and said wow and hugged it and me, and as she was holding it, blushing and wondering what to do with it, a black woman approached the counter and said to Marisa, "Oh, somebody gave you a rose!"; and Marisa froze up and said nothing for a long time, and finally looked the black woman up and down a couple of times and said, "Yes, it's a *white* rose."

When the health inspector came to Bouncer's and didn't like her tiles, she punched him in the mouth. The inspector turned off the gas range. "You're closed."

Marisa was known sufficiently well that if you went and stood at a bus stop round about 10:00 in the morning you might see a blonde with dark rings under her eyes drinking beer in a paper bag, and she wore a black leather jacket; and if you asked her what time it was she'd laugh and say, "Oh, God, I don't even know what *year* it is," and there'd be a silence and she'd say, "Just kidding," and she'd say, "I think it's 8:30 or 9:00; you see, I just got out of Juvenile Hall; today's my eighteenth birthday," and you'd go (if you were nice), "Congratulations," and she'd go, "Now I'm out, I gotta stay out," and you'd say, "Yep, that's right," and there'd be another silence, and you'd go, "Maybe you know a friend of mine, a skinhead girl named Marisa," and she'd go, "You mean the one that's not quite a skinhead, with the stubble on her head? Sure, I know her," and at that the world would become a brighter place. Yes, she knew Marisa in Juvenile Hall, Marisa who was locked into her room every night, which was all concrete and echoey; and early in the morning the loudspeaker echoed: "*Wake up!*", and Marisa had to get up then and go wash and eat breakfast; and then for three hours she and the other girls sat doing nothing in the court-appointed "school," and then they had lunch; and in the afternoon they sat around and then after dinner the ones who'd been good were allowed to watch TV, and the ones who'd been bad had to do nothing; and then they all went back to their separate concrete rooms to get locked up again. They weren't ever allowed to go outside, but if nobody had fucked up, Juvie showed Walt Disney movies on the VCR on Friday night. They showed "Bambi" over and over. *

One of the reasons that Marisa hated blacks was that she'd been in Juvie in Detroit (how old would she have been then—thirteen, fourteen? Probably eleven, because she still had some of her baby teeth); the only white girl in Juvie, and they had to put her in isolation because all the other girls kept beating her up for being white, seven or eight black girls at a time (one on one Marisa could have handled them); and you must be informed of the final scene, when one of the girls got a pair of pliers from a guard (the guards were black); and in the cool wet unwholesome echoey darkness the black girls gathered around Marisa screaming and hitting her, and the black girl with the pliers banged Marisa's head down and got her mouth open and the black girls held Marisa down while she screamed and tried to punch them and the girl with the pliers pulled one of Marisa's front teeth out.—But when I first heard this story I misinterpreted one detail:

"So the girls held you down?"

"No, the guards did."* *

A Cold Sunday

Dee was a thin bootwoman with big teeth. She had a tall, egglike head and angular eyebrows. Her head was shaved to grey stubble. She had a way of smiling which bent her lower lip down and exposed her teeth, making her seem candid. Her right arm was tattooed. So was her back. When she took off her shirt to show it off you could see a horrid monster whose head was all eyes bulging out like pustules, except where its mouth was (it had long teeth); and below its lips writhed an array of tentacles lost in each other. On her left shoulder was her brother's name and the letters R.I.P. (He had died in an accident.) Her bowed head, the stubble cropped in a zigzag at the back of her neck, furnished her with an intentness appropriate to her boots.

---

* "Were the other girls nice?" — "*Nice!*" said Marisa in astonishment. "They were in Juvie! We were locked up!"

* * "There will be some," wrote Major W. E. Fairbairn in his commando manual *Get Tough!* (D. Appleton-Century, 1943), "who will be shocked by the methods advocated here. To them I say 'In war you cannot afford the luxury of squeamishness. Either you kill or capture, or you will be captured and killed. We've got to be tough to win, and we've got to be ruthless—tougher and more ruthless than our enemies." This is undoubtedly what Marisa's dentists thought.

"I have a gun," she said almost shyly the first time I met her. "I'll show you. It's only my first one." She fumbled under the bed and finally dragged out something wrapped in a dusty garbage bag. It was a crude long-barreled .410 pistol without sights, almost resembling a musket. "I'm gonna kill some coons with it," she laughed. "Just kidding." —The gun had never been cleaned. It didn't look safe to fire.

In a skinhead face, as I have said, the eyes become of prime importance. She had strong, calm eyes. Dee herself was strong and calm, intelligent and practical. She was always cleaning up, "keeping the house together" she called it, feeding other Skinz who came and stayed and stayed, unlike my roommate's discarded girlfriends who would sometimes come here because they had no place else to go, as in the case of Parisian Mathilde, whose uncle brought her here with a pair of suitcases, saying, "She'll be staying only a week," and Mathilde with her melancholy timidity interjected, "And it's a very *short* week!" —No, the Skinz were nothing like that, for many of them had no way to pay rent; Yama, for instance, slept for a long time in his car out by Kezar until it got towed. Late at night you could walk down Lincoln Street along the border of the Park, and there were always cars and vans and buses parked there, their windows blackout-curtained by plastic, by stacked up boxes, by junky possessions, and sometimes you might see a light flash briefly inside one of those carcasses, like a firefly inside the mouth of a dead horse; but when decomposer bacteria such as towtrucks finally disposed of the charnel there was no place for the fireflies to flit unless they had someone like Dee to help them. She let them stay and kept cleaning up, making what had been the living room into the bedroom again, the bed up against the window. Even Yama's dog Rebel got fed while Yama was in jail.

When Dee first came out from West Virginia she thought the S.F. Skinz were a bunch of assholes, because Blue, Chuckles, Johnny Beast and Dagger were younger then, wilder, more punk-rock, and the punk rockers were going nowhere new. The Skinz hadn't split off from the punk rockers yet. But now they were family. Dee shaved her head because that was very clean.

"Awright," goes yellow-toothed Tully, shaking out the sofa cushions, "so we found that little ole plastic spider Marisa lost and was bitching about. And here's Hunter's extra weights."

Dee was cleaning out the closet. "Nova," she called to her daughter. "You want a little purse?"

"No, thank you," said Nova moodily. "But is there anything in it?"

"Just my old health card. It's expired."

Nova didn't answer. She was a big blonde whose mother had died, and whose father wouldn't have anything to do with her once she got a Mohawk. For awhile she lived in a squat in San Francisco. Finally Dee took her in. (Marisa would have liked to be taken in there, too.)

The Skinz all stood around kicking the floor. One of them had hair. —"Oh, I'm a skin, see?" said blond Cam. And he rolled up his sleeve to show a tattoo of a skin being crucified.

"Why did you let your hair grow, then?"

"Well, I had to. That's all. I'm a non-traditional skin."

"Hey, *crucial!*" said Hunter. "My old V-necked green rugby attire." He worked with cement, as you may remember, setting up rebar, digging and pouring.

"Well, you wanna go play football?" said a new guy, standing there holding a pair of Hunter's moldy old boots from the closet. Hunter had given them to him.

"No," Hunter said.

"Then we can go looking for that guy with the green beret again," the new guy said.

"I'll bet he took off," Dee said.

"That sonofabitch," the new guy said.

"He said he'd cut up my dog and feed it to me," Hunter said.

Dee kept throwing things out of the closet. She was the only person working. "You know," she said over her shoulder, "I was thinking about putting our firewood in the fireplace to make it look like it was really burning in there."

"That's hilarious," Hunter said.

"This one person I know," said Cam, "if you can believe it, she cut cardboard up and made it look like flames. Cardboard on top of wood in an empty fireplace."

"That's fuckin' *hilarious*," Hunter said.

"It's real cold in here," Dee said. "I've been cold all day."

At night in November it got so cold that you could see your breath, and the Skinz holed up in bars watching the Niners game. — "Fuckin' go for it!" they yelled. "Well, they took three last time, they took three this time, that's six. Forty fuckin' yards and they can't fuckin' make it; I feel like putting a foot up their fuckin' ass." — "Hey, don't sit there!" they yelled at the others. "Your hair's in the way.' —And the tramps leaned forward wide-eyed at every pass, grinning cautiously in order not to get thrown back out for not buying beer. — "That motherfucker!" yelled the Skinz. "He didn't even get hurt!"—Some Dumbo laughed *Eee-heh-heh-heh-heh!*

Only Brandi was out with her son, trying to raise some money for dinner or drugs.—"C'mon, I gotta feed him," she said. "Spare some change, twennyfive, fifty cents?"

"No."

"Aw, look, you can do it," goes a white lady. "I have four children, and I still gave her a dollar."

"That's right," said Brandi eagerly. "Thank you very much, Ma'am."

"How about all the money you already owe me?"

"I see you later," she said brightly, moving away.

"Hey, you got any change?" went the tramps, leaning up against the streetwalls, and if you said no they dismissed you and went back to their talk: "Oh, he's got a connection, all right; I mean, *mango!*"; and if you give them money then they take it and do the same thing; but if you say to them, "No, I'm broke, do you have any change for me?" then they get all worried and say, "Just eight cents, I tell you, I can't give you anything," and THEN they dismiss you and go back to their talk:—"Yeah, well, if he's got mango how come his snort is *lousy* like *piss?*" —"Because he don't get everything he wants like them skinheads, that's why!"

And two Skinz went by, wearing grey canvas jackets, with American flags on the back. On the wall by the anarchist bookstore was written THE POWER & THE GLORY: U.S. SKINZ. The skinheads sat smoking and shaking their heads when the Niners lost a play. "We're gonna get you, motherfucker," they said. They could not believe that nothing was ever going to happen.

A police car sat parked at the curb. The cop walked nervously around it a few times, trying all the door handles and shining his flashlight in the window-cracks. As the night went on, the guitar-playing vagabonds packed up and left their doorway, bereft. A man came running by, his breath puffing like smoke signals, but he stopped short when he saw the police car, and strolled affectedly for half a block. Then he began to run again.

And the cop came back and laboriously double-unlocked his car. Then he locked it again. Skinheads went by in camouflage pants, jerking their heads back, puffing cigarettes between their lips. One of them came back, very dignified, with his bootwoman at his side. They ignored the police car, whereas the woman who walked by next turned to give it a fake salute. At the number seven stop, old people got on the late-night bus, shaking their heads slowly; the young strong ones shot their arms up against the ceiling rails in a Sieg Heil parade.

And in the November nights, the December nights, with the cold deep enough to make the insides of your ears hurt, the flags still flew high on Haight Street, the American flag whipping unconsoled beside Nova's Irish banner.

Preparations for Death in Ireland

Nova was an ice cream scooper at Bud's. She'd met Dee when Dee was a panhandling punk. Nova had panhandled with her, lived with her at the Golden Eagle on Broadway. In the afternoons, when the skinheads started coming back from work, rubbing their tired eyebrows, Nova sat in her room and listened to records. She didn't like going out because it was so boring.

"I have nothing to do with their sayings or nothings," said Nova sullenly. "They're just like my family. They're for American causes. I'm more for different causes, like I'm gonna join the I.R.A. But I don't care what causes my family are living in. Everybody's got like their own ways of thinking and expressions."

Strangles came in and sat there listening. He was a skinhead from way back who had his own band, Rich Kids on L.S.D. He worried about Nova sometimes.

"I relate to what's happening about America," said Nova. "It's too damn free. There are weird people running around. Niggers going after clean white girls and stuff. The way I see it, I'd like to go over to Ireland and be like a drummer girl. I'll live there and die there, that's all."

Strangles nodded. "I used to be politically stressed out, like you," he said. "You can take like years off your life."

"Maybe so," Nova said. "But I just don't wanna live here. I just don't wanna be here."

King Yama

"Rebel, you be cool," said Yama to his dog. He had a scary face. "What's this American Front thing anyway?"

"It's just a little thing we have going," Yama said. "We work for our

money, or try to, at least. I'm looking for a job right now. We're just
proud young Republicans who like our President, who'd be happy to
die for our country."

Yama moved quickly, smoothly.

"You *are* an ugly bastard, don't you know that, Yama?"

213

"Yeahp."

Yama had a scar on his nose. "The night I got this," he said, "I was panhandling from a nigger. I said, 'You got some green?', he said, 'Fuck you,' and I saw the blood coming down inside my brain and I said, 'You're gonna die now, nigger,' and his eyes went BLING! and he went running into Cala Foods, and this Cala Foods nigger came running up and said, 'I'm gonna *fuck you up*!', and I hit him three times but he didn't go down. He had a box-cutter with a triangular blade, and he slashed me right like *this*!"

"Well, hell, man," said Anthony, "that's why I wanna hit up south. I wanna go where there's lots of white people."

Yama didn't say anything. He had a way of suddenly glaring at you, as if you were walking along a deserted dangerous road at night and suddenly headlights came around a corner you couldn't even see and then flicked off and then a car ran you over in the dark.

"Yeah," said Anthony, "I made some money off some dudes who're looking for Blue. I said, yah, he's in Canada."

"You writin' this down?" said Yama. "Say Blue and Chuckles are in Canada. Say Blue and Chuckles are dead. Tell 'em that Blue and Chuckles died last summer, you got that? Chuckles died in the summer of 'eighty-five. He got stabbed in the summer of 'eighty-four. Yeah, he got stabbed.:"

Yama and Anthony sat at the kitchen table drinking Bud and looking at pictures of themselves. "There's Vern," Anthony said. "Vern from L.A. He's a dick. We went down, and he wouldn't even let us stay with him. Not a very skinhead thing to do."

"Fuck 'im," said Yama carelessly.

"Yeah, carve him."

Yama didn't say anything.

"There's Rebel when he was a puppy," said Anthony.

"Yeah," said Yama, "I had that picture when I was in jail."

"Boy," said Anthony, "I miss Dagger and Spike."

Yama didn't say anything.

"They're gonna have a kid, get married and stuff," Anthony sighed. "I hope it's a boy, 'cause otherwise it'll be a fuckin' ugly girl. Either way it'll grow up and respect America, man."

"A friend of mine just got out of jail," interrupted Yama, apparently addressing his knees. He preferred the company of his knees to that of many people. "Name of Cowboy. I hate that dude. He's a faggot. He was in San Bruno, too. The last time I saw him, he was in the faggot tier, the Polk Street tier, they call it, the he-shes. Every time I saw him after I found out he's a faggot, I booted him, I fucked him up."

"All *right,*" said Anthony respectfully. "And whatever happened to Butch?"

"He's doin' time in a brig on an aircraft carrier," Yama said.

"That's like the worst," Anthony said. "You get no window, man."

"Hey, Reb, c'mon," said Yama. "Don't kiss me. Just lookit me, dude."

The two Skinz concentrated on Rebel, playing with his ears, frowning and grinning at the dog. — "Rebel, you want some Bud?" they said. — Rebel raised his ears and looked at them wide-eyed. — "I'm tryin' to train Rebel to growl at niggers," Yama said. "At the bus stop today, I saw some, I took Reb by the ears, I said, '*Watch 'em!*'; he started growlin.'"

"Rebel's the best," said Anthony.

"This is my son right now," Yama said, pointing a forefinger at the big black dog. "The only person in the world right now."

"Rebel'll lock onto people when he's scared," said Anthony. "I fight the best when I'm scared. When I see some big bastard coming at me I just start to whale at him!"

Yama didn't say anything.

"Rebel's part Lab and part pit bull," said Anthony to the world in general.

Yama didn't say anything.

Anthony started polishing his boots. He had his arm all the way inside his left boot so that it looked like a black leather gauntlet. "I'm gonna polish 'em up real good and then when I kick someone in the face he'll see his own reflection," he explained, not for the first time. "It'll be the last thing they ever see!"

"Awright," said Yama. "America rules."

Encouraged, Anthony started to tell a story about Albert and some Skinz in Germany but Yama said, "You know Albert's story. You don't want no one to know what it is."

"What're you doin', lettin' your eyebrows grow out?' said Anthony quickly.

"Yeah," said Yama, "for winter. Girls love it, too."

"Right on. Girls love anything."

"I got a date on Lincoln Memorial, right by Lincoln's right leg, on July 4th. You don't know how many girls I've fucked by the reflecting pool."

"All *right!*" said Anthony. "Right on, Yama!" —But a month later

215

Anthony had crossed the Skinz. — "I gave him three chances," said Dickie peaceably, leaning back on the double bed, "and he struck out. If he comes around this house I'll kill him." — "He's just a *shit*!" yelled Dan-L. "He *fucked* with everyone! Tried to steal Rebel, too, after all that Dee did for him! He's growing his hair now, I'll tell you. I'd like to *beat* his *ass*!" — "Yep, she knows," said Dickie with a wink at his Budweiser. On the wall a sticker read: DON'T BLAME ME—I VOTED FOR HITLER.

But as of yet this rupture had not occurred, Anthony was still skull-shaved, and Yama crushed his empty beer can in one hand, while the two skinheads sat smoking and watching Rebel fight another dog. I am wall-eyed. Yama, noticing this, turned to me and said, "Are you blind in one eye?" — "Just about," I said. "I only see out of one eye at a time." — "Oh, yeah?" he said with real gentleness. "Would you rather I didn't talk about it?"*

Yama grew up on a ranch near Santa Fe. Every night his Dad would put marbles in the freezer, and then roll them into his bed at 6:30 in the morning to wake him up. No matter where you rolled in bed, those marbles followed you to get you up. He was born left-handed. His Mom died when he was three, and his Dad came and took him to New Mexico and made him eat with his right hand. Even when Yama was a little kid, his Dad would say, "When you're mad, you just let me know and we'll take it out back." Later Yama was a punk in New York. He inherited $33,000.00, so he bought three cars and plenty of cocaine. Before he knew it, he started shooting up. One day he came into a long dark hall in a burned-out shell on the lower East Side. At the end of the hall was a curtain and three candles. It was five bucks for a C and ten bucks for a D. You set your money in front of the curtain and a nigger's hand reached out and took it and gave you your drugs. Yama came up to the curtain to buy a D. There wasn't a sound in the gutted hallway. Suddenly someone rushed up behind him and knocked him with a piece of rebar. Yama had a .22 in his trench coat. He squeezed the trigger twice, right into the kneecap, and ran into Tomkins Square and had a pizza. He ditched the gun. Later he got a hundred-dollar shotgun from another skinhead.

When Yama's girlfriend told him she'd miscarried, he was sitting

---

*In truth I often worry about my vision, and last night I dreamed that my blue eyes ran like bloodshot mercury-droplets across my forehead, and finally touched, joined, flowed together into a watery Cyclops eye.

with her in his car. He punched the car roof. Later he said he'd missed her chin by *that* much! He knew she'd miscarried on purpose 'cause she thought the kid was somebody's else's. He knew it was on purpose 'cause women could do that stuff whenever they wanted; after all, *he* could *come* whenever he wanted to come.

Yama was accepted for admission at San Bruno because on Halloween night he saw this pretty girl in a haltertop get hit by some guy, so Yama came running up and walloped the guy, because you don't hit women in America. The dude's friends came running out, but a guy ran up in front and said, "Hey, you don't fuck around with skinheads!" At that time Yama was going out with this girl Tania from Berlin, and he decided to drop her, so the night before he gave her the news, he and a couple other Skinz three-holed her. The next day, he told her she was fired. Then Tania snitched on him. The police were on top of him like stink on shit. In jail Yama made a gun out of a toilet paper tube. He packed it full of foil and wet toilet paper to close off one end. Then he ground up a bunch of match heads for gunpowder and sifted it into the tube. For shot he used broken aspirin. That gun could do some damage. Mainly he passed his sentence working out and reading, but he also learned from a little Chinaman how to kill people with his bare hands. Before you learn to kill somebody with your bare hands, you gotta go through all this other shit, but Yama went through it, all clean-cropped and dignified.

The White House

"Each tier is a country," Yama said. "2N, 2S, 3N, 3S. Like, 2N was the tier to be on. We'd have outside clearance, so we got rum and weed in there. You know them big three-liter Seven-Up bottles. They brought those in full of white rum. Being a trusty, you have the privilege of a private shower, and the TV's on twenty-four hours a day. A Cuban nigger had my job, and I took his job, don't matter how. There's lots of land out there; they have a farm crew. I fucked up the farm truck when I was stoned. But that was cool. Now, Dagger and I were in there together. We were cooks. We could sell a hundred packets of sugar for a dollar twenty. Or hamburgers, you'd steal one and fry it up and sneak it in your coat and take it to one of the upstairs tiers and sell it for a buck. I had my neighbors, a white neighbor here, a white neighbor there; I was in a white neigh-

borhood. That was the White House, we'd call it. In the morning I'd
go, *Rring, rring, rring,* like I was on the phone, and somebody would
say, What do you want, and I'd say, C'mon over and party!, and he'd
go, O.K., click!

"Every tier, it says, MAJOR RULES, MINOR RULES. Major rules
are like a page and a half; minor rules are shorter. Minor rules are
like don't change the channel on the TV. You fight over that. Two
people died over that when I was there. One guy got stabbed, another
guy—this five-six nigger—got thrown off a table. The niggers'd put
on a nigger TV show and the white boys and Mexicans'd go back and
play cards. I used to come back between the niggers and watch TV.
The niggers'd go, 'Skinhead, you got heart! We like you! The other
white boys go back; you stay with us.' I'd say, 'You leave me alone, I'll
leave you alone.' They *respected* me."

BACK TO THE PALACE

Yama didn't stay out of confinement very long. All his friends
agreed that he was losing it. There was something the matter with
him, but no one could tell what it was. Dickie and Dan-L tried to be
his friends as long as they could. They could feel themselves losing
touch with him, as if he were dead and his eyeballs were slowly
filming over. One day Yama did a strange thing which I will not
write about that got him put in the psycho cells for a long time. He
may or may not be getting shock treatments. Visiting days are
Wednesdays and Saturdays.

THE OLD LOOK AND THE NEW LOOK

From where I sat watching the Skinz from behind the blinds of an
ice cream parlor, they strode by, scraping their coats and chains
against the glass, not seeing me, I thought, their heads high, shoulders swinging like powerful shark-flippers; while other jobless sat
scowling into their little cups of espresso, legs crossed under the
white tables. Bootwomen went by, skulls sometimes turbaned in
towels or in soft cloths, as if to protect those most sensitive bones
from the world, the way that Muslim women veiled their faces. —
The Skinz turned around suddenly and came back, staring into the
glassfronts window by window until they found the spy; one of

them, the most unfriendly, having a lush blond skull-carpet instead of the usual grey; and he kicked the window meaningfully with his boot. —They leaned up against the grilles of liquor stores at night, making faces and glowering so hard that they wrinkled up the chains and snakes tattooed around their ears. They looked as if they were about to spit burning shit out of their mouths. Maybe Dickie had looked like that when he won the dogfood-eating contest. The other contestants hadn't been able to finish their first can, but Dickie was halfway through his second before he turned green and puked all over the video audience, spraying bile between his teeth to burn and stink on those screaming faces... The Skinz leaned up against fences, kicking the sidewalk with their boot-toes. — "I'll slap her face," a new one said, "and she can just do anything she fucking wants; we're not friends; I'm just *using* her." — Round about eleven o'clock the drifters started sitting on their backpacks in the doorways between Clayton and Belvedere, not panhandling anymore; and inside the ice cream parlor, where it was warm, only the reflections of Christmas tinsel and streetlights could be seen, unless one of the Park People came up against the windowpane to look in. Buses caught the light. —The skinheads lounged in the painted alleys yelling, showing themselves to all as demonic concentration camp traitors. Just as afterimages remain to closed eyes at the end of Halloween night—the transvestites, tigers, bears, vampires, military detachments, half-naked women in fishnets all compressing like coal in the eyes' darkness into half a dozen black-swaddled figures with gold plumes, advancing in silence—so the skinheads left behind them the picture of a single warrior in profile, a man with spiky scalp-grass pricking up proud on his skull, and a sullen all-seeing eye. That was the skinhead look.

There was a new look, too, a black-jacketed, black-bandanna'd, thin-legged look that might supplant the skinhead look someday; or maybe the bearded tramps would be fashionably imitated by folks who used shampoo and moustache wax; all that was certain was that the skinheads WOULD be supplanted someday; and no one would give a damn.

About the Photographer

And up by the anarchist bookstore, Ken the street photographer (who took these pictures, so you might as well know a little about him) was still trying to get rid of his housemates Dahlia and Denise, who were getting on his nerves, so he ate everything they put in the refrigerator and he jumped up and down outside their room early in the morning, yelling, and he taunted the house dog with chains and iron bars until she barked *rrrrRRRAGGH! rrrRAUGHH!* so that the whole flat shook, and Ken threw the girls' mail against the door so that the dog snapped at it; and for weeks the girls laughed uncomfortably, pretending that Ken was joking, so Ken had to get a little more direct, like picking his teeth and rubbing his crotch when they talked to him, letting drool go down his chin, and when they said good morning he'd yell, "What the fuck do you mean, good morning? What's so good about it? Did I say it was a good morning?", and then the girls started ignoring Ken, and when they brought their friends home Ken would say, "What's your name? You're pretty! Can I take pictures of you NAKED? Will you fuck me right now on the floor?', and Denise would say, "Just leave him alone; he's obnoxious," and still Denise and Dahlia stayed, so Ken told Denise she made him want to puke, and every day he asked her if she'd found a place yet, and finally she got the message and started billing Ken when he ate her food, and going around all the time muttering, *"I want out!",* and one day they were both gone, were Dahlia and Denise, so quickly that Dahlia's father didn't even know they'd left, and so he called for Dahlia and Ken said, "Dahlia? Dahlia who?", and Dahlia's father goes, "Dahlia Ackerby," and Ken goes, "Oh, *that* Dahlia. This is her husband. Who the fuck are you?" — "WHAT!" goes Dahlia's father, and Ken goes, "Just kidding," and he could tell it was a long distance call so he dropped the phone for about ten minutes and had a beer and then came back and said, "Mr. Ackerby, you still there?" — "I'm still here," said Dahlia's father grimly, and at that Ken put down the phone for about fifteen minutes and had two more beers and then got Dahlia's number from the refrigerator door and read it off to her father and when her father said thank you Ken said, "You BET, pal!" and hung up, and then he and I went into the storeroom where one of Dahlia's suitcases was and we picked out some of Dahlia's nice clean pink underwear and sniffed it and threw it to the house dog and the house dog snapped at it and shook it so that it fluttered across her chops and the dog decided that Dahlia's underwear must be alive and made up her mind to kill the thing, whatever it was, so she snarled and bit and tore so many holes in Dahlia's underwear that Dahlia would have had to be an octopus to wear them; and the dog tore them some more until they were one long rag whose contours made lots of side trips, and Ken and I laughed and laughed and Ken was revenged for his sufferings.

On the front of Ken's house the skinheads drew a tombstone with the words:

R.I.P.
S.F. Skinz
1981-1985

Some of The Best Men Alive or Dead

and right by the door they wrote: S.F. SKINZ THEY WERE HERE THEY FUCKED YOUR WIMMIN THEY DRANK YOUR BEER.

THREE FUTURES

We are lucky that the skinheads are not capable (as I dreamed last night) of hosting hundred-dollar-a-plate luncheons for their cause, every skin, every bootwoman in business tweed, clinking glasses with their dupes, old farts and young, remarking on the parsley garnish, taking long private walks with bankers until they have the capital to stand smoking one winter's night at the border, *Maschinengewehr* happy and warm under a blanket of gun grease, and the Skinz stand waiting to cross the ice of the Rubicon at dawn. I am grateful that they spend their energies spray-painting schematic skulls-and-bones on the back of Polytechnic High, writing RAGE and STORM TROOPS OF DEATH OR DIE and S.F. SKINZ BLOOD PURE. As to the future, either some one could arm and pay them (there are neo-Nazi camps in Germany and Austria, where boys practice being clean and orderly, with firearms training and mock executions to complete their education; there is a National Front in the U.K.; there is a Nazi printing company in Lincoln, Nebraska); or else they might get tired of being skinheads; or maybe the South of Market gang will carry out the threat which it has written by the freeway ramp: S.F. SKINZ WILL DIE SCREAMING. —There are plenty of people with that point of view: —when I was waiting for my bus tonight in Oakland, over at San Pablo and Yerba Buena, men were standing by the Bank Club Cafe drinking out of paper sacks, and I asked one of the blacks what he thought of the skinheads, and he said, "You want to see a knife that talks?", and I said sure, and he

221

pulled out a knife and told it to to say something, and it went SNICKK! and its blade switched out almost all the way to my chin.

WHAT THE SKINHEADS THOUGHT

"Dude, I want to talk to you about your story," screamed Bootwoman Marisa very rapidly, "because it fucking sucks!" — "Well," said Bootwoman Dan-L, "my first reaction wasn't too positive. You need a lot of work with your grammar. You have a lot of run-on sentences." — "She knows," said Dickie, lighting up his bong. "She went to college." — As for Ice, he buttonholed Ken in private. "I don't really know this guy," he said. "But he seems too poetic. I can talk to you; you're levelheaded. I've read parts of this story, and I think it should be cut, maybe to about a page." Dagger, Spike, Dee, Hunter, Nova and of course Yama had left town.

August 1985 – February 1986

Three Stories
Diane Williams

MY FEMALE HONOR IS OF A TYPE

I DID SOME V LAST NIGHT of a kind I have not done before. I gave myself permission. I said to myself calmly in my mind—on this occasion I will give you permission to do the following—listen carefully to yourself: you are allowed to cut up your husband's money which is on his bureau top, just the single bills, there are not too many of them; cut up his business card which is in his card case, and then cut up a folded piece of paper—you do not know what it is. There, you are cutting paper.

He gave me permission when he saw me, even, even when he saw me leafing through big bills with the scissors and the card case, flipping to choose, and sorting the paper, the opportunity for cutting.

The occasion for this V which I permitted and which my husband permitted was anger of a type.

I said to her, "*You should fear for your life!*" Tonight I said, "Tell *them* you feared for it!" Whereas my husband would have left. He would have walked out mildly and back to home.

They say so, and then their head is in your vision, only their spooky eyes, or their bony nose shaking, not even their mouth is in your vision because you are too close, maybe some of this someone's platinum hairs mixed up with silver and brown and white, and pale pale yellow hairs, antiseptic hairs is what I call it, clean out of grease or refuse.

But not the hairs on *her* head, not the crisply cut card with the credentials she put for me to see, hairy letters on a hairy card, the card of someone who ran the whole show, that I could not even see the name, because of hair, nor did I want to.

"*You've got what you wanted!*" she said so that all the hairs were not enough hairs, or the telephone in the bag she gave me, the black phone. All the hairs were not like the hairs on *her* head which she pinned up or she pulled down which she waved, which she lustered

223

fully out. All the little rings on the black cord to put your finger in, to hold your finger, all the little rings that stretch to ringlets, all the twirlies.

We left. It was between her and her. The husband and the mild-mannered boy behind her, and the husband did not play key roles. We ran the show and when I left something did die, a little something, and later on she will know something teeny keeled. I took that teeny thing, and the fat phone in the fat bag. I took the teeny tiny pathetic, that can climb in between hairs all by itself, that can lay down their eggs to hatch.

I would not do murder for a phone. I would do it for hair.

ALL AMERICAN

THE WOMAN, WHO IS ME—why pretend otherwise?—wants to love a man she cannot have. She thinks that is what she should do. She should love a man like that. He is inappropriate for some reason. He is married.

When she thinks of the man, she thinks *force*, and then whoever has the man already is her enemy—which is the man's wife.

The woman makes sure the man falls in love with her. She has fatal charm. She can force herself to have it. Then she tells the man she cannot love him in return. She says, "You are in the camp with the enemy."

Of course, the woman knew the man was sleeping with the enemy before she ever tried to love him, and the word *enemy* gives joy—the same as I get when the wrong kind of person calls me *Darling*, as when my brother says, "Okay," to me, "goodbye, darling," before he hangs up the phone, after we have just made some kind of a pact, which is what we should do, because I have to force myself to love the ones I am supposed to love, and then I have to force myself on the ones I am not supposed to love.

I got my first real glimpse of this kind of thing when I was still a girl trying to force myself on my sister. I didn't know what I was doing until it was obvious. We were in the back seat of the family car. The car had just been pulled into the garage. The others got out, but we didn't. I thought I was not done with something. Something was not undone yet—something like that—and I was trying to kiss my sister, and I was trying to hug my sister, and she must have thought it was inappropriate, like what did I think I was a man and she was a woman?

I must have been getting rough, because she was getting hysterical. I remember I was surprised. I remember knowing then that I was applying force and was getting away with it.

PORNOGRAPHY

I JUST HAD a terrible experience—I'm sorry. I was yelling at my boy, "Don't you ever!" I saw this crash. I saw this little old man. The door of the car opened and I saw this little old man tottering out. Somebody said, "I saw him!" The same somebody said, "He's already hit two cars."

There was this kid. He wasn't a kid. He was about nineteen. He was screaming and screaming on a bicycle.

Then I saw him, the kid, on the stretcher.

That little old man did more for me than any sex has ever done for me. I got these shudders.

The same thing with another kid—this one tiny, the same thing, on a stretcher, absolutely quiet in a playground, and I was far enough away so that I did not know what had happened. I never found out. Same thing, shudders that I tried to make last, because I thought it would be wonderful if they would last for at least the four blocks it took me to get home and they were lasting and then I saw two more boys on their bicycles looking to get hit, not with any menace like they wanted to *do* anything to me, because I wasn't even over the white crossing line, not yet, and the only reason I saw either one of them was because I was ready to turn and I was looking at the script unlit yellow neon *1* on the cleaner's marquee which was kitty-corner to me, when just off that *1* I saw the red and the orange and my driver's leg struck up and down hard on the brake without my thinking, even though I think I was ready to go full out at that time, because where was I going, anyway? back home to my boy?

My car was rocking, the nose of it, against the T-shirts of those boys, first the red one, and then the orange one, and they each of them, they looked me in the eye.

Back home, my boy, he's only five, he's going to show me, making himself into a bicycle streak down our drive, heading, he says for my mother's house, heading for that dangerous curve where so many horrible accidents have happened or have almost happened. What I did was yell at him DON'T YOU DO THAT! but he was already off, and then this goddamn little thing, this animal, this tiny chipmunk thing races with all its stripes right up at me, but not all the way *to* me, and then the thing, it whips around and runs away, like right now with my boy—I can't—there is no other way to put it—I *can't come.*

Across the Kudzu and Way Down Yonder Under Algamila
Jonathan Williams

Photographs by Guy Mendes

FRIDAY, NOVEMBER 27, 1987: What better place to rendezvous with the poet and cuisinière, Ellen Patterson (whose literary moniker is Ford Betty Ford), than the Mall at Lenox Square in Buckhead, Atlanta, on the busiest shopping day of the whole year! If you can find it, there's a very agreeable place for lunch called the Fish Market, with decor in the Hispano-Mooresque, Day-Glo, Rocococacola Style. It is filled with ample ladies dressed by Neiman's and stoop-shouldered brokers à la Brooks Brothers. Bizarre, perhaps, but both the food and the waiters are fresh. "Hi, I'm Gary, I'm going to be your waitperson today. Copies of my auto-biography (signed) are on special at the desk when you leave. Besides Blackened White Fish, Blackened Blue Fish, Blackened Red Fish, and Blackened Black-Eyed Peas, we are featuring Blacken'd Decker..." Drink enough and it's all just what you need to forget the 3,000,000 automobiles on the loose in Fulton County, Georgia.

A quick visit to the High Museum of Art to see a Frank Gehry exhibition. South on I-85, past the airport, to check into the La Quinta Inn and await the arrival from Lexington, Kentucky, of G. Mendes, the guy with the eye. We're going to "bag" some Visionary Folk Artists before every picker, curator, collector, and urban preda-tor east of Gnome, Alaska, gets there. Or, so we think.

Later on, back up I-85 to the Chef's Café, at the La Quinta on North Piedmont Road. This is the recommendation of Bill Cutler, the *literatus arcanus* of the city. The son of the eminent Edward C. Aswell (Thomas Wolfe people, please note). Bill edits an insider restaurant guide to Metroland called *knife & fork*. The other hot place in town is the Sierra Grill (nuova cocina), filled with Yups and long lines impatiently waiting. In Atlanta grits have been demoted and polenta is the dish of the season. Excellent, if you like imported cornmeal mush. Ms. Patterson, for one, did not agree. "Puppy poo-poo," she exclaimed to our collective distress. But, the waiters were, again, fresh—you take what you can get on Piedmont Avenue du Nord.

Saturday: Breakfast at Denny's, in the company of dozens of prison guards, flown in from all over to help cope with the Cuban Uprising at the Atlanta Federal Penitentiary. We three aesthetes ate our country ham and scrambled with the best of them and talked loudly of the glories of Kentucky basketball. Tom Meyer, unimpressed by the thought of eight days in the Fifth World, departs for Hartford, CT to work with James Sellars (Fort Smith, Arkansas' Very Own Composer-Feller) on their four-year project, The Turing Opera. Mr. Guy and I load up "Okra," the VW Rabbit, and head west. ("Okra" is the color of blanched spinach—you can't call a car Blanch Spinach. At least I can't.)

There's nothing remarkable on I-85 to see all day except one sign. In Coweta County, on a gray metal shed set in the pine trees, are big industrial letters that spell out:

HEAVY YELLOW EQUIPMENT

On the south bypass around Montgomery, Alabama, we lunched at one of those suburban grunt-pits with a name like T. J. Tripps. It was filled with big jocks from Auburn who sell tires (tars) and State Farm Insurance and run Motel 6s. The waitresses have muy big garbanzos, wear frilly skirts and black silk stockings, and smile endlessly (but pleasantly) as they serve up ice-covered schooners of Bud Lite. The 50-inch TV features the Ragin' Cajuns of Southwestern Louisiana State vs. the local boys, the Troy State Trojans; i.e., little black scatbacks vs. white Baptist hulks—the true National Game in just 60 minutes.

At 6:05 p.m. we arrive at 1433 West Howard Avenue, Biloxi (B'luxi), God-hep-us-miz-sippy, and seek sanctuary from the Harrison County polymath, Orcenith Lyle Bongé. Lyle is the very best and surely the laziest photographer *ever* from the Gulf Coast. He is also a builder of fiberglass yachts, a topper of trees after hurricanes, a sculptor, a jeweller, a raconteur, a chef, an investor in gold, and a macho-hohoho devotee of the fleshified female bod. What is a refined and seasoned connoisseur of *coq de garçon* in the highest Athenian tradition to do at table in Old Biloxi when two crazed heterosexualist photographers begin yacking it up about tits and ass? Mercy on us! I supped resolutely at my shrimp bisque and sipped heavily at my Maker's Mark and branch water...

Sunday: After a couple of hours photographing around town with Le Mâitre, we cruised on into Nawlins. Stayed on St. Philip Street in the Quarter with an old friend, Alden Ashforth, composer from UCLA, working on his history of New Orleans music. Dined at the most memorable place I'd been in for many months: Le Bistro at the Hotel Maison de Ville, 727 Rue Toulouse. A friend of Guy's named Susan Spicer was in charge of the kitchen. One of those nights when nothing remains clear, but I have dream-images of rolled oysters on a bed of spinach in a cosmic sauce, followed by a filet of beef stuffed with Roquefort. Gewürztraminer and Merlot—what else do you need to know?

Monday: a leisurely day checking out friends who either knew about Visionary Folk Artists (from now on: VFAs), or about art with a capital A, or about jazz, or about food, or about sex, or about something good. So this included Bill Fagaly, at the New Orleans Museum; Dick Gasperi, who runs the excellent gallery devoted to Outsider Art (831 St. Peter Street); Bill Russell, the St. Francis of Crescent City Music; John Lawrence, photographer, a curator at the Historic New Orleans Collection (533 Royal Street); the sublimely *sui generis* Estill Curtis Pennington (between jobs running museums under the magnolias); the artist and catbird and sight-and-a-half, George Dureau; and Kenneth Holditch, professor and local maven, who can show you precisely where Sherwood Anderson and

229

Lafcadio Hearn and Bill Faulkner and Roark Bradford did this and that.

Nonpareil Two-Line Bumper-Sticker, Rampart Street, Nola

IF YOU DON'T LIKE MY DRIVING DIAL 1-800 EAT SHIT

Tuesday: Woke up to National Public Radio's "Morning Report," doing a spot on our new book *St. Eom in the Land of Pasaquan*. A very nice, nine-minute awakening indeed. How lovely to hear the voice of Eddie Owens Martin (ST. EOM himself) greeting us on tape from the pine woods near Buena Vista, Georgia, a couple of years before his death and giving a clear warning: "I told Jimmy Carter that Reagan's got just what this country wants: a good head o' hair and a mean line o' talk." Guy and I had a (poor) shrimp omelette in what used to be the Café du Monde in the French Market and headed out of town, headed for another eventual oasis in Greenwood, Mississippi.

Found Haiku (Back of Tanker Truck, I-10, Louisiana)

TECHNICAL ANI-MAL FAT. NOT INTENDED FOR HUMAN CONSUMPTION.

Along about McComb, hunger o'ertook us. We searched out Franchise Row and finally spotted a scabrous barbecue joint that looked "local" if nothing else. The villains of David Lynch's film *Blue Velvet* might have munched in transgalactic stupification—we were transfixed by the misery of it all and expected to throw up in 20 minutes. Oddly, we didn't. If you ever travel the Deepest South, please take a respectable guidebook with you. May I suggest John Egerton's *Southern Food* (Knopf, 1987). Open it, there it is: The Dinner Bell, where the venerable Elise Crosley is still cooking real food: chicken and dumplings, catfish, turnip greens, fried okra, and sweet potato casserole. Farewell, McComb. If it is ever my fate to go there again, I'll know where to go.

Up I-55 we finally got to some VFAs. On the south side of

Hazelhurst you see the home place of Mary Tillman Smith. The collectors have pretty much taken it all away. Mrs. Smith is 84, has had strokes, cannot speak or make more of her startling and poignant messages on pieces of tin. She obviously loves for people to come and visit. When we'd try to tell her how much we enjoyed her garden, she'd smile and open her arms and say something like "IT'S ALL!!! IT'S ALL!!!"

Proclamations on Tin in the Garden of Mary Tillman Smith

MY NAME IS SOMEONE THE LORD FOR ME HE NO

HEAR I AM DONT YOU SEE ME

I LOVE THE NAME OF THE LORD 123456

I LIKE A GARDEN THAT IS A GOD

A DOG BARK & MOTHER AROUND LOOK OUT

I WAS IN A RAKE THE LORD WAS FOR ME

I DONT NO NO BITY

HERE IS 1980 TIM GON BY

The next stop was at Luster Willis's place. He lives about six miles out of Terry, in the country. Again, he's had strokes, is in a wheel chair, and cannot make anything new. There was not one piece of art left in the house. His kindly wife said: "They came and got it all. They got the fish tails and they got the rat tails . . ." We left them smiling wistfully, and a lot of dogs barked at us from the edge of the woods.

Luster Willis, of Terry, Mississippi

> why luster
> well first it was gonna be
> donis
> then luster was the first thing
> fell out of their mind
> i never did find out
> what it mean
>   like in china the chinese
> they don't give them chirren no real names
> they just drop a pan on the floor
> and name'm like it sounds
>   ping ding bang
> bong

232

Distances in Mississippi are deceptive. Night came as we sped on through Yazoo City and finally got to our destination, Greenwood. Would you really expect to spend your evening in Greenwood, Mississippi, talking about Catullus and Martial, Hadrian and Antinous? Not unless you knew the one and only J. Norwood Pratt and his wife Charlot. Most of the talking was next day six hours after the George Dickel and the Hermitage and the homemade peach ice cream . . .

Wednesday: Norwood is one of those amazing Delta creatures who can charm the skin off a snake and doesn't seem even vaguely plausible in our drear agora. He knows all there is to know about wines, all there is to know about teas, and has books under his belt to prove it. He looks like a cross between Vincent Price and Zachary Scott—which ain't bad—and he manages (with the help of Charlot and his young sons) to live in one of the most austere tophets of our bookless republic. And live sanely and vigorously. After a phantasmagorical breakfast of beaten biscuits, country ham, grits, pecan waffles, and much more, we piled in their station wagon and headed west to visit the eminent James "Son Ford" Thomas, sculptor and musician, in Leland, Mississippi.

204 Ninth Street is hard to find. Keep asking. When we got there, there seemed to be lots of folks about, including several better-class vehicles from 'away'. The owner of one turned out to be the collector, Bill Arnett, of Atlanta. He was in the process of putting the latest still-wet clay skulls of Son Thomas's into the van. We had to beg in order to photograph the artist with a piece of his work. Bill is controversial. He thinks that most of the Southern visionaries are being ripped off, ruined, and exploited to death by carpetbaggers from all over. He is building vast collections himself and so filling his neo-Georgian house in Buckhead, Atlanta, with the findings that you have trouble finding a place to set down. Some people hate him (he says it goes with the territory), some people think he is the best thing that has happened, i.e., someone from the South who knows what all this work is about and who is conserving it from outside predators. I'm not sure yet, but I've invited Bill to come see me here in the mountains next month and we will certainly sit down over food and drink and spend a weekend coming to terms we both understand. Based on one quick visit to his house, he has convinced me already that he has the best eye of anybody who has looked at outlandish work. What, if anything, he is "up to," that's another question.

233

Son Thomas? He was feeling poorly, it was no time to talk to him, we let his children take him off to the doctor. Hope he's feeling better and is not always so beleaguered by the likes of us.

Back in Greenwood, we all talked folks, talked High Art, drank whiskey, ate lovely food, listened to Medieval and Delta music, and eventually collapsed in a happy and foolish state. What superlative hosts. Better to go to Greenwood than Prague. The Mississippi Delta provokes extraordinary powers of conversation from some of its artists; viz., Charles Henri Ford, the poet, from Midnight; and that elusive figure, V. E. G. Ham (a.k.a. Artemis Rat Okra), from somewhere down in there. These folks rattle away as quickly and brilliantly as the Oxbridge-trained gentlemen-critics on the BBC, like Frank Muir, Clement Freud and Julian Mitchell. Another very late night.

Thursday: After breakfast we went with Norwood and Charlot to see the restoration work being done on the old mansion they're moving into next spring. It's within view of the famous Tallahatchie Bridge, from which Billy Joe McCallister jumped in Bobbie Gentry's song. And then it was time to head east to Tuscaloosa. Sadly, we missed some of the most memorable little places in the state (Sledge, Alligator, Itta Bena, Money, Rolling Fork, Hot Coffee, Improve, Arm, Maxie, Red Lick, Learned, Lemon, Why not, Bewelcome, Toomsuba, Energy, Prismatic, Noxapater, Tishomingo, Petal, Splunge, Wamba,

Strong, Zetus, Hushpuckena, Sunflower, Walls, and Panther Burn),
but along Highway 82 we passed through Carrollton (home of the
novelist Elizabeth Spencer) and Mathiston (home of the Fastest
Mouth in the South, painter Bill Dunlap). Our host in Cottondale,
Alabama, just to the east of Tuscaloosa, was Richard-Gabriel Rum-
monds, printer of the fine *Ex Ophidia Editions*, and director of one of
the few graduate programs in book arts in this country, at the
University of Alabama. Gabriel comes from the days of Jack Spicer
in San Francisco and has perfected his craft in many places, particularly Verona. Tucked away in his studio in redneck heaven is a
master-printer that you would not find working with such devotion
at the Certosa di Pavia. Guy asked him why he had a metal tag on the
front of his truck's bumper that said TRASHMAN? "One of my
droller students gave it to me. He says it's because I bring it home." A
simple, very good Bolognese meal with a couple of bottles of
Amarone and all have an early night. A lot of VFAs are planned for
tomorrow.

Friday: Up Highway 43 to Fayette. Here's a poem about our
encounter at 809 First Street:

A Jocular Visit to the Man Who Paints with 32 Colors of Mud

        can we come see you this morning
        mr sudduth

        of course you can
        i'm just hangin around
        like a rusty fish hook

        you ever been to fayette before
        just ask at mr davis's printshop
        they know me
        everybody in fayette knows me
        they all look
        when they drive by

        •

        how do you
        pronounce your name
        jimmy lee

        s-u-d-d-u-e-t-h,

just like the southern
railroad

•

i love
makin people
happy

everybody likes my paintings!
this is
something somebody
ain't got

•

had a show
down in tuscaloosa

made 1400 dollars
just one weekend

that's easy money yes sir yes sir
that's easy money

Next, a few minutes out in the country near Bankston to visit the Hartline Church of Brother B. F. Perkins. The venerable and amiable Brother Perkins spends his days painting gourds red, white, and blue, praising God and the Republic. He has built his version of the Holy Sepulchre at Jerusalem and covered it with admonitory inscriptions. He has also built a number of earthen bunkers, in case of cyclones. He diligently feeds the birds. I can't remember what species he said would hover over any poisonous snake and warn him. I found Mr. Perkins a bit hard to fathom. He can't spell *Heartline* and yet he assured us that he had once sold real estate in Washington, D.C., and has worked for the CIA in the Middle East. Still, he seemed a genuinely happy and contented soul in his retreat in the Alabama pine trees under a brilliant late autumn sun.

Last stop of the day: Fred Webster, Box 105, Berry, AL 35546. Mr. Webster is the retired principal of the local high school. He carves and whittles figures in wood. Some might call him a hobbyist, but there's more to the work than that. He likes visitors and he loves to sell things. Most of his work went, he said, to a gallery in Tuscaloosa, but Guy bought a Daniel Boone with six-shooter and I bought a little tableau of Adam & Eve, the Tree & the Serpent. Very charming. I was a little surprised to learn from Mrs. Webster that now and then they'd make trips to the Holyland, Mainland China, Tokyo, and Rio. Fred said he loved to see what folk artists in those places were making.

Saturday: The heaviest day of all, in all respects. First, to Prattville, home of not one but two VFAs. Charlie Lucas, who calls himself "The Tinmens," was off in town shopping, so all we could do was wander about his place and look at the ingenious dinosaurs and figures he has contrived from old bits of cars, tractors, stoves, you name it—anything metal that's been thrown away. He is certainly as inventive as Alexander Calder on a good day.

Re-enforced with a Big Mac and a Quarter-Pounder With Cheese, two large fries and two medium cokes, we repeatedly asked directions to an ominous place indeed: THE MIRICAL GAREN OF W. C. RICE. For those of you who like to visit concentration camps, here are directions: northwest of town about three miles on Highway 82. Pass the Prattville Golf and Country Club (on left). Go over the crest of a hill. First paved road (left) is Indian Hills Road. Soon you'll see on both sides of you an assemblage of thousands of hand-painted signs on wood and tin: MEN IN HELL FROM SEX...POP IN HELL FOR SEX...MOM IN HELL FOR SEX...SISTER IN HELL FROM SEX...ALL KIN IN HELL FOR SEX USED WRONG WAY...NO NO NO WATER IN HELL...IN HELL FOR SEX...Everything is covered in barbed wire and the edges of the tin are left jagged to cut anyone who tries to touch them. It is both staggering and very nasty. The godly old devil who made this garden was locked in his house with

the television on (Jimmy Swaggart? Jim Bakker? The Pope?) and wouldn't come out to see us smart-ass, secular sinners. Guy took his photographs and we left quickly, ready for a six-pak.

Into Montgomery, with nerves more or less soothed. We sought out a contact in Micki Spiller, a sharp, stylish young lawyer. Had a few drinks and went to visit with Mose Tolliver. Mose looked like he was still feeling the effect of too many the night before. But, for once, his house was full of paintings. He paints on everything, with anything. Maybe ten a day! A lot of his customers ask him to do this and to do that. He does, but not happily. Let him tell it:

Mose Tolliver Amongst the Carpetbaggers

> they come and say
> mose you makin too
> many trees and too
> many flowers we tired
> of trees flowers
> make some animals make
> some dogs some hogs
> some gooses & some
> moose women moose women
> yeah women with them

239

> funny antlers for legs
> we not tired yet
> of green moose women

We checked into the Sheraton Riverfront Station late in the afternoon, at the intersection of Coosa & Tallapoosa. They've made a
interesting restoration of the old Western Railway Freight Depot.
Guy got some ice and I turned on the TV. Amazing! Caught the last
30 seconds of the Kentucky/Indiana game as King Rex Chapman
sank a 3-pointer and tied it. Kentucky won in overtime. W. C. Rice's
place had so bemused both of us that we'd forgotten this epic battle
of jockish inanity. Go Cats! That evening we dined in the restaurant
inserted into the Romanesque confines of old Union Railway Station. Mr. Mendes had them re-make his Manhattan three times and
complained that the fish was off. The waiter wasn't fresh either, just
slow. Long miles in the Fifth World were getting to us.

Mammonite Totem Near Loachapoka, Alabama

Sunday: I pointed "Okra" east and we high-tailed it back towards
Metro Atlanta. Took the back road to Auburn (which enabled us to
see the fine sign in fine-sounding Loachapoka). US 29 between
Auburn and Opelika takes the cake for just Pure Ugly—it's not to be
missed and not to be believed. From there, I-85 into Georgia and
within an hour and a half we were parking under Colony Square in
Atlanta and taking the elevator up to Harry & Eleanor Callahan's
condominium. Eleanor's cooking is like Harry's photography: good,

simple, comforting. We spent the afternoon telling tales of the World Beyond K-Mart. Then back to the airport. Citizen Mendes had finally escaped having to listen to a week's steady diet of Frank Bridge, Lou Harrison, Poulenc, Delius, Percy Grainger, John Lewis and that awful Russian, Rotyorkockoff. It's hard traveling with eccentric, epicurean poets, smoking Royal Jamaica Double Coronas in small VWs. Guy got on Delta at 4:54. And Tom came in on Eastern at 4:57. Everything worked. It was time to head for the Blue Ridge.

SHIT HAPPENS!

—Herakleitan bumper-sticker, New Orleans ...

DOO-DOO HAPPENS

—Simpering, mealy-mouthed bumper-sticker, Atlanta

EXCREMENT OCCURS, POSSIBLY

—Imaginary bumper-sticker, London

One later note: Over the Christmas Holidays, Guy went back to New Orleans to visit his brother and his family. Dick Gasperi took him to Morgan City, Louisiana, to see the 94-year-old David Butler, whose cut-tin constructions are one of the real delights of VFA. Once upon a time Mr. Butler's little cabin in Patterson was surrounded by decorative pieces. Now there's nothing. The scavengers have cleaned house. The old man said to Guy: "Don't call me an artist. I did all this for me to look at and for the Lord. I'm over with it. I don't want to think about it. I don't want you to take my photograph, because people will just come and take everything away from me." Guy mentioned a prominent Louisiana collector and a handsome catalogue we'd just seen that included David Butler. It seems the gentleman in question had been to Morgan City and handed the book to Mr. Butler: "This is for you." David Butler looked at it, handed it back and said: "No, this is for *you.*" Should Guy have taken the photograph? Should I even be mentioning David Butler's name? With all the attention and the collecting, Butler and Luster Willis and Son Ford Thomas and Jimmy Lee and Mose are living dirtpoor as ever in shacks with mattresses sagging nearly to the floor. And considerable amounts of money are being made weekly amongst people who sleep on BeautyRest. Maybe that's the point? O ye Mammonites, leave people's beauty at rest. Uncle Iv Owens once told me: "You may think you're doin' good—but don't fergit the bad part."

Four Poems
Michael Davidson

LORDS OVER FACT

I come to the letter eight
and start over
I come to the letter sixteen
it is the same thing

the same as one
done fifteen times
until the wings work by themselves
which is the letter two

and with this I take up the card
and write "two"
never again to begin for the first time
though the cards are new

and the colors familiar
I continue the precession of four
doubled and redoubled
until I am almost not myself

so much a part of time
that number is only a tic
an old habit of one in its disguise
as three and the shape

it takes among leaves and the lame
and then I meet the abject nineteen
unable to go on to twenty
who returns through hedge rows

their turnstiles a mark of egress
into between or beyond
like zero the impossible one
partly the figure at the window

who has always gone and partly not
and you look out
it is six and seven the letters
form a windscreen against prayer

that the ground might have something left
that water will be allowed to stay
where it gathers in pools in the rock
nine

the sound of it roaring below the horizon
so that only dogs know
what is coming
they won't print this

because it is written by a dog
I speak for him
and translate eleven through fourteen
as quarters of the yard

ten is the forbidden zone
and even I draw a line around it
as it draws around me
something of its solitude

rain grows in it
as it folds the layers one
on top of another
and becomes stone

so that to invoke the letter five
is to begin life again
feet form around it
and stars become points

that only eighteen can destroy
anything more than itself
is excessive and possibly necessary
ten plus seven plus

the one we will have forgotten to pack
the minus that opens cans
or bottles or doors
or the script that tells of old weather

the time before weather
when the letters began to coalesce
and one thing entered another
often quite alone.

SONNET

One who speaks of the multifariousness of voices
one through whom the voices speak speaks twice
once through rapt inflections breath on fire
once as metal fathers rising in the blood
the voice becoming wire and things said through it
thinner still so that
one who standing on the outside of a logos looking in
is one who sits within and reaching for the phone
arrives at speech his own by way of voices
he but replicates and theirs ventriloquized in him
he later writes it down: tundra, reindeer
polar silence that lives beneath the breath
all Spring partly vocable and partly simply cold;
the witness is unspeakable someone dead
who speaks the name a footstep leaves ahead.

Michael Davidson

The Last Word on the Sign

"contingency is correlative to a necessity"
—Husserl

Some things have to be sitting on four legs
to bear the weight
of one
who could sit anywhere but prefers

where he is
was never forced
happened to come along this way
followed a pointing finger

and sat
one part plasma
one part what he sat
to think about

what he thought
was in
the red of in
and how it blushed

becoming something more
than "out"
the blue without which
water is a table

between them
difference forms on a slide
like a chair made out of flesh
in the phrase "I'll think on it"

which not to sit perfects
though I was here first
and have my receipts
I needed just this much

to explain it to you.

Michael Davidson

THE SECOND WORD

He enters the world wordless
discerns a tree through the eyes
of the world tree
and they give him a chair

made partly of wood, partly of air
the first is a shell
for the S that points at itself
and sounds like there

the next is not outside, not
core nor cloud but not one
or more
the chair has not to be himself

to sit in
in which the idea of a worldless I
takes up the winter and by the spring
is a convention of weather

the word the weather needed
just to be himself
and the protective outer clothing
necessary

satisfaction marks the agreement
between rain and water
which falls today
in both forms equally

equally filling
the empty dog dish
this is the sign
of something extra

to which I am attached.

From Hidden
Ron *Silliman*

"Lucky"

My ears 'pop' at the hilltop.
Stoic half-frown on the man's face

being wheeled up to the ambulance
in blue cotton pajamas. Green dice earrings

and blue sunglasses — the large woman
picks her nose. The cop leans forward

before he spits. It's not a neighborhood
people pass through going to work

or shopping, or to visit a park.
Yellow-brown wall-to-wall carpet,

optometrist's outer office.
Think here: you are reading a poem

—already this defines you. Hyperopic
boy makes good. Off-rhyme by iambs

hidden in the flood. Willingly I'll say
there's been a clear rip-off. No ideas

but in drugs? No teeth, bad back
don't make Ted a bad boy.

Bright pink scarf against turquoise jacket.
Out of print, out of mind. Woman

with pocked cheeks (sequence of alternate details
by which to triangulate image)

pulls up her jeans. Hear the loud chewing
in one's own head. Penis minus bonus.

Dan White is dead also. Sleeping pigeons
atop power line. Tar-heater

like a caboose linked to roofer's truck.
From sacred to salsa: a woman

in nurse whites carries three purses
into her place of work. Truck double-parked

on residential street. Face moved by muscles
of the jawbone as it chews, teeth sliding

side to side. What is the social content
of a poor night's sleep? Between terms

thought moves through a process
of distraction. Syntax slides

over a rough surface. Noses slope
or rise or spread (sometimes twist)

across the face. Hardware wholesale house
next door to machineworks (big sheds

of corrugated metal), since we're clanging anyway
any way we can. Thought into action

divided by social constraint (terms repeat).
Teams don't. Soft earth absorbs the fog,

spongelike, until the sky clears. The air
is not the mind nor a reflection of it.

Ironing board juts out of dumpster.
Refrigerator upright

in the back of a pick-up. Shadows
in a dense fog, headlights barely cutting thru.

Weight is relative to height. Fate
correlates to sight. Each place waits

for the right stress. I thought
in D.C. to head south for a visit

tho what had I to show? Vacant lot
turned into community garden

bulldozed as site for new video mart.
Song: (oh no) don't say nothin'

bad about my baby (oh no).
Thought replacement technique.

Shag knit sox cover golf clubs
(only the woods). Touch of rouge

to shine up cheeks. Writing by the light
of a kerosene lamp. Stomach rumbles

during group meditation. Pants pockets
are hidden holsters. Cricket buzzes

alone on a deer trail (further,
solitary woodpecker

knocks on a tree)—big horse chestnut
impossible to eat. Even here

in the high chaparral, the shining monarch
lands and is still on a rock amid dry grass.

Blue jay, descending, fans its wings.
Old pine, having fallen, forms both bench and path.

Oh that world, the real one. Potted cactus
oxymoron. North of Calistoga

a car that's rolled and burned: semi-circle
of ambulance and fire trucks (no hope here).

The world is all that is your face
isn't it exactly either. Try to write

as the bus turns (the body pulled
is the body). Lunch or lurch,

which one? Sea and shoe, which
is the foreground, which the rear?

Sky perceived as the object, against which
land's the margin. Who, what, when, where, how

are there also. Trochee's trick (again
twitch): protagonist. I, I, I

take you out on others, old pronoun,
cleft chin. An image (as in a dream)

of being held aloft—that fear
of not falling (which it's since become).

Boredom in the eyes of women
at a laundromat, class specific,

against the restlessness of their children,
men absent, constructs a world.

Ambit
Peter Cole

In the milky,
  pre-dawn air,

the spine of
road and flashing
      signals

sound the
shape
of
last month's
  understanding

   around me:

a kind of bitter,

a rind.

———————

The lambent
nearness there in the flaw

        of truth

  the act is:

where everything
     offered burns,

where most
  of what's withheld

begins

its decay.

———————

Green tufts of slope

and mustard flowers—

stork's beak, pea,

and the
(pale veronica)
February

angle to walk through:

the triple
piston of soul rattling...

———————

Where love is stalled:

Better a dinner of parsley
and care,

A hymn to the soft
exact middle of evening

and error.

Better the sparrow-like
provisional measure.

———————

Peter Cole

Before shame—

or simply a place to assume—

    at his shoes,

    and the others.

Standards of canvas and leather,
  warps of gait and various

  weathers a
kind of pride—

or pact, also before shame,

which is kindness excused

  repeatedly.

Of mud and heel.   Lace.

A place to scrape, not to polish.

————————

    But
    that spirit is
      aware of

    Hananiah said

   the waters

   rushing the channel
      entrance;

  or Samuel—

   not that the body

is actually

distinct
from soul—

the sound of a
rope used to moor
a swaying
ship

threading its porthole.

———————

Or the April-musk
of pittosporum

pinning the
small, smudged moth-
wings

of person
back toward the
language

along us—
a fence

approached to clutch
and stare through,

or climb.

———————

Up toward where the
orange
car and patch
of cloud

Peter Cole

deflect us—

as spirit crushed
in a parallel body by chance,

or tangled in the woman
across

at the table—

form
we talk our way
around with:

vodka,

to eat at the ego

into one's heart.

———————

First fruits and the
fine

quiet of
flour the hand
proportions;

adjustment,

and cord to the fissure
of aspect
reason too

earnestly
accomodates—

will,
actuarial,

contracts

to ignore.

———————

The 6 a.m. air easy to step
                    naked out to—

as bleached fields straw between us sign

    what was principle   now
        something I thought I'd wanted
                    to say, or said,

        inside our confusion and givenness;

        the false limits we verge on,
    repeatedly—horizons—displaced by love,
                    not only fortuitously

        and language in its nature

        which,
    chipping the infinite,

            holds it in its glass,

                as ground.

———————

Cadiz?

            Familiar hills and people,
    exponentially, streets, one's own speech,
    the rhythms of conversation, pressure along time

not epiphany   or slope, or manner—

Peter Cole

threshold set within habit

toward, not essence, but ambit,
(neighborhood: a dwelling in nearness)

risking insufficient prescription.

Early orange's green on bright
yellow with light pouring in from behind it
is one moment's equivalent; mauve suffused
through ochre, scored, another.

Between two pillars, requiring language.

Constellation as gear to the swarm.

———————

Also the chain
-geranium

angels of
    thick
antiseptic scent
and leafage,

nausea
salmon-pinks
  and scarlet,

  magenta;

abundant

of childhood
and on...

the muffled stink
  of facticity—

stalk of mute
thrownness increasingly;

utterly
other, moebial disgust

through memory

arrived at
itself opposite;

a favorite flower.

———————

Grace: not just

what the eye has hold of.

A place
          beyond
     of his act.
The boundary
     marked
          only in having
               crossed it:

          jacaranda
               petals

     scattered
     like sidewalk
               marbles

     on the shade—
pointed
     out by a friend
          from the car

     in passing.

Peter Cole

Invoking the rope.

Grace.

What waiting's afraid of.

———————

A place gone
back

toward?

A future the
visits were

estranging;

a small
wind stirring the verdigris
shoots and purple

of oregano—

geranium—

a year;

she was bitter in
his mouth like an olive,

she was gentle,

or true

to how they had known it.

———————

Truths within time;

or a kind of

  home-
  town elastic cinch
    at the waist
   and levelled

 zero to eight, as infinity.

 Adjacencies,

and floor to a chorus of figures—

  voices,
    and music to voices, turning
   their longing through measure.

      . . .

    Lords of failure,

  Lords of cure—

 break the day's pain across us

  through blindness or poise.

    ————————

 A flatness like video—
to an almost
    pious receptivity;
  or passive, irrelevance—
the empty ground for threshing made smooth,
   and Thamyris lame.

Peter Cole

Each music is a necessary
refraction.   The mottled pinks
                        through white
leaf and stalk greens crushed
of hollyhock—
                  impasto.

... out of, and into balance;
the risk
            an element of the rhythm;
the mass of being lifted as
if borne through the air, momentarily,
returned,

      ...

to keep the deity pure and maintain
distinction is
      specifically our problem,
so that, and a great deal depends
on it, neither penitence nor a misconstrued sign
invoke the judgement prematurely.

Pressure to only the extent it's perceived.

The song in its aspect.

———————

Kunstsprache.

Basil.

An August
  thickness

      along
the arms

262

and wind.

Vermilion streaking
   stars, etc.

Cypress and fruit-bats;
   oak, and small moon.

   Genital.
          Palm.

   The upright
   soul at its treadmill

   angled at its fuckmates

    at their own.

———————

Pansy
   yellow
   over

    gray
swirled

  blue
bull's head
   Shechinah;

    clotted
    blood ghost
      attendant.

Smudge of presence.

Pigment.   Wing.

Shoe box—

even cardboard

under glass;

crease,

and silver
naive scrawl

TO CAUSE HIS NAME

TO DWELL THERE

The onenessing
           sued for an open...

       And the needle of singular
       will
                   splitting
           into a
           suddenly innocence
           of also

                   learning—
           behind itself,
           closed,

       to be threaded;

       traced through stitch,

       not always design.

For example,

and the new   Elul of moon,

"to another tape, fifteen minutes long—
   this one of rain noises—

   two girls stood or ran in curves..."

———————

The world 'as if'—

or as though their hearts

were air,
            it seemed

to him seeing, bright-metal

burrs, like motes,

over the lawns

      were falling.

Zero to

      one as prime-

differential patterned

a safer, other

      engineering;

one to

   Bet was blade,

   into their day

Peter Cole

as 'as,'

turning—

it seemed

to him walking—

flaking

the sunlight,

across

all seeming...

If hearts were air,

as it seemed to him seeing.

Scenes from *Bouquet Rag*
Gilbert Sorrentino

GIN CITY, A SCULPTURE WHICH IS NOW usually attributed to Annie Flammard, has a history of ownership the details of which have to do with the curse of glossolalia. At present, Annie is smoking the last of a pack of Gitanes, a morale-booster designed to strengthen her for a look into the envelope where she keeps her cash. There is no cash, and Annie knows this. She seems rather distracted and a little dowdy, the result, perhaps, of life, coupled with the unwanted bi-weekly visits of a clubfooted man whose wheezing outside her door is always followed by his demand—never acceded to—that she tell him the secrets of the yellowed newspaper. Annie unfailingly sits in silence, and waits for him to go away. She knows nothing of Maureen Cullinan's "athletic tricks," either, another of her visitor's subjects of inquiry. After a time, the clump and swish of the desperate man's unspeakable foot moves away down the hall, and she relaxes, but awaits his inevitable parting sally: "A sense of humor, for Christ's sake, is no bar to advancement, you unfriendly bitch!" On this particular morning, the gimp is almost banjaxed in the street by the rushing figure of Glasyalabolas, the Murderer, summoned by the Lard Goddess to punish the woman who currently impersonates her. Glasyalabolas, who has no sense of direction, soon finds himself not in Agapa, but in a neighboring town, Gnatville. He promptly joins a barbecue-in-progress.

"...badly burned *chicken* for God's sake...Stekel and *whose* boots?...and only vegetables you say...charming old jalopy...could eat you in that white dress...need refueling...perverted rock stars' what?...in the *fucking* chicken coop yes...then the refurbished pillow...Oaky Doaks...a *frisson* of icy terror ..."

Glasyalabolas soon determines that the counterfeit Lard Goddess is not located in this burg, but decides to linger. A young woman who introduces herself as what his demonic ears take to be "Saybuddy," is wearing a short, tight, crocheted dress which, as Viña Delmar might say, leaves little to the imagination. The striking young woman is going on about a wonderful club, really hip, really

267

fun, called the Gold Coast Bar and Grill. "Kind of a *boîte*," she says, getting very close to the infernal visitor, who can't help but wonder what she'd do if she were to see him as the winged dog whose form he usually favors. "What do you say we go tonight?" she smiles, coquettishly waving an incredibly charred chicken leg at him. Well, as coquettishly as possible, considering. Glasyalabolas, who is slightly deficient in the art of small talk, and ignorant of flirtation, replies, "I teach all arts and sciences simultaneously, incite to bloodshed, am the leader of all homicides, discern past and future, and make men invisible." He beams, more or less, at her, and she is a little surprised at the size of his canine teeth. "You are really a cute guy," she titters while mincing. Then she lowers her eyes, raises them, and licks her lips. Glasyalabolas, unable to interpret these signs in a civilized manner, frees a monstrous red phallus from the constraint of his seersucker trousers, and at the same moment reaches a hand, on which the wiry hairs are crackling with blue fire, toward the young woman. So much for this jovial gathering.

The Gold Coast Bar and Grill is a joint on the Brooklyn waterfront. Once frequented by stevedores, longshoremen, and merchant sailors, it is now a chic watering place for people with little time and too much money, a murderous combination. They delight in the atmosphere, rigorously preserved, and the nightly entertainment, always of minimal talent. The patrons think of this entertainment as camp, and are thus ennobled in their lives. It doesn't take much, does it? The current entertainment comprises two acts: the Gold Dust Twins, who bear an uneasy resemblance to Barry Gatto and Annie Flammard; and their "opener," a skinny, middle-aged woman, her face leathery from the sun, in a fifties-style puce cocktail dress. The Gold Dust Twins specialize in dramatic readings from little-known plays, and at present are offering scenes from *'Tis Ruth the Whore's Dead*, by Thomas Ballantyne. To give you an idea:

CAZZO (*discovered alone*):

> Now dread varlets hold the welkin dear,
> Wherein doth, marry, phials incarnadine
> Fume so that a king may felter'd be;
> Yet all the glories of that drear assemblage
> Lack physick and the puling of a maid
> Whose mincing mows pricketh th' ebon Saracen!

Meet that, an't be a shining poniard
Pluck'd from the massy comet that dread Jupiter,
Blanch'd ere he wrapp'd his corse in finest lawn,
Shall grin the bony skull whence fled the fiend.
But soft! Keep venoms sealed up tight,
'Twas ne'er a lady pecked at asp so bright.

PUTTANA (*entering*):

Yet methinks sweet Cazzo in his license
Vents our news of most strange things, that, seconded,
'Twill be brutish to th' extreme of unguento.
Still, his ducket and this blizzardy wet look
Belike unto an apeish picture out o' wax
Do crown the common bawds and ruffianos.
(*To* CAZZO):
How now, my lord? Doth blood run pure as babes
In the painted honours of dissembling coins?
Or doth my breast, blue as the spicy carbuncle
That prov'd a pomegranate of worse favour
Drop, as it must, thou know'st, unto chill sooth?
My soul, as the curious lizard o' far jousts,
Blinds my womanish nature like the frightened whelp,
And speeds me to a doom of mummery.
(*Dies.*)

Miss Golden Delicious, the aforementioned opener, warms up the customers by showing slides of the Golden Gate Bridge, Construction of; Repairs to; Renovations undertaken of; Calculations concerning; Romance of; Legends about; Suicides of; Moods of; etc., etc. These arresting photographs, many in full color, are accompanied by Miss Delicious's enthusiastic, if unlearned, commentary. Nevertheless, in the last few months, surprise raids on the *boîte* have been carried out by the more radical members of the Golden Rose Fellowship, the action wing of the Immaculate Syndicate, a group dedicated to the eradication of public and private restrooms. The organization feels, as its literature indicates, that the restroom is an "area in which men and women" alike "loosen, open, and dishevel" their various "garments" and in the process "expose" themselves, this "activity leading to sin or thoughts of sin." The "Goldie" chant, chilling to many, is well known throughout the city, and illustrated copies of its verses are currently on view at the Gom Gallery in its controversial "Corners of the City" exhibition. One chorus, especially, has caught the public's fancy:

Chorus:	Oh Jesus sweet and fine,
	Oh Jesus strong and pure,
	Oh Jesus so sublime,
	Oh Jesus will you cure
	These sinners who should burn in Hell?
Response:	Sure!

It may be obvious that the city is no longer the one that Zuleika Dobson tells us of in the "Girdle Story," lines 116-172, despite its electric atmosphere, vital people, and numerous interesting activities, many free of charge. Still, no one, as thousands regularly point out, can know its heart.

Lincoln Gom, whose hair has turned to silver, yet some love him just the same, admires his pictures, as he does whenever he has a moment. He can almost hear them appreciating before his eyes, or ears, and both organs, though not as attractive as they once were, are still sharp. He is especially delighted with himself today because a piece in the newspaper on the "downtown art scene," which you've all read before, has a flattering reference to him as a "shrewd connoisseur" in the "ecology of the thriving art world." Odd how ecology, in all of its vainglorious manifestations, has always been a big part of Lincoln's life. He's elegantly dressed today, for "lounging." He takes another survey of his pictures, which he calls holdings, among the more valuable of which are *Connecticut Condo*, *Silver Mercedes*, *A Cool Million*, *Vintage Port*, *Fake Diner*, *I Want It All*, *Trump*, *Studio Apt. $3000*, *More Skyscrapers*, and his favorite, *Koch's Paradise*. He sighs, and makes a mental note to read more poetry like the one about killing men rather than hawks. Hawks! He used to read a good deal of poetry until, well. There's something wonderful about how it makes order out of chaos, and he needs a little order in his frenetic life. He cannot "lounge" for *too* long, not with all the sharks in the water. Sharks!

"Babs" Gonzales, who occasionally travels under the name "Boobs" Consundays, tired of reading Mrs. Browning, who can be tiresome indeed when in her amazed mode, "marches" into The Good Company to return her "Cute Cop" outfit, piqued because "Muffin" is currently featured as the model for this costume in the latest issue of *Cults and Coteries*. Of all people, "Muffin"! She must be forty-five if she's a day, the bitch, and she's running to Anglo wrinkles.

So much for sisterhood.

"I don't like much these holester," she says to the man behind the counter. He is a *bored salesclerk*.

A little verisimilitude to truly depict life in our time.

Check.

So that it's as if we're living it ourselves.

Check!

"In what way don't you like these holester?" the bored salesclerk says mockingly.

"It is bumping me in the wrong personal intimate place, coño," Babs says. "Makes the bruises."

"I'm afraid, Madam," he says, *yawning elaborately*, that we can neither take in exchange nor accept for refund any costume that has been worn. Your best alternative would be to go to the Good Will and donate it for a tax deduction."

"Can I change these holester maybe, only? For a peg leg?"

"I'm afraid not, Madam," the clerk says, *studying his fingernails*. "That peg leg is part of our new Long John Silver ensemble and cannot be sold separately."

"Babs" walks out, cursing Michael Cullinan under her breath. He's the one who really objects to the holester! She doesn't really give a damn about it, it's "Muffin" who makes the costume odious. What she needs is a double Gordon's gin, no ice, and so she enters a dim saloon, the Gotham, and puts her shopping bag on the bar.

An epiphany from *Treasure Island*

"Har, har, Jim!" Long John Silver laughed, his salty earring trembling as if schooner-rigged. "Keelhaul me if I don't be struck blind as Pew! H'isted in a wicker basket, ye say? Har, har."

The boys, exhausted by their courageous climb, sat across from each other in the rear of the little country inn, its rough-hewn pine walls sending forth a rich, spicy aroma that soothed their spirits. The day had brought its share of agonizing worries to the chums. Taking a long swallow of his sarsaparilla, Dick Witherspoon vigorously banged his glass down on the crude wooden table, then laughed joyously.

"Well, old man," he said to Buddy, "I 'spect we won't be reaching Misty Crag *this* evening," he opined. "Might as well batten down here for the night."

"I'm afraid you're correct, Dick, as is sometimes the case," Buddy confessed, his cheeks peculiarly flushed. "And yet that priest, Father Graham, seemed like a regular sort, despite his suspicious complexion, broken compass, and odious religious beliefs." Buddy set his jaw with determined vim.

"'Pears he took us for a brace o' yokels, Buddy," Dick nodded. "I thought for certain that we'd be hallooing on the dangerous crags long 'fore now. Maybe even scaring up some chuck and c'lecting dead wood for the fire. I pondered something was mighty odd when the Romish galoot told us to foller that bear trail." Dick raised his schooner to his smiling lips.

"Had I but paid attention to my father's woodland tips," Buddy said softly, his eyes bright with the memory of old Mr. Buddy's plaid mackinaw, "now gathered, at last, under the title *A Grain of Salt*— and how good it is that we now have them all together—we would certainly have directed ourselves toward the sought-for crag. By means of moss-growth and other such lore."

"Well, my friend," Dick replied, retying his colorful neckerchief, "there's no use to spoiling the milk now. Let's wrestle some hot grub and bed down."

At that moment, a young lady, her dark eyes glowing with health, walked into the inn and sat, her nether limbs modestly crossed, at the long serving bar. Buddy and Dick, with an exhibition of youthful pluck, leaped onto their chairs and stood respectfully upon them, watching her drink a large tumbler of gin, neat.

"She must be dusty o'throat," Dick remarked, "like the little pals we...left behind."

"Indeed," Buddy whispered admiringly, "she does seem too much disposed toward strong spirits, and yet there is something refined about her carriage, something naturally superior in her bearing. I would not be at all surprised to learn that she occupies a position of some importance in the business community."

"There sure isn't nothing of the Dago about her," Dick commented, and then, jumping lightly to the floor, he continued. "Say, Buddy, do you remember the strapping feller who used to join us when we held our feral clambakes?"

"Indeed I do!" Buddy replied. "Dick Grande was the lad's name, I believe. A tall boy, slightly but not unpleasantly hirsute." He

quickly joined Dick on the floor, and stood, a slight smile of nostal-
gia on his lips. "But why do you inquire?" Buddy continued, an
expression of hesitant longing playing over his chiseled features.

"Well," Dick said, biting his lips together one at a time, "do you
remember his...sister?"

If Buddy remembered anything of his fifteen years on this ter-
restrial globe, it was the beautiful tease, Jeannette Grande. She had,
on more than one occasion, made him doubt the advice on personal
hygiene given in his weathered *Handbook for Lutherans*. Beaming
jovially, he bounded again onto his chair so as to gaze at the young
woman at the serving bar.

"Well?" Dick inquired anxiously, "is she ...?"

But Buddy, with a cry of pure brawn, had fallen heavily from his
chair into his comrade's arms, his eyes rolling nervously about. The
young woman had gone, and at the place where she had been lately
sitting, there lay a bulky shopping bag, and, pinned to it, a letter on
daintily scalloped, lilac-hued stationery. There would be, Dick
Witherspoon guessed, as he smoothly laid Buddy's insipid head on a
nearby dado, no meatball sandwiches for them tonight!

Although the wind seems about to blow up, and the trees on their
quiet street threaten to sough at any moment, a lady of unchaste
proclivities, Edith Granger, stern in the cruel, iron-ribbed foundation garment that is "doing its job" beneath her purposeful tweeds,
and her newfound friend, Lady Granjon, are putting the finishing
touches on their amusing ad. Not to reveal the verbatim copy of
what the ladies considered an "appeal," it may be noted that the
message contains promises of mutually enlightening cross-dress-
ing, mirror larks, Greek interludes, *tableaux vivants*, discipline *à la*
the Greengage School, and stimulating episodes featuring cooking-
oil and Green Goddess salad dressing. "It has to be good for *something*!" Lady Granjon quietly jokes of the latter. There is also a
reference to a Greenwich Village masque, depending, and quite
properly so, on the weather. So they continue to polish their verbiage
as carefully as Mamie Morsett polishes her clam poems; perhaps
more carefully, since so much more is at stake.

Then too: Richard Gross, Bart., Will Return to Prison, DA Says;
Author Claims *Growing Dark* Basis for *Dark Victory* Screenplay;
Swiss Tourist Board Admits Gstaad Does Not Exist; "The Guards"
to Take Acting Classes; John Crowe Ransom "Secret Structuralist,"

Eloise Stephanie Gump Reveals; Russell Gunge, Inventor of Insolent Pompadour, Dead at 87; *Guns in Action* May Hire Michelle Caccatanto as Cultural Editor.

Gusion, the Duke of Those Who Discern, is sent to rescue Glasyalabolas from the barbecue, which the ingenuous sprite, as one might have guessed, has reduced to a shambles, the exact nature of which will be discreetly passed over in silence.

"Are you crazy?" Gusion says, mucking through broken glass and Christ knows what else. "You're *supposed* to be looking for the counterfeit Lard Goddess, so that we may send storms of flies and lice, fire, and poisonous winds against her. You are *not* supposed to be wreaking havoc on these professional persons here (indicates clusters of abandoned barbecuers) strewn about. I'm going to have to put this *faux pas* in my report."

"What does 'cute' mean?" Glasyalabolas asks.

"You haven't heard one word, have you? Let us go and find Agapa," Gusion says, levitating slightly.

"All right. Say, how come you don't look like some big fido-head today?"

"*Here?*" Gusion shakes his head at such a display of naïveté.

The two slowly fly off, scattering bits of garbage and carrion, and marveling at the bodies writhing in various pleasant combinations on the emerald lawn below. Slabs and gobbets of dead animals send up thin plumes of smoke.

Eddy Beshary definitely decides to buy the lissome yet muscular Bertha a drawing by Philip Guston, if the charming maid promises to stop walloping the unfortunate tourists who sometimes surprise him amid the flowering shrubs.

"Who?" Bertha asks suspiciously.

"Never mind on it," Beshary says, hanging up rudely on a mogul. "Suffice it to proclaim that it is of a pulchritude to emboggle the mind's eye. It also promises seriously to attain monetary values sufficient to enable you the ability to purchase plethorous ruffly aprons and bewitching caps when old age shall reft your earning powers from off of you."

"So you say," Bertha replies. "I'll ask 'Guts,' the savvy bartender, about this guy before I promise to play the coward or the regular guy 'mid the blowing foliage."

"As you wish, my enchantress of a fellow," Beshary smiles. "Now, if you will permit me to create an excuse, I must open a deal on the telephone which waits obediently on this cheap wicker table."

Bertha pushes wisps of silken hair under his bewitching cap. What he doesn't know is that "Guts" is about to throw up his job at the hotel bar, for he is in possession, by means of a delicate ruse, of a rare bibliophilic item, *Gusty Ghetto Tales*. This famous anthology, on which all others of its genre are modeled, is actually entitled *Gutsy Ghetto Tales*. The misprinted item, which contains the error on its spine, half-title page, part-title page, full-title page, and in the running heads throughout, is but one of a rumored 17 in existence. In his delight, "Guts," in defiance of hotel rules, mixes himself a celebratory Banana Amaze, "the drink that made Bermuda laugh." The heretofore secret recipe follows:

Banana Amaze

1½ oz. Gypsy Rose wine
1 oz. banana absinthe
½ oz. mastiachi pepper extract
Shake well with cracked ice and strain into a frosted cocktail glass. Decorate with two thin rounds of ripe banana and a sprig of pink brilliantine.

"Guts" takes a sip, rolls his eyes, and grins. To the bar at large, he proclaims, "*Habits and Wimples* has nothing on this, despite its clear and complete index and exemplary notes."

Habits and Wimples?

The, ah, reference is obscure. But that's just like "Guts."

The Bluebird Inn, a small roadhouse specializing in fox-trot contests, lies just outside Hackettstown on the road to Budd Lake. It may well be the "little country inn" in which Dick and Buddy are playing yet another scene in the mundane drama of their prescribed lives. Did they only know it, Misty Crag is but a two-hour walk from the inn. But they are confused, and Buddy is still semi-conscious. The possibility that they may not reach the somber heights today is very real. Their predicament is made even more complex by their map of the area, for it shows Hackettstown as Haddam Neck. This transmutation may be the work of Hagenti, Maker of Gold, sometimes, because of his penchant for pranks, called "the Halloween Kid," and his vicious thug of a comrade, Halpas, Burner of Cities, who likes to go by the name of "Hans," a kind of acknowledgment made to his old Nazi pals. But why they should decide to toy with the map used by Buddy and Dick is an unanswerable question, and besides, Halpas does not take kindly to interrogation.

Wisdom as Such:
In Respect of Robert Duncan
Robert Creeley

MUCH AS IF ONE had stumbled upon an immense simplification of difficulties or a sudden opening of seemingly blocked way, Duncan's instance and reflection were always of great use to me. When I felt secure in my own conduct, I would at times patronize his larger view, his boredom with the immediate demands of my own intimate associations—as, for one, life then in Bolinas, with all its insistently exercised freedoms. I can't now recall his having come out more than once or twice in the five years I lived there. But he was hardly above the daily or the topical. In fact, it was there he specifically located, as poems such as "Santa Cruz Propositions" or, alternative in its intimate preoccupation, "The Quotidian," make very clear. It is the web of articulate associations, the resonances, the apprehensions that define the human and all the world "leaning in," that he made so sounding a rhyme. I think of various of his essays, "Poetry Before Language," "Notes on Poetics Regarding Olson's *Maximus*," or—most determining here—"Towards an Open Universe" with its quotation of Carlyle, ending: "See deep enough and you see musically; the heart of Nature *being* everywhere music, if you can only reach it."

His death on February 3rd of this year was anticipated, simply that the nature of his illness and the battering of its effects gave no grounds for some prospect of recovery. No one ever looked at things, as one says, with a colder eye than Robert. It was hardly a fact of being objective but rather that he loathed the pretensions either of euphemisms or of ignorance. He wanted to know what was happening—one thinks of Pound's "we must understand what is happening" in "The Venice Poem"—for the factual value of that information, and by reason of its being one's own life to live and to die in. That cannot be done by proxy or convenient absence. That life was "all the time" was one of Robert's emphases, and so when he first had to deal with dialysis, I'm told, he would go through the process while teaching, the students thus witness to his very real life—but really far more, to the specificness of all such life to literal body. The poems of *Groundwork II: In the Dark* again and again are this articulate emphasis: "in the physical body."

"Wisdom as Such" comes from the title of a piece of Olson's years ago, "Against Wisdom as Such," a curious fear, in some sense, that Charles had concerning Robert's predilection towards lore, call it, or what Charles in that note characterizes as "Ojai," that is, his imagination of southern California's appetite for mystic cults—or so a New Englander would think. Possibly it was even some tacit competition that prompted Charles, but in any case the qualification stuck in Robert's mind long after it had shifted in Charles's, for whom Robert became an unequivocal master of the art. These two are an intensive congruence, I feel, a place in our art wherein an extraordinary range of potential and instance gain locus, so that either reads or writes beyond the habituated boundaries of contemporary conventions of whatever kind—and yet are not apart, or isolated, or simply sports of singular potentials. Robert is especially common, of the "many," in his imagination and practice of community, and as he writes of Whitman, so one may say of him: "The poet who exists close on the vital universe then exists close on his Self. All the events of human experience come as words of the poem of poems—the confidence stays with him..."

It is characteristic that, in thinking of Robert, one thinks of more and more and more. I loved his "Wisdom," it was like having a very humanly blessed and absolute source of information always at hand that could somehow field the most various range of concerns. It was he, for example, who first gave me active sense of Jack Kerouac's writing in Mallorca, gave me active introduction to Zukofsky and H.D., who once helped me tape a sequence of records to give me some grounding in music of this century—and so on, to matters far from the arts. I was fascinated by his use of information coming from linguistics back in the fifties, and he must have known well before I did that Trager and Smith were at Buffalo. Last time I saw Jess and Robert in August, they talked of an article they'd read in *Scientific American* concerning dyslexia, and of how the distance, call it, from the sign to the sounding, the abstraction so effected, intensified the brain's disfunction in this circumstance. So Chinese speakers had far less of a problem in the use of that language than did English speakers or others of this western world. What a charming echo of Pound and Fenollosa!

But it was Robert's "Wisdom as Such" that is finally the point here, the literal wisdom of his life and art. In a letter dated February 8th Duncan McNaughton writes: "...I think of Whitman and of Olson as being conspicuously American creatures, with commensurate mystery of their genius, their immense and mysterious coherence of mind, as *mind* was, finally, the agent of and the outcome of their achievement. But Duncan, as Olson repeatedly noted, was another sort of American wonder—the purest, and oldest, thing we know as "poet," the living lore of it. That lore had gathered in Duncan as in no other American I know of, not even Zukofsky. I think Yeats was something like that too. That tremendous capacity to inherit the lore of the poem, and to apply it.

"But it's the American mind of Duncan that seems to me to kick it outside the set-up. No more elegant blend of elements than R.D."

As Duncan writes,

There is truly no direction   no "center" to the "center"   our sounding
    goes out as we go out   no circumference to the "circumference"

        perilous then   time and space   as we reckon

    we but follow a beckoning   in measure   haunted

"without actually performing any true computation at all"

That one so lives in the world without relief, that we are only the lives given us to live, that there is no measure save in the community we constitute and must learn to admit, are wry contractions of my own, given the ample disposition of what Robert both recognized and proposed as human. Most to be remembered is that "With Dante, I take the literal, the actual, as the primary ground. We ourselves are literal, actual beings. This is the hardest ground for us to know, for we are *of* it—not outside, observing, but inside, experiencing."

So it is then, in memory, in fact:

Wisdom as such must wonder   for sortilege   is all.   Thruout
    the magic-loving tongue speaks and tastes

        thunder   the radiance of the sun upon the leaf.

    And among the poet's chimeras of an afternoon   the moth's
        ephemeral existence   take key in mystery
            translates...what?   The event   courses direct

        comes "from"?

Robert Creeley

To volunteer   *ite, missa est*   my life when's done the feast I offer you   plunder
   my excess   but what's sweet and true I've meant to be the office
                   the vowels in sequence   rime's offering
   the trumpet voluntary imitates the soul's release   Will's   not forced
nor reaches but   upon the ayre's promise   frees itself.   Entirely
   what we see, taste, hear, balance and   let go from balancing,   hear to pace,   feel
     the presence of   its scent   the fearful transport in every sense we know
     is given   we come to ourselves wherein   as if

           recovering,

born by the Virtue of this thing…

R E A D I N G S: *Reviews and Criticism*

ROBERT DUNCAN. *Ground Work II: In the Dark*. New York, New Directions. $19.95.

'Tears will not start here.' Nor here. The lament must take another form. But the acknowledgement, and the tribute. "Now we have no poet", said John Moritz at the news of Robert Duncan's death (3 February 1988—Gertrude Stein's birthday, and also Simone Weil's— and Trakl's, someone never named by Duncan in his constellation, and yet—where we look into that 'face of stone in black waters'). For him who in his work and life most showed us what poet is. He once praised Robert Creeley's novel *The Island* because "it tells us what it's like to be a Creeley!" And to be a *Duncan*?! Yet in the work it is the *share*, the commonality, our commons, joined—'the one ground . . . a life / to live / —the Word Itself   has no other foundation.' 'There is no art that is not chaind in its joy, Comedian, to the sufferings of the world!' 'There is no ecstasy of Beauty in which I will not remember man's misery.' 'What works in me is not mine but / ancient survivals'—'one alone and yet entirely given over to the many movements beyond saying the man I am no more alone than that '—'this adventuring of a soul' 'where / / mutualities awaken' 'more than you bargain for'. 'The writer's having lived in the writing the reader in turn lives in.' But it is through *this* particular life, and this particular experience of age and the coming of grave illness, in this particular poet, against these ravages now, written with all the accomplishment of a lifetime's mastery, dying his life, living his death, beyond, fully, in the imagination, reached, unto the end, the 'eternal arrest' of the last words of the final poem. Yet even there not to forget: 'What is complete but rests in the momentary illusion.'

•

'Tears will not start here', the book begins. Not to shed *this* time, now. Later, *this* here, for they will come more and more easily. But have already *been*, from the beginning—the waters of the soul, to shed again, unto the pool (it is also the reflecting mirror, and on beyond reflection) that is utter stillness, and from the rock break

281

forth—the current, in all things, sea, river, blood, house, electricity, language, earth, music, turning, time—forgetfulness and memory—where we find, the 'Me, Myself, and I' of self, who we are—and know we go back to, 'this still water / / we thirst for in dreams we dread'—by which the gods swear, by which they are kept honest. Is this, this 'black water', this Styx, to call it by but one name, by but one 'known' presence, the light of day is not so bright as, the guarantee of the faith of the universe?

•

The book is most prominently established by the five larger sets, *An Alternate Life, To Master Baudelaire, Veil, Turbine, Cord, and Bird, The Regulators*, and *The Five Songs* (to which "Structure of Rime: Of The Five Songs" is but a preface), but amongst which, and as intensely, individual poems (for instance, "At Cambridge", in its romance of language from the babblings of infancy to 'the threshold of another language as it were Heaven . . . the New World, before me, drawing me', and "At the Door", bringing the powers of Voudou into the work), and smaller suites (such as "An Eros/Amor/Love Cycle", with its great phallic hymn, and 'Illustrative Lines', to be read with Kitaj's cover drawing of the poet in mind), and pairs of poems which reach to one another, even across the distance of intervening other poems or inclusions (as "In Wonder" and "In Waking", "Whose" and "Close")—but *all* the poems most *closely* linked, most intricately and richly interrelated, calling and responding, surely more closely and intricately so than in any other of Duncan's books—to the culminating finalé of "After a Long Illness." To cite in these a few of the many notable moments of the poetic craft: the complexity of crosscurrents held in suspension yet kept in flow of the second stanza of "In the South"; the elusive and compelling logopoeia of *alternate* (and *you*) in *An Alternate Life*, in rime then on through the book; the weavings of word play in "Whose" and also, and of other languages, in "In Wonder"; the long, multi-counted lines of *The Regulators*; the rigor in taut measure of the alternating lines of the first Baudelaire homage; the calling forth and enacting, to then name, of the "uprising" in "Whose". Not to diminish any of the poems here nor anything else Duncan has written, but *The Regulators*, in all its dimensions, most particularly strikes as of the greatest American poetry—poetry at a pitch of such high, intense seriousness it is almost too much to sustain, and yet demands and sustains the engagement. That set, and "After a Long Illness", where the direct, quiet immediacy of personal distress, love's affirmation, and the exactitude of vision lure and carry us on, enthralled, even to the the chilling, motionless end. They star the crown of all of Duncan's work.

•

Ground Work II: In the Dark forms a continuous whole with the earlier *Ground Work: Before the War* (covering together work from 1968 to 1984) and should be read and thought of with it. The direct link can be felt immediately from the last poem of *GW I*, the Rūmī set, to the opening sequence here, in term after term (including the Australian Connection, earlier by reference to the star Fomalhaut, alpha Piscis Australis, 'splendor of the other "sky"', here as actual locus of "In the South"), both poems passionately addressed to the poet's life companion and love. The same central themes, essential foci, numinous *noeuds* recur throughout the two volumes: the sets of four (the four elements, Fire Earth Water Air, through many transformations, becoming suits of cards and the seasons but also echoing others, Reiteration Retribution Restitution Refusal, Love Law War Will, the up down strange charm of quarks—and then for each the fifth, the hidden element, quint-essence, as Beauty in 'The Dignities' is hidden in those nine powers to make ten, two sets of five—and so the hand(s)); birds (how many here! but most poignantly the Nuttall song sparrow at the end of 'After Passage'); angels ('No, I do not speak of Evils or of Agents of Death   but these Angels / are attendants of lives raging within life'); the mind; the abyss; the self and the other; love; the lover; sexual passion; stars; romance and lure; enthrallment; the alternations of night/day, sunset/dawn, sleep/waking, early/late, youth/age, dark/light; the orders of the cosmos; stupidity; denial; war; destruction; dissolution; death; and more and more, the letting go, the giving over; and in all, always the *questioning*. So the two books form poles of one another, that polarity of ourselves Emerson tells us we can only obey: the Light-Fire-War of *GW I*; the Dark-Cold-Rest of *GW II*.

•

[The reader who has seen both books will note that *GW I* was reproduced from the poet's typescript while the present volume is set in type. The reasons, various and complex, for Duncan's concern with and unequivocal preference for a typed text and the exact equality of one space-one letter—followed then under his supervision in *GW I*—can be found in his preface to *Maps* 6 (1974) and in brief summary in this reviewer's notice of *GW I* in CONJUNCTIONS:7 (1985). The text of the present volume has been very carefully and handsomely set, with clear intent to correspond faithfully to the typed ms. As almost unavoidably there would be in a book of this complexity, there are some errors and difficulties. Most notably these include: on the acknowledgement page, 'Illustrated Lines' should read 'Illustrative Lines'; in the table of contents, *The Regulators* is referred to simply as *Regulators*; in both the table of contents and the text the title of 'Structure of Rime: Of The Five Songs' is set in a larger type which makes it seem the title of the entire set, *The Five Songs*, rather than just of the prefacing poem it is; 'You, Muses' in the table of contents should read 'YOU, Muses'; the text of that poem lacks the designation [*Passages 22*] which it should have and which the table of contents does provide it, and in the body of the poem the imprint of much of the Greek (at least in the copies seen so far) is unclear and difficult to read, and there is one

misprint (p.73): $\mu\nu\eta\sigma\alpha\iota\alpha\delta$' should read $\mu\nu\eta\sigma\alpha\iota\alpha\theta$';

in 'Et' (p. 44), $O\delta\upsilon o o \acute{\epsilon}\omega\varsigma$ should read $O\delta\upsilon\sigma\sigma\acute{\epsilon}\omega\varsigma$;

throughout there is the problem of keeping clear the careful gradation of type sizes and forms for all the variety of titles and subtitles that the ms. does precisely establish. (There was at one time also a prefacing poem for the whole book, 'In Passage', provided this reviewer by the poet when he last visited Lawrence in Feb-Mar 1983, whatever may have happened to it since.)

None of this amounts to a great deal. But the question must remain, notwithstanding the illness of the author and his own inability to type the final copy, and whatever allowances he may have agreed to, why this present volume, which does use the same page size and shape, has not followed the presentation of *GW I* established by the writer (someone else, for instance, could have typed copy from the ms. as readily as type was set from it)? Should the central importance Duncan clearly attached to this matter, arrived at carefully, in the full power of his consideration, be passed over, whatever compromises in illness may later have seemed expedient? It is, to stress again, a handsome volume, and most readers (this reviewer included) may *aesthetically* find the printed text more attractive. But isn't it reasonable that both volumes of *Ground Work* should appear in the same integral format, and that the one the poet believed in?]

.

Duncan's prose is always worth reading in connection with his poetry, as well as simply for its own sake, and in the case of *Ground Work*, especially the essays collected in *Fictive Certainties*. There are two pieces that might particularly be mentioned as valuable here. The first, one of his most striking works, "Properties And Our Real Estate", has strangely never been reprinted since it appeared in the original issue of *Journal for the Protection of All Beings* in 1961. Its relevance is in counterpoint, presenting concepts of soul, body, spirit, sun, heaven and hell, love and the lover, revelation, the gift, which question and add complex dimensions to the later work, and which, again so far as can be established, have yet to be considered integrally with such similar concerns, and the *ground* and the *work*, in these books. The other, "The Self in Postmodern Poetry" (first published in 1983), to be found in *Fictive Certainties*, speaks directly to what is before us:

> I work with what is the matter with this life in an alchemical operation seeking not the overthrow of the matter—though increasingly the theme of letting it all go comes into the works—but the transvaluation of that matter. I read and write, gathering darkness, I would say, deepening the rift. . . . I work only in question; mine is a questionable work.

. . .

> The Self . . . I also would undo the idea of, let it go. The theme increases in recent years, and back of it hovers the dissolution of the physical chemical universe which I take to be the very spiritual ground and body of our being. Something more than Death or Inertia comes as a lure in this 'Letting go'. . . . Self—a Sublime Undoing.

.

No, not death is at the heart here—felt, but not just death, and not the fear of death at all. 'The fullness of the creative imagination demands that rigor and painful knowledge be the condition of harmony; that death be the condition of eternal forms'. It is a 'specter'— an image, an appearance—but no more than is the lover, the companion of his life: 'you that other / specter of my actually living is'— for 'Death is the Lord of a Passage that unites us'. And even there the poet embraces also the possible return: 'and, if the wheel so return me, I shall embrace again birth cord and pang of this animal being and come into whatever desires and delusions in memory of you and

285

this passing time in your care.'

In all this, too, is the kinship with other poets, the company of the work and the spirit: Homer (citations from the Catalogue of Ships in Book II of the *Iliad* in "YOU, Muses", the actual *Passages 22* we have been waiting for since "In Place of a Passages 22" in *Bending the Bow*); Hesiod (in "Styx"); Rūmī, Stein, Zukofsky, Pound, Rilke, many another; but most especially, and throughout, Baudelaire. Not so much the Baudelaire of debauch, sin, guilt, nor even really of death as "vieux capitaine"—though overtones of all those as well—but of the life and death in the heart; the depths and despairs, and the grandeurs, of the soul and spirit; the immense compassion for all misery; the angels; the living torches; the abyss; the longing for nothingness—and the cat, and the owls. In all, the poetry. And with these, not named but implicit, heard within, there is Williams: 'The descent beckons / as the ascent beckoned / ... / endless and indestructible'. And there is Lawrence: 'If there were not an utter and absolute dark / of silence and sheer oblivion / at the core of everything, / how terrible the sun would be, / how ghastly it would be to strike a match, and make a light.' And there is Emerson: 'Why should we fear to be crushed by the savage elements, we who are made of the same elements?':

> And on his mind, at dawn of day,
> Soft shadows of the evening lay.
> For the prevision is allied
> Unto the thing so signified;
> Or say, the foresight that awaits
> Is the same Genius that creates.

•

The matter, the deep matter at the heart here is vision. Vision, not what one would want or decide to see, but what one is given and cannot avoid seeing—what, as Duncan would say, you don't get not to see, to experience. The Angel Syphilis (he did not yet name the Angel AIDS), the Angel Cancer, the Angel of nuclear disaster, the Jesus who comes forward 'not to heal but to tear the scab from the wound you wanted to forget. / May the grass no longer spread out to cover the works of man in the ruin of earth', and the condition of knowing these, all speak of a malaise felt at the very heart of the society and nation, of mankind, as well as the poet's individual being. And the questioning. 'What Angel,   what Gift of the Poem,   has brought into my body // this sickness of living?' 'You think I have some defense for it,   in it?' But part of the vision also is love, is the 'flower of song / / this lingering of a scent in every thing', is the Dignities.

Poetry, the poet has told us, is not the repository of dead things but the place where eternal things emerge (what follows here is based on notes drawn from Duncan's introductory remarks to a reading of *The Regulators* in Buffalo in Feb 1982, a tape of which was kindly provided at the time by Robert Bertholf). What the social, the political, the civic/civil world has surrendered from itself, has given up on, goes then into the realm of the imagination. There is only one place for these visions of what has been thought possible, of what has come to be seen as lost in the actual world, to come true— Christendom for Dante, Kings for Shakespeare, Democracy for Duncan and us all—not just as survivors of history and of being disowned in the public realm, but as regulators and accusers of what is happening. It took Kings to betray Kings, Kings being Kings, and the idea of Kings. So as participants in Democracy our eternal yearnings are for the nature of what we have betrayed. Here these are a litany addressed to the Dignities themselves, those nine divine attributes Ramon Lull named, consonant with all religions, manifest on all levels of Creation (Frances Yates, the poet's source, sets forth in *The Occult Philosophy in the Elizabethan Age*): Goodness, Greatness, Eternity, Power, Wisdom, Will, Virtue or Strength, Truth, Glory. In the poems then come forward propositions of these Regulators: what might regulate—direct according to a rule or governing principle—the depth of how to live in the face of the massive lies and betrayals in which we do live—not for the first time in man's history. A poetry of the Spirit (the Spirit, not *my* Spirit, stresses the poet)—the Spirit, which is more than an other than the Mind, so they can coexist. So Duncan makes his testimony: Language is pure Spirit, and more than eternal: I cannot account for my experience of it—and in Language I encounter God. (So the effort over and over is to try to account for that experience—to account for the unaccountable by means of the unaccountable, which effort is then its experience of the unaccountable experience.) That there be a poetry both of prophecy and vision which does not seek to resolve or idealize away any of the profound trouble in which it works, but entirely to accept it: that which *is* too much for us to deal with. The prayer: not to quiet the trouble, but lift it so that it can be seen as it is, a divine gift —'brightning mind / lifts soul in to its arms let love but regulate.' And two and a half years later, after the onset of the illness that

287

was with him to the end—'the failure of systems' 'the kidneys' / condition is terminal'—and the first congestive heart attack: 'the prayer / —I didn't have a prayer—   your care / alone kept my love clear.'

This legacy! "Where does sex *come* from?!" the student asks incredulously, starting forward, never having thought the question could be asked and for an answer. 'Out of love, the light *came*.' The cry, the asking!—'the breath flows from— / / whose then the resident identity?' 'Who then   is this passion / / that returns for me/ who then / that remembers and goes back for me?' '—your sudden call'. This life work now given to us—'to face what Man is in'— which in the very depth of its anguish and darkness—which are *our* anguish and darkness—and in its questioning, affirms and renews faith in the Spirit in Language in the Imagination in Poetry. And, oh, most profoundly, in Love. And makes a home. And to leave. 'Love comes to Grief to strike a light / again, and Dark increases to enhance / the pathos of a brief humanity time allows / not easily.' It is a book of sublime poetry.

—Kenneth Irby

Δ   Δ   Δ

Georges Perec. *Life: a User's Manual.* Translated by David Bellos. Boston, David R. Godine. $24.95.

Jacques Roubaud. *Our Beautiful Heroine.* Translated by David Kornacker. Woodstock, The Overlook Press. $17.95.

Our Beautiful Heroine is the loveliest, lightest serious book you're likely to read in a long while. Jacques Roubaud, one of the most arresting French poets of our day, known for a lyric work sensuous and muscular, has here written a short novel of grace, modesty, elegance and wickedness in measure; the narrative is pleasantly stuffed with asides and by-play and literary reminiscences—characters' names, allusions, typologies from here and there, muffled cannon shots, veiled and naked accolades to Queneau, Mathews and others of the OuLiPo, and to their ascended master Raymond Roussel. And, of course, there are a few tributes to Georges Perec, whose present novel, like zany shareware, provides Roubaud with the plan of arranging the narrative of a novel according to the real estate of a detailed, unnamed city. Nimbly Roubaud turns this trope, and allows the actions, coded by address and floor plan, to spill out into the street in a light-heartedly criminous romp.

Life: A User's Manual, on the other hand, is massive, compelling: a Dostoevsky without punishment, a Balzac without remorse, it is an explosive girandole of a book, whirling everywhere, sparkling relentless insights into the crazy syllogisms of behavior that warp our actions into what, at the end of things, we presume to call 'a life.' Perec cares amorously about antiques, warfare, decor, advertising rhetoric, the hidden life of objects, the dark logic of furniture that constrains the ways we live. I think this book is one that people will in time come to call great.

Every house is a haunted house, I think, scarred by the ghosts of its past dwellers, poignant with the pleasures of those who have not yet come, but will come, to be shaped in their day by the house's order. No one has shown better than Perec, less sentimentally, more vividly, the sad, glad dialectic of the house: the mind's lock on place, and the place's lock on mind.

A naive American reader, like the undersigned, is impressed by how French Perec is, with his earnest tabulations of peccant behavior (like a Balzac), the joyous self-involved catalogues of reified nonsense of a Rabelais: impedimenta, books, words, images. Perec's sedulous avoidance of any employment of the object as an item in a psychological code is itself a backhanded testimonial to the 'meaning of things' school (Mme Aubain's clock in the form of the Temple of Vesta.)

But just as emphatically does *Our Beautiful Heroine* feel British—it seems set in the France of Chesterton's Flambeau, in an era of artful, pleasing narration, and it plays with a sense of *innocent crime* that might have come out of *The Man Who Was Thursday.* And before that, and above all, Roubaud reminds us again and again of the very different sensibility of Laurence Sterne, founder of the novel, of all possible novels. When we remember that the author of *A Sentimental Journey* learned his manners in France, a gentle circle is closed.

Roubaud sets a winningly austere abstraction-loving detective on the trail of an elegant criminal. The presence of a narrator—sometimes reduced to a mere character—allows Roubaud some acerbic fun making light of libraries, logic and love. Every act in the novel, however sensuously or playfully reported (and some of them are quite nifty), seems shadowed by some mathematical or other rigorous dimension. I feel as if a set of closer re-readings would provide me with a different conception of the way events criss-cross to produce new narrative lines. (The author's reference to Pappus's Theorem gives me the confidence to make this observation.)

The primary trope of *Life: A User's Manual* is the jigsaw puzzle. Bartlebooth (in whose name we read Melville's obsessed scrivener, Melville's own sea wanderings, and Valery Larbaud's mythic American millionaire-poet Barnabooth) is that stock-figure of French comedy, the eccentric English zillionaire. He travels to paint watercolors of seaside views all over the world. The paintings are converted into puzzles, which must be solved, then dissolved, turned back into blankness, into nothing: this is the rigorous, complex and funny conceit that orders this huge book.

The story is told room by room, a big apartment house in Paris; room by room, item by item within the room, we are conducted through the real-estate of life, and the movables that shape our lives. (One of the last of the many score of discrete narratives in the book is a sobering fabliau about the godly intervention of a bedroom suite in the life of a young couple—furniture as deity).

In both books, the novel is the world, the very specific world (the only one possible to inhabit), a house-world. We live in numbers, and the urban geography of Roubaud is shaped by numbered-bus lines (which are rivers), and the forests of numbered apartment house addresses, inside which the polity of staircases, floors, and numbered doors assorts our fates. We live in the determinants-of-action that numbers are. In Perec, the last work of the painter Valène (who, as "the oldest inhabitant," is as close to having a god's-eye view as the novel gives us) is a bleak canvas sketched lightly in charcoal with simple squares that represent rooms of a house. It is in such a specific sense one claims these as 'mathematical novels,' their reliance on the primacy of geometry and logical array as signifiers of moral energy.

Of course as in any dream (any book is a dream, as we learn to our peril when—if not before—we fall asleep while reading, and the ennaration goes on), a house = the mind. The geography of the house is the geography of the mind.

Now imagine a book turned to the world. (The world is the sum of what we say about ourselves and manage to remember for a while. Or: the world is whatever you think when you hear the word "world;" such reactions will include the annoyance that metalinguistics and other forms of Being Clever usually produce in the honest reader.)

Imagine a book turned to the world. It examines the world "because it is there." A novel is an x-ray machine that illuminates and transcribes the hidden connective tissue of all-our-lives.

A book doesn't need a reason, any more than a window does. Lenses see. When the lens gets smudged, we call this Time, passing. Or history.

Perec's lens is clear, precise, objective as only a tale told by objects could be. There are pornographically detailed descriptions of inlaid wood, floorboards, abandoned clocks, inkwells, lamps—and the people are ghosts, mere names at times, or tender smells drifting through empty rooms: as if the humans were characters in stories the furniture tells itself in the interminable night of objects.

Now we take this fresh contraption, The Novel, and trundle it around and point it at the mind. The mind is at least everything, certainly everything that is speaking when the word "world" or the word "mind" is pronounced, and probably everything else. The lens is still a lens. The machine is running. The operator has left the room.

The machine records the connections it finds inside words, between numbers. A man is an absence, so the book concentrates on his identity papers, his Visa card, his driver's license, the almost unrecognizable photo in his passport, his fingerprints. His name. A book is an analysis of his name. The documentation left when people are gone (and Perec too is dead) is the world, or world enough for us.

Life: A User's Manual examines the apartments in a huge house (the House as Mind is old as Artemidorus). And the people? The place keeps them alive. Where they lived is called reality (as in 'real estate'). What their names were, and other things they said, is called Language.

The machine (the Novel) examines these (or this). From the shuddering and heaving of its mighty hoses, proposes action. The book turns into a novel. The lens speaks.

Life: A User's Manual is funny, moving, full of epenthetic narratives (107 of them are itemized by title in a separate appendix—though these titles do not occur as such in the text), nuggets of fantasy, true history, feigned history. Perec was an immensely generous writer, who believed in approaching the reader with full hands. He is the charlatan who tricks you by giving you a thousand real diamonds in which you are free to pick out and claim the one false. There is richness here, a kind of closeness of detail, a dense specific

291

documentation of the imagination unheard of, almost inconceivable, in the shallow American novel.

Both Roubaud and Perec remind us that in the deepest level of our reception, beneath the jovial or saturnine ever-branching narratives, every novel may in fact be a kind of *sutra*, exploring the *pratitya-samutpada*: the endlessly shifting, endlessly proliferating web of dependent originations, the interdependency of all things.

(Is that why the Church condemned on its infamous Index all novels of its target authors, all novels, not because they were *fabula amatoria* (love stories—what love story could they read wilder than the Gospel of John?), but because they, novels, deny the philosophical safe-house of Coincidence. In the novel, everything *means*).

For the novel, everything causes everything else, and there is no such thing as a neutral action. (Long have western institutions rested comfortably on the insupportable notion of the neutrality of a vast class of actions—business, warfare, sport—whose pleasant and profitable continuance excites no scruple from State or Church.) Here it is just this *absence of any neutral action* that makes the novels of Roubaud and Perec so tender, so finally (may I use this word in this century?) ripe. Confronted with the array of things, the mind must decide it all means nothing, or that there is some element, some dignity, some moral semiotics it can embrace.

Read these two novels, one lightly, one solemnly advancing the theory and practice of the puzzle. In both you run into pictures, captions, events and even characters' names that seem like punch-lines to jokes you will never hear. You engage a text that compares the art of writing and reading to the bizarre process of cutting images into intricate puzzles, reassembling them, and bleaching the images back into nothingness again:

> Let us imagine a man whose wealth is equalled only by his indifference to what wealth generally brings, a man of exceptional arrogance who wishes to fix, to describe, and to exhaust…a constituted fragment of the world: in the face of the inextricable incoherence of things, he will set out to execute a (necessarily limited) programme right the way through, in all its irreducible, intact entirety…a single project, an arbitrarily constrained programme with no purpose outside its own completion.
> *Life: A User's Manual*, 117

And yet, and yet. Seldom have I seen wit, cleverness, brittle numerology, arcane detail and intellectual grandstanding used so compassionately, with such a fine, generous sense of time and human feeling. Reading the last pages of this vast but moderated chronicle, I found myself thinking after all that the multiplication table (with its greeds, aspirations and converse divisions, losses, dreams) is the most sentimental thing we have. It is the very hardware of *Life: A User's Manual* that makes the book so moving, its ability to reckon so many human cliches and transform them by their tender, durable possessions. In Chapter 74, the aged Valène, unnamed, stares down on all the heaps of accumulations in the store-rooms of the house. To such debris and detritus and stowed gear all our history tends to stick. How can we tell it from ourselves?

—ROBERT KELLY

Δ   Δ   Δ

PAUL CELAN. *Collected Prose*, translated by Rosmarie Waldrop. New York, P.N. Review/Carcanet. $14.95. *Last Poems*, translated by Katherine Washburn and Margaret Guillemin. San Francisco, North Point Press. $20.00.

So much has been written about Paul Celan, so many poetries posited as his, so many personalities tendered for him in his name and for his benefit, that one might think that his was an exhausted myth. It isn't though, because the "myth" of Celan—admixture of speech, suffering and silence, of hermeticism and encounter—exerts a positive influence on American poetry and on what kind of importance we are going to attach to it in the future.

Born into a German-speaking milieu in Czernowitz, Rumania, in 1920, son of Jewish parents who would be deported and shot by the S.S. in 1942, Celan was rooted in a unique historical reality, that of the holocaust, and in his double identity as German-speaker and Jew, as survivor (physically) and victim (in every other sense). No book makes the specificity of Celan's situation more clear than the *Collected Prose*, skillfully translated from the German by the ever-reliable Rosmarie Waldrop. The volume is slim, but inclusive of all the occasional prose pieces—essays, speeches, letters with a bearing on the poetic—which Celan wrote between 1948 and 1970. While they don't shed much light on him as a person, they do reveal another side of Celan's work, as intellectually demanding as the poems, but more accessible since more theoretically direct. The most important of these is "The Meridian" (with its evocation of a poetic act akin to Lucille's cry of "Long Live the King" in the face of the King's executioners in Buchner's *Danton's Death*), a speech

293

given on the occasion of Celan's reception of the Buchner prize in 1960. Here, the crucial notion of *Atemwande* is introduced, glossed by Waldrop in her brief introduction to *Collected Prose* as referring to a moment in which "existence is actually threatened, when [the poet's] breath fails, when silence literally (if momentarily) means death—at this moment a poem may be born." If the poem *is* born, then we have uttered Lucille's "counter-word" again, and the poem becomes an act of liberation, a reclamation of existence.

"Conversation in the Mountains," included in this volume (it appears as well in *Last Poems*), is the prose work Celan apparently thought of as his most significant. For this reason, however, this parable of the Jew *Gross* and the Jew *Klein* has been overrated by many critics; it is not on the same level as his other writings, though it might be of some value if read biographically or in an effort to evaluate Celan's Jewishness. On the other hand, "Edgar Jene and the Dream about the Dream" is essential to understanding Celan's surrealist side, while the "Letter to Hans Bender" should serve to distance Celan from any formalist aesthetic of either the "well-crafted" or L-A-N-G-U-A-G-E variety: "Craft means handiwork, a matter of hands. [But] only truthful hands write true poems...And then there are, at every lyrical street corner, experimenters that muck around with the so-called word material. Poems are also gifts to the attentive." Indeed, what these prose pieces ultimately show is that Celan was a romantic, in the same sense that the surrealists were romantics, in the same sense that religious thinkers like Buber were romantic, in the same sense that much great poetry has been romantic: they uphold the expectation that subjectivity, if plumbed deeply enough, leads to a discovery of the Other.

Celan, then, submerged himself in his materials not simply in order to explore them, but in order to reconstitute through them, in a plausible modern way, the two terms of the romantic equation: the lyric ego and the Other. This is true even of his last most difficult books, all of which are represented in *Last Poems*: *Lichtzwang* (*Force of Light*, 1970), *Schnee-Part* (*Snow-Part*, 1971) and *Zeitgehëft* (*Farmstead of Time*, 1976). In her outstanding introduction to the volume (the translation itself was also done by Margret Guillemin), Katharine Washburn discusses many of the facts central to the experience of reading Celan. A private lexicon of words—hair, sand, eyes, stone—appear throughout his poetry, and serve to unify first to last poems; at the same time, as she points out, all explanation is eroded from those words in the later poems, leaving the words alone, as if they were stones themselves. Celan's must be seen as a *willed* decomposition of poetry, an all-out attempt to destroy that which preceded it, with the secret hope that only the purest of stuff might survive. But a willed decomposition is only necessary due to destruction undergone. In Celan's own often quoted words, "language had to go through its own lack of answers, through terrifying silence, through the thousand darknesses of murderous speech. It went through." For Celan, something *did* survive all the forms of negation, both willed and undergone.

For all of its opacity, *Force of Light* can upon occasion be remarkably clear about its desire for transcendence:

> DISCUS
> starred with premonitions,
>
> throw yourself
> out of yourself.

In poems such as this, one sees the reflection of Celan's insistence that his poems were not hermetic but rather "messages in the bottle." But the title of the second collection—*Snow-Part*—is a typical Celan paradox, literally meaning a part (of music) written for the snow, in its silence, to play. Celan's condition was one that might just as well have blanketed the mind under a deathly silence. He was a displaced person, a German-speaking Jew living in Paris, and, in the end, a suicide. In the poems silence and light, object, sound and the illusion of object and sound are interwoven in such a way as to crease the veritable emptiness and leave instead wrinkles of memory and perception, nightmare and lost subjectivity.

A poem from *Farmstead of Time*:

> FROM THE SINKING WHALEBROW
> I read you—
> you recognize me,
>
> heaven
> hurls itself
> into the harpoon,
>
> six-legged
> our star crouches in the foam,
>
> slowly
> someone who sees it hoists

a scrap of comfort: the
strutting Nothingness.

That, in the person of Celan, words could encounter the horrible
and retain such beauty for themselves—without granting beauty to
the horror itself—is Celan's first-order achievement.

—LEONARD SCHWARTZ

Δ   Δ   Δ

ALISON ARMSTRONG. *The Joyce of Cooking: Food and Drink from
James Joyce's Dublin.* Barrytown, New York, Station Hill Press.
$18.95.

In this era of serious cooks, gourmands, and food writers who handle
their subject as culinary anthropologists and historians, the recipe is
more than a means to a meal. Alison Armstrong's *The Joyce of
Cooking: Food & Drink from James Joyce's Dublin* is a rich, joyous
culinary Baedecker. The author—cofounder of the *James Joyce
Broadsheet* and coeditor of the Irish *Literary Supplement*—introduces her well-researched and -written recipes with quotes from
Joyce. "High tea. Mayonnaise I poured on the plums thinking it was a
custard." *Ulysses* is cited, and the page number given (in addition to
indexes and an appendix of weights and measures, this cookbook has
a bibliography). "Plums in Custard, No Mayonnaise," a recipe for
stewed plums with custard sauce, follows. Like the best cookbook
authors, she is specific about ingredients, utensils, and procedure.
"Greengage plums are more popular in Ireland than Damsons; the
former is a sweet fruit—while the latter is an oval purple fruit of
Syrian origin which, unless very ripe, can leave a bitter aftertaste
until cooked," and in the same recipe, "Whisk in the top of a double
boiler or in a heated round-bottomed copper bowl."

The *Joyce of Cooking* is classic in structure: chapters follow the
natural sequence of a meal, from "Fat Soups" through "Meats and
Inner Organs" to "Sweet Sins & Other Trifles." Vegetarian meals,
home remedies, and beverages, "Off the Drink & On the Drink," are
not overlooked. Many of the recipes are the author's creations;
others are from her Irish grandmother or adapted from dishes of Irish
chefs and food writers. All are representative of early 20th-century
classic Irish cooking. As Anthony Burgess states in his foreword,
"Out of *Ulysses* you can reconstruct the entire Dublin cuisine."

Armstrong's wit and attention to authenticity ensure that the reconstruction results, for reader or cook, in a feast. She frequently offers serving suggestions—for candied violets and marzipan roses, "serve in a beautifully appointed drawing room"—and menu ideas. "Bloomusalem Artichoke Soup," for example, is "good with a main course of kidneys, nutty gizzards, or roast heart." Aside from enriching the character of the book, these suggestions are helpful to the cook who wants to create a Joycean repast.

—SARAH BELK

Δ   Δ   Δ

JAY CANTOR. *Krazy Kat.* New York, Simon & Schuster. $16.95.

People have said many unkind things about William Randolph Hearst, and I am no exception. I suppose my snottiest remarks concerning him were made during a limousine visit to his isolated mountaintop mansion, and they mainly concerned the surprisingly second-rate quality of the art works displayed and embedded in Hearst's bizarre eyrie (always with the exception of the blue tile pool, a beaut), considering the outrageous amounts of money which, my guides assured me, over and over again, he had spent in order to accumulate the stuff. I think a mediocre Titian, hung in a high, dark corner as if in shame, got me going: poor old Hearst could never be given any serious consideration as a patron of the arts. It all made me feel quite grand as there are few things more satisfying than putting down the intolerably fortunate of this world, especially if you're part Irish. But later on, being driven down the hill from that comic place, I grew increasingly mortified (another satisfying emotional state for one of Celtic extraction) as it dawned on me that, whatever his failings, Hearst had indeed been one of the great connoisseurs of all time, and would surely be listed among the most revered of the kings and popes and whatnots who have encouraged things artistic, for it was he who spotted and supported George Herriman, and it was George Herriman who created *Krazy Kat.*

There have been many satisfactory comic strips—*Little Nemo* with its beautiful nightmares, *Dick Tracy* and his ugly adversaries—but they all pale compared with *Krazy Kat,* which told, in spellings and images unforgettable, of Krazy, a dear, mad, saintly/lustful cat who forever interpreted the bricks heaved at her by an infuriated mouse, Ignatz, as messages of love, and of how their relationship was persistently misunderstood as a morality problem by her less appreciated, but no less dedicated, admirer, Officer Pup, and how wonderful it was that things could never be worked out between the three of them.

The readers and editors of Hearst's papers seem to have been a dim lot so far as Herriman's magnum opus was concerned. Krazy's sweet generosity went completely over their heads or alarmed them or both, and if it had not been for Hearst's personal intercession, the strip would many times have been dropped. Hearst insisted that it be printed, even if it had to be moved out of the comic pages and given a special place of its own in the entertainment section; the American public would take Krazy's special message of joy and love, he declared, and be damned. Eventually monuments such as Gilbert Seldes and E. E. Cummings let it be known in print that they loved Krazy back; after that the editors had to let Krazy run or never again be respected by their wives, and the hoi polloi once more had to learn to live with something on account of it was art. Krazy was safe and sound until, in 1944, George Herriman died, leaving, as a good cartoonist should, a number of strips all finished and waiting for the printer.

Now comes along Jay Cantor, fresh from his wonderful first novel, *The Death of Che Guevera*, to write a book based on the strip and called, sure enough, *Krazy Kat*. The editor of this magazine hit upon the notion of having a cartoonist review the thing, and he asked me to do it, and after some thought, and more than a little hesitation, I said, Yes.

I hesitated because I'd noticed it lying around in various bookstores, and been mildly irritated by it, to be frank; by its cover, to be specific. It wasn't the content of the drawing that irritated me— Krazy and Ignatz standing atop a mesa and looking out at the mushroom cloud of an atomic bomb—I rather liked that. It was the drawing itself. It attempted to mimic Herriman's style of drawing, but in an coy way, as if to say, "I'm not *really* trying to imitate this fellow." I would be unhappy with anybody who did that with me, and so might Herriman. The drawing was toying around with a talent way out of its class: its line and color and composition— everything about it was just so so, whereas Herriman was great.

In the book are reproductions of panels from the strip itself, and they are superb (if a little lonely by themselves), but then there is a bad drawing, *not* by Herriman, repeated atop each chapter heading. The dedication is enclosed in another brick done with the same lack of success and essential concern as these other interloping drawings, and while all that might be a small point in another sort of book, in one trying to do what this one is, I'm not sure if it's a small point at all. However, that's not Cantor's fault, just his bad luck, I thought, settling down to read. Though, I thought, he'd better be good.

The book starts with a cute enough concept: the cast of *Krazy Kat* and Coconino County itself, have survived and merely retired from the comic strip biz, from the public gaze. Krazy herself is quite content to loll around in the sun on the design of her Navajo rug and gaze out at the ever-changing landscape (as in the strip, cacti change into moons, moons into mountains, mountains into clouds, and each shift may lead directly from midnight to high noon or the other way around) and drink this and that from her set of Zuni eggshell-blue tea cups. Ignatz the Mouse, on the other hand, burns to return to the spotlight, but he knows he hasn't a chance without Krazy, so he is constantly devising plots and strategems to nudge her back into Mr. Hearst's newspapers. Fan mail arrives daily, signed with names more than a little suggestive of "Ignatz" or "Offissa Bull Pup," extolling Krazy's past glories and urging her to take up her art once more. She is touched, even moved, but she remains retired. Then Ignatz, in a mad, bold move, tells Krazy there is something he wants to show her, and she follows him trustingly (being Krazy, she knows no other way to follow him) and soon the two of them arrive at an isolated spot in the desert, near a place called Alamogordo. They come within sight of an odd-looking tower with a football-shaped something hanging from it. Krazy puzzles sweetly over what that might be and then her heart pounds with love when her imagined solution comes with a rush: Dear, tiny Ignatz has built her the ultimate brick!

Of course *we* know what it *really* is, and so it doesn't come as all that much of a surprise to us when Krazy realizes that a nearby cactus is not a cactus at all but a human being, the first one she's ever seen. The human's incredible three-dimensionality brings home to Krazy her comic-strip flatness, but that does not depress so much as thrill her because she knows he is the most beautiful thing she has ever seen. The man has kindly, sad eyes and is none other than J. Robert Oppenheimer—father of the atomic bomb—himself.

Following the explosion, there is a very funny exchange of letters between a transparently mouselike Oppenheimer and the Kat. It starts out eminently well but ends with Oppie ("please call me Oppie—all my friends do") blaming her and her passion-arousing

299

art for inspiring him to use his terrible device. Unable to bear the burden of her guilt sober, she, poor thing, takes to drinking more tiger tea than is good for her, which eventually causes her to howl out that "BECAUSE OF MOMS MEN ARE ANGRY AT THE WOMEN THEY LOVE...AND WOMEN ARE ANGRY AT WOMEN, TOO!" In response Ignatz makes up a mouselike version of psycholanalysis: this section is full of insights and hilarious images entirely new to me. I will ever be grateful to Cantor for it. I don't know how much Cantor has had to do with the poor, suffering bastards who make up our movies and television dreams as they wander along from one story conference to the next, but he shows, in his depiction of an insane monster known as the Producer—an individual who drops into Coconino County via helicopter in order to talk about shooting an on-location movie with the locals—that those he's seen he's observed beautifully. The producer comes up with one nifty idea after the other, ready to drop them all if he doesn't sense immediate approval from his viewers. It's genuinely scary humor.

All of the above is done stylishly and cleverly, even though the book does begin to wobble and flop a mite so far as using Herriman's world and creatures is concerned. There continue to be bright insights and clever turnings, but the project seems to be adrift, turning from a novel into a presentation of various theses. Cantor abandons poor Krazy for an intellectual trick and it's hard to feel kindly toward him then because up until now you thought he loved her.

By slow degrees, poor Krazy and Ignatz finally make it into the human race, as does Offissa Pup, who dies of cancer. The final result of their tedious struggle to achieve membership in our species I found remarkable for its mediocrity, as Cantor (who must be a man of little mercy) has the two become a team of saloon singers with Ignatz at the piano. When we last see them, they are relaxing at the Plaza Hotel, reading reviews of their work. I had hopes that this might be a final joke on Cantor's part and read through this last part of the book again, searching for some evidence to that effect, but I'm afraid he wasn't kidding. —GAHAN WILSON

Cantor, as cartographer of *Krazy Kat*'s hallucinatory landscape, recalls the scholar's siting of the *Tempest* isle in our Atlantic waters, neatly locating genteel—and, germane to the novel, gentile—New Country ideals of cultivation, culture and the noble savage: "We're not animals. I mean we *are,* but we're *not.* We *talk."* Imagine Miranda discovering, after her sea passage of longing, hag-whelped humanity, exchanging her innocence for dark knowledge. America, specifically the desert of Alamogordo, is the brave new world, where all the characters are refugees, constructing a new land—and landscape equals character—of splintered boards and bent nails washed up along the coast. Ignatz, putting aside bricks for the flotsam of mankind's sharp theories and passions, is Prospero, Sebastian and Caliban conflated into one shrewd mouse. Krazy in fact is not much of a rhetoritician. She can't lie, can't swear, can't express sophisticated ("softfisticaked") ideas. Through the innocent feline speak Pound, Stein, Lewis Carroll, Sterne (down to "FADE TO BLACK" followed by the new chapter prefaced by a Shandean black page) and a host of other guides and guardians of self-interpretation.

By virtue of turning within the confines of its buff covers, *Krazy Kat* goes on forever. Composed of change it is eternal serpent, tail hooked in its mouth, each scale reflecting ad infinitum both stars and scales. The image is Cantor's: there isn't a sentence that doesn't echo, twist, repeat, distort what has gone before. No character possesses a single identity; no word has a simple meaning. The old Shaker hymn—first line, "'Tis a gift to be simple"—introduces the novel. Cantor's punning on the last line, "Til by turning, turning we *come round* right," as Krazy and Ignatz attempt three-dimensionality, much of the assault in the form of elaborate sexual fantasy, is not off-handed witticism. Puns are portents.

Actors on their newsprint stage ("Strut it out horns!" as Krazy exclaims), they are constructed, quite evidently, of societal dreams—religious inheritance, history, comic routines which they flesh out and, of course, language. The culture of the Old Country, as well as the oldest country, pre-Coconino desert with its Law and bitter herbs, is at conflict with the new, inhabited by the demigods Fred and Ginger. Goldberg's friendly gadgets make way for the bomb. Ink blot cat and mouse move through a glorious inhabiting of old showtunes, through pagan German rites of purification, through Freudian analysis and the lessons of Hollywood, suffering the changes each world view imposes.

They finally achieve, aided by imagination's power but incarnated through free will, humanity. Ignatz, always proud of his handlike paws, manipulates. Krazy, as (and like) Kate, has been tamed: she wears the time-honored upholstery of the pet—a collar, silk stockings, garters. In the chapter of sexual fantasies which propel them toward mortality, they enact the dreams of anonymous and pseudonymous authors, repeat the tales to their analyst, return to the drama with new interpretations and players — and begin to flicker around the edges, to recede from the yearned-for new dimension. The hand that holds the vibrator is translucent, like developed film. Cantor's brilliant parody of the analyst, inflicting on the patient his own traumas and terrors, concerned almost exclusively with his own theories and deductions, leading the (female) analysand to fulfill his post-diction of events resuscitated from his own past, concerns all relationships, which invent desire and then imagine into being the thing they have invented. We've been taught to regret the loss of innocence, as a sorry passage to adulthood. We keep our darlings ("dollinks") flush-cheeked and cherry-lipped as long as possible. No pain, no death, no sex. One does feel sorrow at the translation of the cheerful-mad cat to the complicated person Kate becomes. It is passage — change introduced by the nuclear age — and leads to an acceptance of responsibility for beliefs hitherto unthought and actions unconsidered, making living with the impossible bomb possible. —Elisabeth Cunnick

Δ   Δ   Δ

Tom Patterson. *St. EOM in the Land of Pasaquan.* Highlands, Jargon Society. $30.00.

Here music can be painted on the walls as Osolomios icons on the side of breathing gypsy mud pictures a castle for a tea breathing card finagler flim flammer pin roller who discovered the basement of hair and beards in a gallery from the other side of life...the desire to be in the feeling of being out as artists are in and out so was St. EOM...my advice to all readers read this book forget the curriculum and look at the pictures.

—Robin Winters

THEODORE ENSLIN. *The Weather Within.* Milwaukee, Landlocked Press. No price given.

One way of reading Theodore Enslin's poetry is as an ongoing conversation or dialectic. In the past, for example, he has often cited the names of those, quick or dead, who have made contributions to this conversation in the margins adjacent to the poems. In *The Weather Within*, there is a single citation for the entire poem in the form of its subtitle: *In Memory In Homage: George Oppen 1908-1984.* This, then, is a conversation with one primary partner, with the voice—as remembered, made part of Enslin's own voice, though not always merely assented to—of George Oppen.

It may be useful to identify the reference of the poem's title. This is given in part no. 20, which I quote in full:

> There is rightness
> a standing up
> rectitude
> in integer vitae
> we will not claim
> all of it
> that is settled
> outside us
> yet a conduct
> a weather within.

The weather is inside, internal, something to be maintained—"a standing up"—against our own vicissitudes and those of the forces, physical and spiritual, outside us. Concern with "rectitude"—and an awareness going well beyond past or present received notions of correct deportment—sets both George Oppen and Theodore Enslin apart from many of their contemporaries. Like some of their diction, these two poets can appear old-fashioned, perhaps deliberately so, in this concern. In an age typified by hi-tech nominalism and an all-pervasive irony, an irony which while once functional threatens to become a disease, both these poets stick out in their standing up. In such an age, both are relatively out of place, though precedents—in Pound, in Zukofsky—can be found. What could be more incongruous than presuming that some modes of behavior, beyond self-interest and "enlightened" pragmatism, are to be preferred over others, than presuming the presentation of one's work has something to do with one's life, than presuming one will be held accountable for how one conducts both activities. At the UC-San Diego

Oppen conference this past spring a not-unintelligent critic asked how students could be helped past the barrier of Oppen's constant "wisdom seeking." One can understand the question, and one can understand that it begs the question.

There are forty-eight parts in *The Weather Within*, two to a page. The parts are numbered, e.g., 3-4, at the upper outside corner of each page. (The parts appear in the same order, though in a somewhat reduced format and without numbers in the offset edition put out by the Membrane Press.) Some mention should be made in passing of the Landlocked Press first edition as a handsome job of bookmaking. The typeface is large and readable, the paper is Ingres-Fabriano (cover and text), there are front and back drawings by Kim Wilson. It's a pleasure to hold such a volume, which will lie open, flat, on a table and which avoids the ostentation of much small press work.

Of the poem's forty-eight parts, I single out three sets of two each from the beginning, middle, and end, each of the three dealing with age. The parts on each page do and do not connect with one another. At the same time it should be noted that they aren't given, antiphonally, as separate statements from Enslin and Oppen. Both are from Enslin, both have "intertextual" allusion, directly quoted in some and only hinted at in others, to Oppen's work. Reading the parts, one overhears and is made aware of Oppen's voice through that of Enslin. In a variety of ways it shows through. Beyond "conversation" generally, perhaps the more specifically accurate analogue for the dynamics of the poem is a two-part motet, the "given" part coming from Oppen, the added and somewhat more "frontal" part from Enslin. We hear the whole of the motet at once, the one part showing ("bleeding") through the other. (For a more formal working out of this particular analogue see Enslin's "Motet" poem in CON-JUNCTIONS:9.)

In the first part we're told that consciousness, in relation to the life around and outside itself, is "out of scale." There is more of it, more going on in it than in the rest of "life." The problem, given this out-of-scaleness, is how to deal with it. And, as the work of both poets has demonstrated over the years, there is no "deal," but only the trying to deal. Or as Enslin drily comments in the final part of the poem, "I suppose/it is the human condition." It could also be called tragedy. Even out-of-scale consciousness "flickers," it is both the "make and brake" of our lives. Oppen appears in this first part through the use of space breaks within lines, a practice that became more and more pronounced toward the end of his work, and through the reference to the consciousness as "the engine," which will be recalled from the serial poem "Image of the Engine" from *The Materials*. While consciousness can be a machine making for "clearing,"—understanding—it is at best "seasonal." It is at once not in proper sync with the world around it and yet subservient to the alteration of that world. It is this root contradiction which is tragic.

In slightly shorter lines part no. 2 then takes up what can be done, granted such a condition, what can be done from the perspective of age. The given, either of consciousness or of the phenomenal world, is no longer a major concern. There is no gesture of dismissal with regard to what can't be dismissed, but simply: "Age is more adventurous." This is a marvelously free line, not flamboyant, but free and intrepid. The question then occurs as to what, having relegated the given to a less-than-privileged position, is to be done. Part no. 2 doesn't provide an immediate response. What follows, instead, defines and qualifies age. We read that this quality of adventuresomeness beyond the given is its gift to us. This is so much the case "We might almost wish/that it were not so." For we crave as others have before us the known, the stable, the familiar. It is even more comforting to be confronted with the constant alteration of the given, which is at least constant in its alteration. For all its brevity this part is full of careful qualification. Age is not simply presented as superior to all that came before it, an invalidation of those "prepatory" years as it were.

Having declared that age is more adventurous, it's noted that that is its gift to and from us. Without being overly grim, the poem denies any external benefits as part of the "human condition." Rather, we're reminded that all we can have, what we must have, is time, but that time is a gift *from* ourselves; what may be realized from or in age comes at the price of our own mortality. Thus it is "we might almost wish/ that it were not so." We find ourselves in such a position because the gift must produce, sought after or not, an increment of consciousness which, as it grows, can only result in the further realization of being "out of scale." (cf. Oppen's "The man is old and—/Out of scale" from "Seated Man," *This In Which*.) Thus age is "poised," but rarely takes "that last flight/above the peaks" that youth had vainly attempted to scale. The nature of the flight isn't further defined. My guess is that it amounts to vision, that awareness of "the big picture," which comes about when one is somehow released from—"above"—the pull of the immediately given. In its relative independence from the given, age can come to vision, a bringing of the world and consciousness into scale, into a kind of harmony. This is a possibility. It is, however, only a possibility, one rarely taken, and if taken, the last.

This bittersweet s'fumato sense of age is something we are familiar with in Oppen, but, in its accentuation, it is relatively new in Enslin. There had been darkness in the work, but it had been counterbalanced by light, hope however qualified, in the ongoing conversation or dialectic of his previous poetry. Now there has been a shift.

> The words themselves   older
> it does not seem so   possible
> that words which we rearrange
> with no difficulty   should be that old
> without an ability to deflect
> our uses   yet in the largest sense
> they do resist   and elude us.
> They make it difficult just at the moment
> when they seem defenseless.
> In measure attempted
> they will assume nobility
> growing from the rubbish
> of our thoughtless assault.
> Oh   the words.
> Words live lives of their own.

There may be attempted measure, there may be nobility, but the nobility belongs to the words living lives independent of us, their unthinking users. The poem may be read as a motet's counterpoint to the heartlessness of words in Oppen's "Route" (*Of Being Numerous*). It is hard, even given the age's clichés of relativity, to imagine anything more devastating.

We encounter restatements of the same "themes" in the parts of the middle set. We are back to consciousness, this time to an awareness "that all has aged around us/we alone remain young." We're told this is the only way of looking out, that what is within does not age. At first glance, then, flecks of light against the darkness. Yet the reservations all but extinguish them. For if that is the only way of looking out, what we find is "only on the surface"; if what's within resists aging, we still know only "our own part" of it. Our "youth" remains caught up with the superficial; our consciousness continues to be out of scale and inharmonious.

The musical expression of this paradox of increasingly aware and increasingly delimited consciousness is developed:

What may be sung   well sung
may we be sung   it is
that pitiless singing   changes
as the bells insist their tones
again   the ringing in stages
many stages   one after another
ways in or our down corridors
long stopped with dust   the
velvet of neglect   done
well done   may well be done.

The part begins with the closing lines of Oppen's "Song, the Winds of Downhill" (*Seascape: Needle's Eye*). That poem is of course one of affirmation. Out of a deliberate impoverishment of the tradition, great or otherwise, one makes one's way, by "handholds" and "footholds," beyond the residential suburban plots of the anthologies, toward the poem "which may be sung/may well be sung," the supposedly originary condition of the traditional lyric. Yet Enslin turns the affirmation of Oppen's poem around: "it is/that pitiless singing." Oppen celebrated the possibility of making one's way, of a kind of progress toward composition which, it's implied, is enough; i.e., that the struggle to arrive, make something from the barest means can be undergone and that the result will be somehow satisfactory, even to the point of casting some doubt on the tradition's mostly honorific gestures toward an origin in song. It *will* sing. Enslin accepts the possibility of singing and produces in true contrary motion a song of darkness. It is as though Gesualdo had reworked Thomas Tallis's "Spem in alium."

What has been won through—and this should be understood neither as an argument with nor as an ironic dismissal of Oppen—is a further realization which happens to be "darker": the song of our struggle for composition is, finally, not our own at all, but that of the words with their own autonomous lives. It is, indeed, a change, an instance of changes, playing on the chords of the older poet. But the playing, like the change-ringing of bells (clangorous relative of the motet), only serves to produce an image of darker and darker darkness. The ringing in stages leads to corridors "long stopped with dust   the/velvet of neglect." From Oppen's image of bareheaded struggle with the outside world (cf. "Carpenter's Boat," *This In Which*) we have come to an antithetical, curiously interior scene. One thinks of the steps in Kafka's insurance office, of Bartleby's law office and prison walls. What has happened is that we forsook the givens of tradition, struggled out in "the elements" only to find ourselves back on those steps and within those walls. Indefinite postponement and ostensive acquittal, indeed. And the little play on the vowels—from Oppen's "sung" to Enslin's "done"—is chilling. And even further, the free floating syntax of the final "may well be done" phrase means this interior scene may very well be *the* scene of our existence.

I want to connect the change-ringing with "that open song." In the latter, the song is described as a single line which, with an added voice, would strengthen to cadence. The purpose of change-ringing is to come to something else, adding to a given or inherited subject, not simply further elaboration, but that elaboration *and* something else. (This is how discovery is made in music and poetry.) Confronted with anyone's sense of limitation, whether or not the weight of tradition is felt as an actual mass, there has to be some expectation that the addition of another voice will help, both for the immediate job of getting along in composition and for the desired end result of something distinct and "new." This expectation, however, is denied twice. Having posited the possibility of cadence, Enslin insists that it still remains a single line and that "we must allow it all to end/without conviction." The poem circles back to the opening of song and the conjoint cadential line. The line is not so much denied—after all, this poem is fair evidence that it can be made—as is its ultimate "discovery" found wanting. "This little trickling melody is all we have." A cadence is a progression of chords, usually two, which gives the effect of defining and closing a "sentence." Here the chord changes, the words have been attended to and put together with skill, only to close with a literal line (melody or sentence) of failure. What we have, what we've made, is not enough.

The final set begins with a reference to "But So As By Fire," one of the poems from Oppen's series "Some San Francisco Poems" (*Seascape*). That poem concludes:

> We have gone
> As far as is possible
>
> Whose lives reflect light
> Like mirrors
>
> One had not thought
> To be afraid
>
> Not of shadow but of light
>
> Summon one's powers

Enslin's reference to Oppen's line, like his other references, is indirect, more a variation than a quotation per se; and, importantly, the poem begins where Oppen's ends. Enslin, then, is not saying the same thing as Oppen. In this poem there is an awareness that not all shadows are threatening or, if so, that their threat may be truly insubstantial. "Yet/power does appear." We can read "power" here, following the reference to "But So As By Fire," as one's capacity to bring about vision (or perhaps the cohering power of vision in itself). Working with words in composition, *some* vision *can* appear. There can be melody, there can be "sense." There is qualification. For that power of clarity and resolution, power of light, may well only "summon shadow/long after the fact has vanished." What would be achieved by the power of vision is, in effect, an incapacitation, a haunting which would prevent any further discovery, if not any motion beyond our old fears. Our very capacity proves to be nullifying. We remain old men, out of scale and seated, stuck.

The final part of the poem returns to the image of the mind "in age." In this condition, as suggested toward the end of no. 2, there is a power beyond what was possible in youth. Now there is flight beyond mere aspiration, there is actual ascent and hovering. There is complication. Once detached from the pull of the given, the mind "cannot come down." It is the tragic, unlooked-for opposite of Icarus. (cf. Oppen's "Daedalus: The Dirge," *The Materials*.) There is further complication in developing the image. "The turns are silent wheeling   shadows/high above the landscape." The shadows that had been simply ominous, instances of generic danger, turn out to be not true "signs" for threatening facts, much less the Erinyes, but the illusory products of our own minds. (And it is difficult not to think of predatory birds in reading these lines, the power of the mind preying upon itself.) The problem of scale, of integrating an ever-enlarging consciousness with what it's conscious of has been resolved. "All that/bewildered us" has been resolved by the vision of age. There remains yet another problem, one revealed—in this rather disheartening process of revelation—as of distance. Just as things come together, the mind and its objects in "mensural" scale, their unity is found to be too distant, "so far off it does no good." At this point Enslin's voice gently, but meaningfully interrupts the less "vocal" flow of the poem. "I suppose/it is the human condition." The very flatness of the statement is affecting. Having come so far in the process of age and of composition, it is a finale made all the more final for its quiet flatness. This is the human condition: that there is vision, coherence, "only at that place/where the fit is powerless." I first misread the last line to be somehow benign, a last "testament of acceptance." That *is* a misreading. Undemonstrative as it may be, it would be difficult to be "darker." The unactionable vision, product of the art so long to learn, exists as a design that is "perfect in its just   repose."

Earlier in the poem both words and axes are identifed as things that cut. The words of the poem's penultimate line, so quiet and flat, could not be more cutting. They are not used as agents of revenge or retribution against another person nor against another politics. Certainly, they are not against George Oppen. The words came, entered composition as the result of vision, the human need for a more than incidental or merely local "given" coherence. In no. 30, symbol, metaphor, synonym are all rejected; more than these, however crucial as language functions, is need: "we are in need/deep need of scene." And with need comes obligation, the poet's obligation to make a scene, an operative or "realizable" design. Once it has realization, however, the mind's own flight in age distances us from it. Whatever perfection there may be belongs to the design in itself. We come to recognize that perfection, that encompassing coherence, only when it is unreachably remote from us, made so by our own need and obligation. The repose is the design's, not ours. The space break between "just" and "repose" in that last line is an instance of the perfection and of the heartlessness of words, of poetry as the art of words.

I don't know that such dark vision of vision can't be found elsewhere in Enslin, in *Forms* or *Ranger* to mention two ambitious earlier works. What strikes me as new is its concentration. It is this concentration which gives *The Weather Within* a largeness of its own. Whether you read it as the inevitable trap that must come of poetry's own self-troping or as tragic vision, the poem is large, not monolithic but inclusive and humanly generous within its inclusion.

—JOHN TAGGART

NOTES ON CONTRIBUTORS

GREGORY AMENOFF shows with Hirschl & Adler Modern, New York.

SARAH BELK's first cookbook, on the new Southern cuisine, will be published by Simon & Schuster next year.

DAVID BELLOS's translation of Georges Perec's *Life: A User's Manual* (Godine) came out earlier this year. He is a Professor of French Studies at the University of Manchester, England.

Mace Hill Remap, by NORMA COLE, has just come out with Moving Letters Press, Paris. Forthcoming is her *Metamorphotsia* (Potes & Poets).

Rift, PETER COLE's first book, was published by The Grenfell Press in 1987. He lives in Jerusalem.

ROBERT COOVER's *Whatever Happened to Gloomy Gus of the Chicago Bears?* was published last year by The Linden Press, Simon & Schuster.

ROBERT CREELEY's *Collected Poems* and *Collected Prose* are available in paperback from the University of California Press.

ELISABETH CUNNICK is senior editor with this magazine.

MICHAEL DAVIDSON is the author of *The Landing of Rochambeau* (Burning Deck) and *The Analogy of the Ion* (The Figures).

Sun & Moon has published BARBARA GUEST's new volume of poems, *Fair Realism*.

JOHN HAWKES's most recent novel is *Whistlejacket* (Weidenfeld & Nicolson). It will be issued in paperback next year by Collier Books.

KENNETH IRBY's books include *To Max Douglas, Catalpa, A Set* (Tansy), and *Orexis* (Station Hill).

ROBERT KELLY's *The Doctor of Silence* was published this spring by McPherson & Co. He teaches at Bard College.

KARIN LESSING lives in Provence. Her first book, *The Fountain*, is available from the Montemora Foundation.

HARRY MATHEWS's novel *Cigarettes* was published last year by Weidenfeld & Nicolson. *The Way Home* is out with The Grenfell Press in a limited edition.

JOSEPH McELROY is the author of *Women and Men* (Knopf). His new novel—*The Letter Left to Me*—whose opening pages are printed here, will be out with Knopf this fall.

GUY MENDES's first book of photographs, *Light at Hand*, came out with Gnomon Press in 1987.

KEN MILLER lives in San Francisco. These are his first published photographs.

LAURA MORIARTY's recent books include *Somber Reptiles* and *Persia*.

BRADFORD MORROW's first novel, *Come Sunday*, was published this spring by Weidenfeld & Nicolson.

YANNICK MURPHY's first collection, *Stories in Another Language*, was published by Knopf last year.

GEORGES PEREC (1936-1982) won the Medicis Prize in 1978 for *Life: A User's Manual*. Author of everything from lipograms to plays, recipes to riddles, univocalics to heterograms, his novel *La Disparition* was written without using the letter *e*.

Atlas Press in London will issue ARMAND SCHWERNER's *Tablets I-XXVI* this winter.

ILIASSA SEQUIN's "Three Quintets" (#10-12) are from a series of twenty, recently completed. She lives in Beverley, England.

LEONARD SCHWARTZ's criticism has appeared in *Central Park*.

RON SILLIMAN's newest book is *What* (The Figures). He is executive editor of *Socialist Review*.

GILBERT SORRENTINO's *Rose Theatre* is out with Dalkey Archive Press. He lives in Stanford, California.

JOHN TAGGART's *Loop* is available from Sun & Moon. A collection of his essays is due next year from Duke University.

WILLIAM T. VOLLMANN's first novel, *You Bright and Risen Angels*, was published by Andre Deutsch and Atheneum last year. His first collection of short fiction, *Under the Rainbow*, will be out in 1989 with the same publishers.

DAVID FOSTER WALLACE's first novel, *The Broom of the System*, was published by Viking in 1986. *Girl With Curious Hair*, his first collection of short fiction, will be out this fall with Viking.

Overlook Press issued PAUL WEST's collection of stories, *The Universe and Other Fictions*. His essays, *Sheer Fictions*, is out with McPherson & Co.

DIANE WILLIAMS has published stories in *The Quarterly*, *Epoch*, and elsewhere.

JONATHAN WILLIAMS continues to work on his *Walks To The Paradise Garden*, a collaboration with photographers Guy Mendes and Roger Manley on Southern "Outsider" artists.

GAHAN WILSON's cartoons have appeared in *Playboy* and elsewhere.

TREVOR WINKFIELD exhibits at Edward Thorp Gallery, New York. His collaboration with Harry Mathews has just appeared in a limited edition with The Grenfell Press.

ROBIN WINTERS shows at Brooke Alexander Gallery, New York. He recently installed an exhibit for the visually impaired and physically challenged at the Wadsworth Atheneum, Hartford, Connecticut.

New Poetry and Prose from
HANUMAN BOOKS

Bob FLANAGAN:
Fuck Journal

Allen GINSBERG:
*Your Reason &
Blake's System*

Max BECKMAN:
*On My Painting:
Essays & Diaries*

Alain DANIELOU:
Fools of God

David TRINIDAD
Three Stories

Willem de KOONING:
Collected Writings

Cookie MUELLER:
*Fan Mail, Frank Letters
and Crank Calls*

Edwin DENBY:
Willem de Kooning

Gary INDIANA:
White Trash Boulevard

Jean GENET:
Rembrandt

Sandro PENNA:
Confused Dream

Vincent KATZ:
Cabal of Zealots

Hanuman Books are published and edited
by Raymond Foye and Francesco Clemente.

All titles $4.95 post paid. Printed in letterpress
and handsewn with dust jackets by the
Kalakshetra Press, Madras, India. Bookstore
inquiries may be directed to Sun & Moon
Distribution, P.O. Box 481170, Los Angeles, CA
90048, or Small Press Distribution, 1814 San
Pablo Avenue, Berkeley, CA 94702.

HANUMAN BOOKS
P.O. Box 1070
Old Chelsea Station
New York, N.Y. 10113
(212) 645-1840

burning deck books

ROBERT CREELEY
The Company
New poems. "No poetic theories are required to support such art: [Creeley's] achieves its own permanence by relating at once to our own groping, semiarticulate wonder." — Joyce Carol Oates, *The New Republic.* "Creeley has brought a brutal and at times even incomprehensible honesty to American poetry." — *Choice.*
52 pages, 2 colors throughout, LP, sewn, paper $10, signed $20

LISSA MCLAUGHLIN
Troubled by his Complexion
The tension between the stories that wants to be told and the limits of words creates an almost physical space of loss and worldlessness. Landscape and gesture take on the functions of plot and character to disclose strange drifting correspondences between feeling and meaning — all resonant with her extraordinary cadences. "The voice is ironical, austerely beautiful and strong... To be reread" — *Reality Studios.*
120 pages, LP, sewn. paper $8, signed $15.

Seeing the Multitudes Delayed. 76 pages, offset, signed
cloth $15, paper $4

Approached by Fur. 28 pages, LP, handmade paper, signed,
with a drawing by the author $20

DALLAS WIEBE
Going to the Mountain
New stories by the Aga-Khan-Prize winner. Quirky inventiveness and grotesque satire lights up the potential terror of everyday life, but also its humor and exhilaration. "The unique poignancy and brittle humor of Weibe's fiction proves disturbing and authentic" — *Gargoyle.* "Insights float like amoeba in a bath of mythomania... To complain of his inability to tell a story is akin to criticizing spaghetti for bending around a fork" — *New York Times.*
160 pages, LP, sewn, paper $10, signed $20

The Transparent Eye-Ball. 114 pages, LP, paper, $4

JAIMY GORDON
Circumspections from an Equestrian Statue
A novella by the author of *Shamp of the City-Solo.* General Burnside, the only Northern general to lose battles in the Civil War, gets entangled with a doctor of gynecology. "She moves the language of the novel into new territory" — *Margins.* "Something new in the great free-wheeling tradition of Petronius, Rabelais, and Swift" — Hayden Carruth.
76 pages, offset, signed cloth $15, paper $4

71 Elmgrove Ave. #1C
Providence, RI 02906

Burning Deck has received grants from the National Endowment for the Arts, the Rhode Island State Council on the Arts, the Rhode Island Foundation, and the Taft Subvention Committee.

TEMBLOR

C O N T E M P O R A R Y   P O E T S

edited by Leland Hickman

ISSUE NUMBER SEVEN:

Jackson MacLow *8th Merzgedicht* In Memoriam *Kurt Schwitters*
and *Pieces o' Six XXXI & XXXIII* with Six Computergraphics by Anne Tardos
Jerome Rothenberg from *Khurban*   Bob Perelman from *Captive Audience*
Gustaf Sobin from *Voyaging Portraits*   Rachel Blau DuPlessis *Draft #6: Midrush*
Gerald Burns *Socrates Dying in Widener*   Jed Rasula *New Rev. on Cell. Path. Porn.*
Claude Royet-Journoud *A Descriptive Method* translated by Michael Davidson
Joseph Simas from *That Other Double In Person*   Marc Nasdor *Treni in Partenza*
Stephen Ratcliffe *spaces in the light said to be where one/ Comes from*
Peter Middleton *Portrait of an Unknown Man*   Barbara Roether *The Formulations*
Rae Armantrout from *Necromance*   Duncan McNaughton from *The Pilot*
Norman Fischer *Working Title & other poems*   David Chaloner *Tongues of Light*
Paul Christensen *A Noble Wave: On Gustaf Sobin*
George Hartley *Sophist & Sentence: Bernstein & Silliman*
Bruce Campbell *Four Poets: Gansz, Coolidge, Andrews, Bernstein*
John Shoptaw *Saving Appearances: On John Ashbery*

ISSUE NUMBER SIX:
Susan Howe: *Thorow*
David C.D. Gansz: *Sin Tactics*
Barbara Guest: *The Screen of Distance*
Clark Coolidge: 20 poems from *Literal Landscapes*
Denis Mahoney: 3 sections from *Black Pig*   Ronald Johnson: *The Fireworks Spires*
Keith Waldrop: from *Transcendental Studies*   Fanny Howe: *Torn Parts: A Novel*
Dennis Phillips: 7 pieces from *A World*   Mei-mei Berssenbrugge: *Recitatif*

Six Writers on Eshleman:
Paul Christensen • Rachel Blau DuPlessis • Jed Rasula
Gerald Burns • James Hillman • Karin Lessing
Clayton Eshleman: *Golub The Axolotl*
Georges Bataille: *Guilty* translated by Bruce Boone
Bob Perelman: 5 poems from *Face Value*
Bruce Andrews: *Be Careful Now & other texts*
Diane Ward: 4 poems from *Concept Lyrics*   Marjorie Perloff: *On Steve McCaffery*
Michael Blitz: *On Jed Rasula*   George Hartley: *On "In the American Tree"*
Linda Reinfeld: *On Susan Howe*   Stephen Ratcliffe: *Two Hejinian Talks*
Pasquale Verdicchio: *Winter Insect, Summer Grass*
a complete novella: Rosmarie Waldrop: *A Form/ Of Taking/ It All*

SUBSCRIBE:
Individuals: 2 issues/1 year $16.00 ppd — 4 issues/2 years $30.00 ppd
Institutions: 2 issues/1 year $20.00 ppd — 4 issues/2 years $40.00 ppd
Single issue $8.50 postpaid

TEMBLOR: contemporary poets
4624 Cahuenga Blvd. #307, North Hollywood, CA 91602

George Robert Minkoff, Inc.

RARE BOOKS

////

*20th Century First Editions, Fine Press Books,
Letters, Manuscripts & Important Archival
Material Bought & Sold
Catalogues issued*

Rowe Road, RFD, Box 147
Great Barrington, MA 02130
[413] 528 - 4575

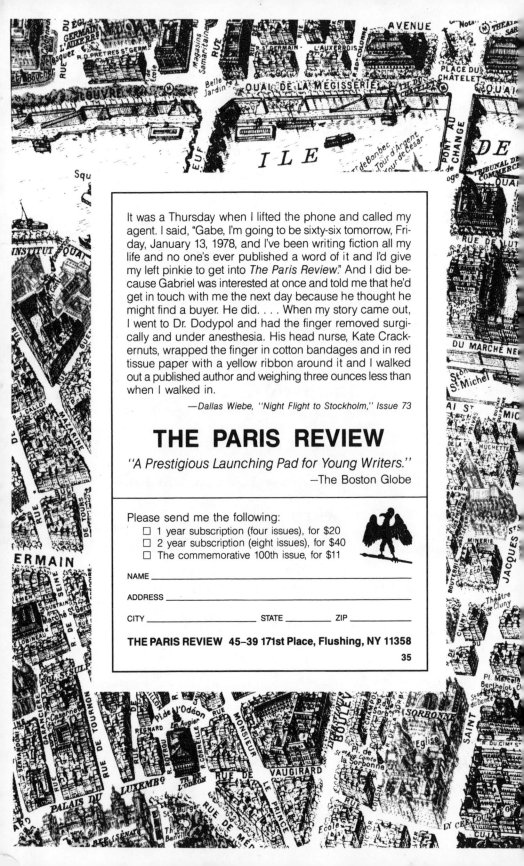

It was a Thursday when I lifted the phone and called my agent. I said, "Gabe, I'm going to be sixty-six tomorrow, Friday, January 13, 1978, and I've been writing fiction all my life and no one's ever published a word of it and I'd give my left pinkie to get into *The Paris Review*." And I did because Gabriel was interested at once and told me that he'd get in touch with me the next day because he thought he might find a buyer. He did. . . . When my story came out, I went to Dr. Dodypol and had the finger removed surgically and under anesthesia. His head nurse, Kate Crackernuts, wrapped the finger in cotton bandages and in red tissue paper with a yellow ribbon around it and I walked out a published author and weighing three ounces less than when I walked in.

—Dallas Wiebe, ''Night Flight to Stockholm,'' Issue 73

THE PARIS REVIEW

''A Prestigious Launching Pad for Young Writers.''
—The Boston Globe